Verandahs of POWER

Space, Place, and Society
John Rennie Short, *Series Editor*

Verandahs of POWER

Colonialism and Space in Urban Africa

Garth Andrew Myers

Syracuse University Press

First Edition 2003

03 04 05 06 07   6 5 4 3 2 1

The paper used in this publication meets the minimum requirements of
American National Standard for Information Sciences—Permanence of
Paper for Printed Library Materials, ANSI Z39.48–1984.∞™

Library of Congress Cataloging-in-Publication Data

Myers, Garth Andrew.
Verandahs of power : colonialism and space in urban Africa / Garth
Andrew Myers.—1st ed.
p. cm.—(Space, place, and society)
Includes bibliographical references and index.
ISBN 0–8156–2972–9 (hardcover (cloth) : alk. paper)—ISBN
0–8156–2997–4 (pbk. : alk. paper)
1. City planning—Africa. 2. Postcolonialism—Africa. I. Title. II.
Series.
HT169.A3 M49 2002
307.1'216'096-dc21
2002151210

To Melanie, Phebe, and Atlee

Garth Andrew Myers is an associate professor in the Departments of Geography and African/African-American Studies at the University of Kansas. His main research interests are in the political, historical, and cultural dimensions of urban development in Africa.

Contents

Illustrations

Preface

"The only real answer to give to these people is an answer in concrete and bricks. . . . The only way of getting things right for the native, and keeping them right, is by cultivation of public opinion on the spot. If ever I am Governor . . . I will devote all my energies to improving the lot of the native in the small practical ways which go to make up life . . . to providing them with the means of improving themselves in mind and body and to trying to make them believe, from what they see with their own eyes, that we are there to help. . . . There are to my mind two outstanding factors in this problem. The first is Rule. Unless the natives are ruled firmly as well as wisely, we are bound straight for chaos. The second is Goodwill. Unless you do get the goodwill . . . you will never get the machinery to work properly."

—Eric Dutton, to Joseph Oldham; Oldham papers,
Box 5, 1930 and Box 7, 1931

This book examines the creation of and struggle over urban order in four cities in eastern and southern Africa, in British colonial and in postcolonial contexts. My focus is on Nairobi, Lusaka, Zanzibar, and Lilongwe, albeit with a greater emphasis on the latter two. I employ research findings from the last decade to assess the attempts by colonial and postcolonial states to use urban planning to shape the physical spaces of city life as a way to create consent as well as domination—or, in the words of the career colonialist Eric Dutton, *goodwill* and *rule*.

The book contributes both to a long tradition of geography research on colonial cities and to a multidisciplinary body of research on the urban cultures and legacies of colonialism. My analysis is centered on the spatial aspects of colonial rule in these cities, but also on the postcolonial inheritance, tracing the legacies of colonialism in different and divergent postcolonial settings. By developing a narrative that moves from Kenya to Northern Rhodesia to Zanzibar in the colonial context, and then to Zanzibar and Malawi in the postcolonial context, my goal is to articulate a middle ground between fetishizing the colonial city and fixating on local differences between cases.

I use themes taken from Timothy Mitchell's concept of *enframing* as a means of articulating how British colonialism and then its inheritor states worked with the physical form of cities to reshape societies (1988). To Mitchell, colonialist enframing was centered on the codification and maintenance of a visible hierarchy of spatial order, of container and contained. He argued that colonial power "required the country to become readable, like a book" (33). This meant not only physically replanning houses and neighborhoods, like those Mitchell examined in colonial Egypt, but changing the way people thought about them. As Eric Dutton put it, British colonialism in African cities sought "an answer in concrete and bricks" for African questions about colonial power, an answer that was explicitly about "cultivation of public opinion on the spot," at once combining "Rule" with "Goodwill."

I document three spatial strategies of enframing in each of the cases in this book. These strategies are, in abstract language: (a) the making of a segmented plan to replace African "orders without frameworks"; (b) the creation of distinctions between "inside" and "outside" at various spatial scales; and (c) the objectification of space via provision of points of observation and places of surveillance. These three themes are examined from a conceptual point of view in the first chapter.

This book differs in its approach from Mitchell's *Colonizing Egypt* on several counts. First, I show how the enframing tactics of and local responses to British colonial rule endure into postcolonial settings, and to do so I examine two apparently very different postcolonial contexts—a revolutionary left-wing socialist state (Zanzibar), and a reactionary right-wing dictatorship (Malawi). Like Mitchell, I examine the roles of the elite among the colonized peoples in the colonial setting. I add to this examination an appreciation of African conceptions of space and negotiations with colonial power in these cities, and of how these conceptualizations relate with the urban-planning strategies of colonizers.

The book is about the urban geographical manifestations of British colonialism and Britain's professional practice of urban planning in Africa, as well as legacies and contestations of these. I look at the first efforts to plan African locations in colonial Nairobi in the 1920s, the program to create a new colonial capital for Northern Rhodesia at Lusaka in the 1930s, and the ambitious but abortive reconstruction of colonial Zanzibar city in the 1940s and 1950s. I then turn to postcolonial revolutionary Zanzibar's equally ambitious and equally abortive reconstruction program in the 1960s and 1970s, and the creation of a new capital for independent Malawi, also in the 1960s and 1970s. In each examination, I not only document the various states' enframing strategies, but also lay out the ways in which African residents in the marginalized urban majority work with, subvert, ignore, or transform those strategies in reframing the spaces of the cities in question.

In addition to the examination of these enframing plans and the African urban majority's responses to them, I trace the experience of the urban-planning process through three different "verandahs of power." This phrase in the title comes from Elspeth Huxley's introduction to the memoirs of Eric Dutton, one of the central figures in this book (1983, i). Huxley said that Dutton was "never far from the verandahs of power" in his career. I like this image for several reasons, some of which I explore at the beginning of chapter 1. But the first and most obvious reason is that it is very spatial and suggests that power and both physical and social space are linked. Huxley's phrase also implies that power, even colonial power, is not absent of real people and their foibles, emotions, and character. I examine and explain each "verandah" in conceptual terms in chapter 1, but let me introduce a few points here.

By personalizing colonial rule and its legacy on these three different levels (which I call *the colonial elite, the colonized middle,* and *the urban majority*), it is my idea also to suggest the threads that tie these levels together. The image of three levels generalizes the variegated capacities of different people within and outside colonial and postcolonial regimes. But the personal stories provide us with necessary complications for the easy simplifications of my levels in the workings of power, by addressing human emotions and experiences of that rule.

The first person I follow in the book is Dutton, a colonial officer who served in five colonies between 1918 and 1952. Dutton was a leader in several aspects of colonial urban planning, siting, and design in British Africa, including parks, gardens, avenue trees, mental hospitals, civic centers, and neighborhood units, beginning with his eight years of service in Kenya. Perhaps most significantly, he supervised the construction of Lusaka in the 1930s and the reconstruction of Zanzibar in the 1940s and 1950s. He was also, in his own words, an "unashamed colonialist" (Dutton 1983, 85). Like colonialism itself, Dutton's manipulative and oppressive agency was both more complex and more influential than first glances suggest. He thrived on the intrigue he helped create within colonial administrations. His struggle with disability (he nearly achieved the second recorded ascent of Mount Kenya just a few years after being severely and permanently impaired by wounds inflicted at Gallipoli) came combined with a mastery of wordplay that made Colonial Office employees seem to dread their "full dress meeting[s] with Major Dutton" during his time in the colonies (Public Record Office, CO 618/83/1–2, 1945).

Dutton served as a mentor for the second person I follow in the book, Ajit Singh Hoogan, a Punjab-born architect who lived and worked for nearly his entire adult life in Zanzibar and Malawi, between 1937 and his death in 1986. Dutton set up Singh in correspondence classes and delegated crucial tasks in Zanzibar's reconstruction to the man he called "the clever artist." As Zanzibar's official architect from the early 1940s until mid-1965, Singh was the designer of many of the city's landmark buildings and ordinary homes. In 1966, Singh became a senior architect in the Ministry of Works and Supplies under Malawian President Hastings Kamuzu Banda. He served as a consultant seconded from the ministry to the Capital City Development Corporation in Banda's scheme to create a new capital at Lilongwe. If Dutton was the stiff upper lip of colonial rule, then Singh provided a voice and a real persona for the colonized people who served the British regimes in Africa as middle-agent functionaries, these often being people who provided key legitimizing tactics for colonialism.

Even though migration and mobility are central to the African urban majority's experiences of urbanism, there is no single African person's experience on which I can draw here as a connective thread stretching from Nairobi in the 1920s to Lilongwe in the 1990s. Instead, on the third verandah of power (metaphorically speaking) in each of the cities, I rely on a variety of voices and sources to provide a picture of what colonial or postcolonial enframing tactics looked like from below and of what happened to African urban majority residential space in each place.

My individual inspiration for attempting to articulate the lifeworld of the urban majority is Juma Maalim Kombo. Bwana Juma was one of Ajit Singh's neighbors in Zanzibar. Juma was a ship pilot and cargo inspector who worked various jobs at sea and in the port city from 1921 to his death in 1993. The views of Juma, many of his neighbors in the part of Zanzibar city known collectively as Ng'ambo (literally, the "Other Side"), and people on the "other sides" of Nairobi, Lusaka, and Lilongwe appear in each chapter about the four cities. These perspectives help to enliven appreciation of the real consequences of colonial and postcolonial planning and the diversity—and yet common threads—of indigenous responses to enframing tactics. I argue that, with the failure of most aspects of state enframing strategies, urban majority residents rely on planning tactics based around local conceptions of faith and custom, set within severe limitations on their own power, to reframe the cities.

Some would have it that "the proper subject of man is quite literally man," meaning that as a male researcher I can be most effective interrogating male views of cities and spaces (Derrick Gregory 1994, 125). Other writings, including Richard Schroeder's (1999, xxii-xxiii) recent work, make a case for cross-gender research that effectively counters those theorists. It is my contention that men ought to find ways of analyzing men's writings, oral narratives, or life stories that ask questions of the dominant position of masculine experiences of place, and this is what I attempt to do here. The fact that so many of the people in power who have planned and built or rebuilt cities in Africa under British colonialism or the power structures that replaced it were and are male also shapes the scope of my analysis. This analysis, however, at the level of the urban majority, makes gender dimensions in African urban experiences of enframing tactics an essential focus.

Part of the inspiration for personalizing the colonial (and postcolonial) experience comes from the outpouring of works in the social history of Africa reliant on the life stories and individual biographies of Africans (Atkins 1993; Bozzoli 1991; Hofmeyr 1994; Landau 1995; Marks 1987; Moodie 1994; Ranger 1995; van Onselen 1996). Where my efforts veer away from these works is that, with one exception (Marks 1987) their narratives are developed deeply mainly at one level of the power structure. Some of the best examples detail the lives of one man (van Onselen 1996), one family (Ranger 1995), or one community (Bozzoli 1991), while Marks (1987) examines the separate worlds of three South African women, one white and two black. I am attempting here to take this peopled approach to three levels in four cities.

Acknowledgments

This book has been a long time coming. In the seven years since the idea first germinated, I have built up intellectual debts and rewarding friendships of which I could not have dreamed. I cannot possibly acknowledge all of the support and the indebtedness, but this is my chance at least to try.

I would like to begin by acknowledging the support of the Hall Center for the Humanities at the University of Kansas, for research travel grants in 1996 and 2000 to the United Kingdom and Zambia. Kathy Porsch has been particularly helpful in guiding me to other sources of funding, as well. The University of Kansas Office of International Programs provided money for the research in Malawi, as did the University of Kansas General Research Fund in the Humanities. The KU African Studies Center and Departments of African and African-American Studies and Geography gave partial support to my travel and work in Nairobi, Zanzibar, Lilongwe, and Lusaka. The U.S. Department of State Bureau of Educational and Cultural Affairs provided support for the work in Zambia, through the University Affiliations grant between the University of Kansas and the University of Zambia. Since some of the material in chapters 5 and 6 comes from research I conducted for my dissertation, I also acknowledge the support of dissertation grants from Fulbright-Hays, the Social Science Research Council, and the UCLA International Studies and Overseas Programs office.

Writing this book, and even more researching it, has only been possible owing to the love, support, and patience of my family, Melanie Hepburn, Phebe Myers, and Atlee Myers—particularly Melanie for putting up with all my comings and goings, caring for me, and keeping me whole. My parents, Bill and Bev Myers, from my childhood onward, have inspired my curiosity about other places and instilled in me a love of learning. Even all these years later, I still depend on their enthusiastic reading of my research.

I could not have come anywhere near to the story I emerged with here without the assistance and expertise of dozens of archivists. In particular, staff at the Zanzibar National Archives, National Archives of Zambia, Society of Malawi, and Rhodes House Library have been very helpful to my work. I respectfully acknowledge the permission of the University of Oxford's Bodleian Library and of Rhodes House to quote from the letters and papers of Eric Dutton, Joseph Oldham, and Frederick Lugard in the book. I also acknowledge the former's permission to reproduce Fig. 4, a black and white photograph of Robert Thorne Coryndon, Eric Dutton, and Palmer Kerrison, from Coryndon's papers in MSS AFR. s. 633 Box 14/1 fol. 1.

My access to the private archive of Ajit Singh Hoogan, held in his former home under the guardianship of his family, has meant a great deal to me, both in terms of my research there and my friendships with Parmukh and Jasjit Singh Hoogan. I thank them both for all of their support and advice. I acknowledge the permission of the Singh family to quote from Ajit Singh Hoogan's letters, and to reproduce from his papers the photographs of Ajit Singh, Eric Dutton, and the Ng'ambo Civic Centre that appear in the book.

Portions of this book have been previously published, in four different articles. Part of "Colonial Discourse and Africa's Colonized Middle: Ajit Singh's Architecture" is herein reprinted with permission of Geosciences Publications, Department of Geography and Anthropology, Louisiana State University, Baton Rouge, LA 70803, from *Historical Geography* 27 (Baton Rouge: Geoscience Publications, 1999): 27–55. Part of "Intellectual of Empire: Eric Dutton and Hegemony in British Africa" is herein reprinted with permission of the Association of American Geographers as copyright holders, from *Annals of the Association of American Geographers* 88 (1) 1998: 1–27. Part of "Making the Socialist City of Zanzibar" is herein reprinted by permission of the American Geographical Society, from *Geographical Review* 84 (4) 1994: 451–63. Part of "Sticks and Stones: Colonialism and Zanzibari Housing" appears by kind permission of the International Africa Institute, from *Africa* 67 (2): 252–72.

In this project, I have had the wonderful opportunity to interview more than a hundred residents of Zanzibar and to interview or engage with a number of residents of Lilongwe, Nairobi, and Lusaka about the ideas in my head. Through these many discussions and conversations with the cities' people, the book has been built but also has steadily changed. Where I have quoted from these interviews in the text, I have generally provided citations consisting of the name of the interviewee and the date the interview occurred. However, for interviews in which the subject preferred not to release his or her name, I have quoted individuals anonymously to protect their privacy. I would especially like to thank the following people for their insights, criticisms, and friendship while in their cities: Imasiku Nyambe, John Volk, Simon Nkemba, Wilma Nchito, Iwake Masialeti, Evaristo Kapungwe, Lordwell Witika, Daniel Nkhuwa, Simasiku Simasiku, Munyindei Masialeti, Godwin Murunga, John Mutio, John Nyagah, Patricia Kameri-Mbote, Parmukh Singh Hoogan, Jasjit Singh Hoogan, M. A. Muhajir, the late Juma Kombo, Abdul Sheriff, Ali Khalil Mirza, Abdulwahab Alawi, Ali Hasan Ali, Zuhura Abdulrahman Mohamed, Mohamedridha Ali Khatib, Badi Richard Wakati, Eidi Suleiman Kideresa, Bimkubwa Ali Saleh, Steve Phiri, Stanley Mazengera, Wilson Godfrey, Felix Sapao, Chief A. Maole, Liz Gal, Catherine Issa, and Deeray Gautama. Muhajir, in particular, has been my confidant and guardian of ideas for a decade now, and I thank him for the great kindness and wisdom he has shared with me. Ali Hasan has assisted and advised me so often in life and work that I hope he accepts me thinking of him as a brother.

So many people have read parts of this book, or have had to sit through my presentations of parts of it, that I really do not know where to begin thanking people. Randy Stakeman, Gerry Hale, Ed Soja, Ned Alpers, and Judy Carney, my undergraduate and graduate mentors, all encouraged me in this endeavor. I would not be doing any of the work I do without their guidance and inspiration. The work of Tim Mitchell has provided me with obvious inspiration here, as have those of Jenny Robinson, Karen Hansen, Maliq Simone, and Debby Potts. Jenny has been a great friend, a font of wisdom, a driving instructor, a fiery imagination to contend with, and an inspiration to think of work and life differently throughout the process of making this book a reality. Maliq and Debby, as well as Laura Fair, Jonathan Glassman, Bill Bissell, Chris Walley, David Schoenbrun, Terry Young, Steve Herbert, Mark Purcell, Chris Brown, Bill Freund, Don Moore, James Sidaway, Jane Parpart, Abdi Samatar, Steve Frenkel, Martin Murray, Sue Parnell, Rick Schroeder, Deborah Pellow, Jim Newman, Misty Bastian, and Miriam Grant—and probably many more people than that—deserve my gratitude for various moments of enthusiasm for my work, for spot-on critiques, or for their companionship along the way to producing it.

My colleagues and students at the University of Kansas, and previously at the University of Nebraska at Omaha and Miami University, have not only kept me busy but pushed me at various moments to think about this work. Tom Klak, Karen Falconer-Alhindi, and students in my Cities of the Developing World courses at Miami and UNO deserve credit for encouraging me to think of starting this book project. Once I came to Lawrence in 1995, the ideas began to take shape. Jacob Gordon, Surendra Bhana, Arthur Drayton, and Peter Ukpokodu—four reframers of British colonial cities—all gave these ideas wings in my faculty seminar in 1996 wherein I first tested the book's premise. Leo Villalon, Fiona McLaughlin, Byron Caminero-Santangelo, Paul Hotvedt, Peter Herlihy, Leslie Dienes, Johan Feddema, Pete and Barbara Shortridge, and the students in my Cities and Development course have lent me their ears in the days since. Keith Shaw, Jennifer Smith-Kastens, Blaine Ray, John Banning, and especially Darin Grauberger of the Kansas Cartographic Services have produced the graphics and made or remade the maps. My students here, especially Jack Livingston, Tom Pratt, Tom Buller, Bjorn Sletto, John Teeple, Craig Davis, Rachel Saifullah, Mohamed Adam, Mark Carper, Cameron McCormick, and Jeremy Lind, have played vital roles in the initial draft and two revisions since by their critical readings, general humanity, and steady encouragement. Jeremy, in particular, has been my lifeline to Nairobi for the past four years, even bringing me a sample of the ground beneath his feet in Eastleigh.

John Rennie Short, Sally Atwater, Brian McCord, Mary Selden Evans, and Irene Vilar-Cuperman at Syracuse University Press have been wise and patient stewards of this project throughout. I would like to thank them, the rest of the Syracuse University Press staff involved, and two anonymous reviewers for seeing to the book's development, improvement, and transformation over the past two years.

Introduction

In addition to introducing the four cities I focus on, I develop in the first chapter the concepts of *enframing* and *reframing* used in the book, and explain the metaphorical verandahs of power that I see as operative (and interactive) in the cities. One of my goals in this book is to highlight the individual agency and human experiences behind colonialism's urban legacy; in the second chapter, therefore, I introduce the key characters followed in the book, Eric Dutton and Ajit Singh. I have followed an introduction to Juma Maalim Kombo with a brief "biography" of Zanzibar's Ng'ambo area. I do so because Bwana Juma and Ng'ambo are exemplary of the similar urban majority communities I examine in the other cities (such as Pumwani in Nairobi, George in Lusaka, or Chinsapo in Lilongwe).

In chapter 3 I discuss the development of urban planning in colonial Nairobi in the 1920s, mainly through the experiences of Eric Dutton during his service in Kenya. The chapter centers on Dutton's work in and writings about Nairobi, and then African reframing of colonial space in that city, particularly in colonial Pumwani. In chapter 4, I turn to the first major colonial urban program in which Dutton was a key player, the construction of Lusaka as Northern Rhodesia's capital in the 1930s. In this chapter, in addition to examining the enframing project from the colonial side through Dutton's contributions, I assess colonialism's attempted balance of rule with goodwill by examining colonial Lusaka from the perspective of Zambian residents and their creation of new neighborhoods outside its enframing order. Where relevant or appropriate, I also refer in both chapters 3 and 4 to the Asian *colonized middle* experience of these cities.

With chapter 5, my geographical focus shifts to Zanzibar, and my biographical scope expands to include not only Dutton's work as the chief creator and generator of the program of reconstruction in that city in the 1940s and 1950s, but also Ajit Singh's experience as that program's chief architect. I then examine Juma Maalim Kombo and his fellow residents of Ng'ambo, including those most directly affected by the reconstruction, highlighting both their resistance to and engagement with colonial urban planning. I conclude with a section on the entanglement of the aftermath of the postwar reconstruction with the political trajectory that would lead to Zanzibar's 1964 revolution.

Chapter 6 is also about Zanzibar. It is the first of two chapters set in Africa's immediate postcolonial era, and in it I examine the revolutionary government of Zanzibar's attempted reconstruction of the city. My contention is that, revolutionary rhetoric aside, this reconstruction project inherited a great deal from colonialism's tactics. On the biographical level, this attempt at creating a socialist city is examined from the point of view of Ajit Singh, who left Zanzibar a year and a half into the revolutionary era but whose family remained behind. I also rely on accounts from residents deeply affected by the reconstruction, including Juma Maalim Kombo. I show both how residents adapted to and transformed the reconstructed area of the city, and how a second "other side" of the city emerged on its periurban fringe, reliant on many of the cornerstones that had produced the first "other side," Ng'ambo.

In chapter 7 I stress a seemingly much different postcolonial setting, Malawi, and in particular the creation of the new capital city in Lilongwe. I begin by contextualizing this capital city project within the trend among many newly independent states in Africa toward creating entirely new capital cities. Once again, though, the spatial tactics of colonialism appear in the landscape of this new city, in their extreme form—indeed, expressing great similarity with apartheid cities in South Africa. The biographical lens here is mainly on Ajit Singh, who was a senior consultant on the Lilongwe project. However, I also examine Malawian reframing of the city, particularly in the creation of its first substantial squatter area, Chinsapo. In the book's concluding chapter I connect the cities and individual stories of the narrative to the main arguments I am making about colonialism, postcolonialism, space, and power in the former British colonies of East and Central Africa.

Verandahs of POWER

Chapter One

Enframing and Reframing African Cities

> "After we came back from the war, they gave us nothing. They had a
> trade school. . . . We were sent there to learn skills . . . and then we
> built houses. . . . [The supervisor] would come by and say, 'no, not so
> much mud, make the stones smaller,' and so on, heh, I finally told him,
> I can't do this. I wasn't born to build houses. I'm a seaman. And so I
> went back to the harbor."
> —Bwana Juma Maalim Kombo, Zanzibar, July 11, 1992

Introduction

The House of Wonders is the centerpiece of Zanzibar city's seafront sky-
line. Zanzibar's Omani sultan, Barghash bin Said, had the palace, replete
with Zanzibar's first elevator, built in the 1880s as a showcase for his elaborate regime. After nearly destroying it in a bombing attack in 1896, the
British Protectorate government renovated the House of Wonders and
used it as administrative headquarters until independence in 1963. Three
wide verandahs wrap around the imposing square building on all sides. A
tall clock tower faces the harbor, beckoning the world to the city.

In 1989, I was afforded the rare opportunity to enter the House of
Wonders. By then, Zanzibar's revolutionary socialist government (in power
since 1964) had renamed it the House of Remembrance and turned it into
the Ideological College of the ruling party. Just inside the House of Remembrance, right ahead of the main doors on the ground floor, the college
leaders had placed a huge, topographically correct scale model of the
Zanzibar islands and Zanzibar city. Colored lights clicked on and off across
the landscape in time to a crackling Swahili soundtrack narrating the geography of Zanzibar's 1964 revolution for the party faithful.

By the year 2000, the House of Remembrance had been forgotten. It
was back to being the House of Wonders again, but with very few wonders

to show for it. Still closed to the public, still surrounded by a huge wrought-iron gate and under armed guard, the building itself was visibly in danger of crumbling, one verandah at a time. Around it on all sides, the living city of Zanzibar swept by its House of Wonders every day. Just across the street, every night, masses of residents from all across the city would gather to share the fruits of informal sector food stalls, have a swim off the seafront retainer wall, or stroll through the kerosene-lamp-lit passages between the crowded stalls that comprise the nightlife of what is called the People's Park.

I begin this narrative of urban plans and contestations of them in four African cities (Nairobi, Lusaka, and Lilongwe, as well as Zanzibar) with this story of Zanzibar's House of Wonders for several reasons. First, although the book's title emanates from Elspeth Huxley's phrase about the British colonial officer Eric Dutton never having been "far from the verandahs of power" in colonial Africa (1983), when I first read Huxley's words in 1992, the verandahs of power I thought of immediately were the spectacular ones that physically surround the House of Wonders. Older Zanzibaris have told me of the trepidation that gripped them on approaching its doors, walking its verandahs, or entering its offices on the rare occasions when they and Africans like them were summoned to appreciate its wonders. To Africans in colonial Zanzibar, and later to those Africans in post-colonial Zanzibar less sure of their revolutionary ideology, this building screamed its connectivity to the dominant power from every one of its verandahs.

Even if an Omani sultan had it built, the House of Wonders serves as a visceral architectural statement of the three principles of enframing that characterized British colonialism's ideal of urban order as Timothy Mitchell (1988) has elaborated them. Long the administrative headquarters of the British colonial regime, it sits in the heart of Forodhani, a neighborhood name meaning "at the customs house" that betrays what the colonial regime and the Omani Sultanate it protected were about—the accumulation of revenue from plantation agriculture. The House of Wonders is deep in the Stone Town of Zanzibar, explicitly the Arab, Indian, and European quarter of the city on British colonialism's highly segmented plan (Lanchester 1923). Its guarded, gated entrance and the heavy-handed control of access to it epitomize the containerization, the separation of inside from outside, basic to enframing the city. Its clock tower is unrivaled in height by any of the older buildings of the city. The memoirs of several holders of the governing post of British Resident in Zanzibar remark on the view the tower provided of all activity in the harbor and the city (Crofton 1953; Pearce 1920). After the building's transformation to the Ideological College's House of Remembrance, the postcolonial government's map model of the revolution also serves as a reminder that power and geography are intimately intertwined, that displays of observational space are intrinsic to the enframing tactics of both colonial and postcolonial states in Africa.

Hence the House of Wonders is both an observed reminder of dominance and power and a central point of observation. Moreover, in thinking of the layering of experiences at three levels that I seek to show—the colonial elite, the colonized middle, and the urban majority—these verandahs hovered in my mind. The image of a British elite controlling the offices that opened onto the top verandahs, a mixed Asian and African middle echelon of bureaucrats on the second level, and African guards and groundskeepers walking the ground-level verandah provides a neat structural image of my approach to colonial urbanism and its legacies.

From these verandahs of the House of Wonders, we can see a colonial city—and then a postcolonial city—enframed. Or can we? Perhaps the three tiers of verandahs provide *too* neat an image. For the attempts to remake this building (and indeed its gradual decay) also hint at the *other side* of my narrative. Enframing strategies in African colonial cities or their postcolonial inheritor cities rarely have had the consequences intended. Instead, quite frequently, we see cities that are reframed in ways never sought by the power structures controlling them. The transient explosive synergies of informal activities in People's Park, the vibrant mobility through it of Zanzibaris from all walks of life, and the irrelevance of the now quite unwonderful House of Wonders to that vibrancy all suggest that an entirely different city of Zanzibar exists for most of its residents, one that has navigated or negotiated its way around many of the frames placed on it. Many colonial cities in Africa had their metaphorical Houses of Wonder. Many postcolonial regimes sought ideological maps like the Ideological College's interactive clay model to display how they would remake those cities and Houses of Wonder. And most of the time, African urban majorities just passed them by outside the gates.

In this chapter, I set the context for my story, locating the four cities under analysis—Nairobi, Lusaka, Zanzibar, and Lilongwe—within the sweep of British colonialism in Africa and describing their contemporary situations. I then lay out the conceptualizations that carry the book, conceptualizations that started for me in visits to the House of Wonders in Zanzibar—the idea of enframing, the verandahs of power, and the ways cities are reframed by the urban majority of the metaphorical lowest verandah.

A Tale of Four Cities

Formal European colonial rule lasted for less than a century across most of Africa, from the Scramble of the 1880s to independence in the 1950s and 1960s (Christopher 1983). Yet colonialism's legacy in Africa is still quite vivid, in political, economic, cultural, or geographical terms. Indeed, the importance of the colonial legacy as a cornerstone for analyses of African current affairs, not only in geography (Jarosz 1992; Bassett 1994) but also across the humanities and social and natural sciences, continues to grow (Comaroff and Comaroff 1991; Comaroff 1997, 163–97; Mamdani 1996; Leach and Mearns 1996).

Britain in particular has had a broad and deep legacy in Africa. Roughly from 1920 to 1960, the British held some form of control over a huge and nearly contiguous block of territory from Sudan to Swaziland, plus five West African territories, and part of Cameroon (Christopher 1988). To some observers, this represented "a ragbag of territorial bits and pieces" (Hyam 1976, 15), but in fact there were numerous commonalties across territories. British rule commenced in these places with direct connections to the metropole's requirements for industrial raw materials or markets and control over their procurement, and colonialists frequently and openly justified imperial control continentwide in these broad terms (Oldham 1924, 97–98; Mill 1965, 693; Havinden and Meredith 1993). While a "colonial trade economy" predominated in the western colonies, most eastern and southern holdings (such as the four colonies whose cities are my focus here) became settler colonies or labor reserve areas for European- or foreign-owned plantations and mines (Amin 1972, 504).

In the four settings of this book (Kenya, Zambia, Zanzibar, and Malawi), four different versions of labor reserve colonialism predominated during Britain's period of rule. Kenya was the most evident white settler colony of the four: Europeans gained access to the best lands in the territory, the space economy of the colony was built around their interests, and Africans were, legally at least, confined to areas known as "native reserves."

Both Northern Rhodesia (today's Zambia) and Nyasaland (today's Malawi) also experienced some white settlement that usurped quality land. However, the broader role of both colonies in the larger context of southern Africa was as labor reserves for white-owned mines and plantations in Northern Rhodesia's Copperbelt, Southern Rhodesia (today's Zimbabwe), and South Africa. Zanzibar, by contrast, was a plantation economy where largely Arab and Indian capital controlled vast clove and coconut groves and Britain's protectorate safeguarded this elite's interests. Indigenous and migrant African communities provided the labor to plantation and port. Yet all four of these colonies experienced the explicitly geographical articulation of colonial power that labor reserve colonialism produced, in what Jennifer Robinson terms "the location strategy" (1996, 2). The spatial separation of Africans in "native locations" set apart from the colonizers and others, most dramatically in towns, became part and parcel of how the colonial enterprise operated. These are four cities that most certainly can be defined as "colonial cities" (de Bruijne 1985, 231–43).

All four colonies consequently experienced some version of the administrative formula known as indirect rule, through which parallel governmental structures ("native" and "European") coexisted (Mamdani 1996; Lugard 1922). The British personnel who instituted and maintained this system made frequent career moves throughout the continent, often meeting and then reconnecting in these four colonies and other territories, further ensuring the patchwork of a common legacy. This legacy of a British colonial imprint is a key commonalty among the four cities I study in this book—Nairobi, Lusaka, Zanzibar, and Lilongwe. It is important, though, to appreciate both the common and the distinctive features of these cities before detailing the conceptual framework I employ in analyzing them.

When one examines them on the surface of things today, the four cities might appear to have little in common. The first two are rapidly becoming major cities with considerably more than a million inhabitants. Nairobi is eastern Africa's principal transport hub, diplomatic center, and business community (Simon 1997). Because there has been no accurate census of its population since 1978, no exact measure of its growth is known. Local planners' estimates of the city's population as of 2000 vary from two to three million, as Nairobi rapidly swallows up the densely populated rural communities that once surrounded it on three sides (Obudho 1994, 198–212; 1997, 292–335). Lusaka, although it is not as globally significant in terms of international agencies or transnational capital, has grown nearly as rapidly as Nairobi. It was estimated to have nearly two million inhabitants in 2000 (Rakodi 1994, 342–63).

Each of the second two cities has fewer than half a million residents. Metropolitan Zanzibar (with a population estimated at 270,000 in 2000) is dwarfed by a factor of ten by its neighboring sister city of Dar es Salaam on Tanzania's mainland. Lilongwe (with a population estimated at 495,000 in 2000) may have passed Blantyre in some estimates to become Malawi's largest city, but Blantyre and Zomba retain central leading city functions. Blantyre is the economic heart of the country as well as its political center of gravity, while Zomba, the colonial capital, is still the place where Malawi's parliament meets and its president lives.

Despite these differences in size and functional importance, however, the four cities do have much in common. Of the four, only Zanzibar predates British colonialism as an urban settlement, and even at that, in real terms barely so. The contemporary city essentially began in the 1690s with the rise of Omani power along the East African coast. It became significant in size and power as an urban center only in the early to mid-nineteenth century, by which time British influence had become quite strong. Both Nairobi and Lusaka grew as a result of colonial railway development in the first decades of the twentieth century. Lilongwe was a town of fewer than twenty thousand people when colonialism ended in Malawi, but, like Nairobi and Lusaka, it originated to perform the politico-administrative functions of British colonialism. By independence, it had even graduated from a district administrative center to a provincial capital.

All of these cities can now be considered national capitals. Lilongwe's status as such is somewhat diminished by the aforementioned failure to relocate the president or the parliament into the city, but it has become recognizable as the seat of the rest of Malawi's government. Zanzibar's capital status may likewise be tainted by virtue of Zanzibar's incorporation into the United Republic of Tanzania in 1964. Indeed, A. J. (Anthony John) Christopher (1994, 413) displays a map of Africa that lists Zanzibar as an "abandoned capital." The wide autonomy of the Revolutionary Government of Zanzibar within Tanzania's union—Zanzibar retains its own presidency, ministries, constitution, and house of representatives—makes such an "abandonment" difficult to read on the ground. Obviously, the function of the capital city "distinguishes it from all other cities" in a national hierarchy, because it is the seat of government (Christopher 1994, 419). Pointedly, in all four cases, then, this means that "government ideology is firmly implanted upon the capital cities," especially given the crucial role of the "urban image" in British colonialism (Christopher 1994, 419). The influence of urban-planning ideas that have their origins in British colonial aesthetic and legal principles is powerfully evident, not only in the maintenance of this urban image, but in very basic features these cities share.

Many authors evidence the fact that historical-geographical analysis of the colonial experience of urban development is vital to understanding Africa's current urban dynamics. Many socioeconomic problems afflicting eastern and southern African cities must be understood as they have emanated from colonial times. In spite of some "momentous changes" with independence, "the post-independence period in African countries has been characterized by continuity rather than change" in urban processes (Rakodi 1995, 8).

Size is the obvious "momentous" change, though. In 1960, East Africa was the world's least urbanized region; of the four states involved here (Kenya, Zambia, Zanzibar, and Malawi) only Zambia had an urban population approaching 20 percent of the national total. By 2000 Kenya and Zanzibar were about one-third urban or more, while Zambia's urban population is sometimes estimated at nearly 60 percent of the total. Even in Malawi the urban population rose from 4 percent of the total in 1960 to 16 percent by 2000 (Simon 1997). By some estimates, Nairobi's and Lusaka's populations were more than ten times larger by 2000 than at independence; Zanzibar has grown fivefold since its 1964 revolution; and Lilongwe surpasses them all, with a population fully twenty-five times its size at independence. Yet even here, colonialism's influence can be seen: one can never ignore that it was the end of colonialism (and its influx controls, pass laws, and other strict laws of movement) that served as a chief catalyst for the burgeoning growth of most cities after independence. Moreover, the end of colonialism did not end the influence of colonial structures in, or attitudes and approaches to, cities.

Enframing Cities

Physical space is a key continuity, a lingering element of colonialism's influence, because cities and towns were built or rebuilt "to create, reflect and reinforce the colonial order" (Simon 1992, 143). The construction of order in British colonial cities in Africa used architecture, landscape, and design features in political ways; shaped space in domestic and neighborhood environments; and gendered those environments, to further, as Eric Dutton put it in a letter to Joseph Oldham, the "cultivation of public opinion on the spot" (Oldham Papers), to make the populace accept British rule and goodwill as commonsense reality.

Robert Young (1995, 173) wants us to articulate the "violent way in which colonial practices were inscribed both physically and psychically on the territories and peoples subject to colonial control." After the initial campaigns of pacification, the "repressive geopolitics of British colonialism" (Young 1995, 173) in Africa were often (though not always) insidious rather than overtly violent. Institutions and rituals of rule that were made to appear as ordinary and everyday by colonialism's functionaries were "crucial in entrenching the supremacy of the colonialist" (Yeoh 1996, 11). Eric Dutton's inscriptions of colonial practices, for instance, through his writings, through physical planning, and through other policies, were only rarely (if ever) directly linked to any overt state violence. However the mundane and longer-lasting impacts of colonial practices bear close examination.

The explicitly spatial dimensions of colonialism's enframing process as "a method of dividing up and containing, as in the construction of barracks or the rebuilding of villages" (Mitchell 1988, 44), is of particular interest to me. Many recent studies of colonialism in Africa discuss conceptions of space and construction of society's spatiality, but most only touch on the real, physical consequences of colonialism's spatial tactics or, crucially, indigenous responses to them (see Young 1995; Said 1993, 1995; Noyes 1992; Pratt 1992; and McClintock 1995). Mitchell's concrete analysis of the colonizing process in Egypt is one of the exceptions (1988). His work represents an important attempt to build a bridge between cultural geography's rich tradition of studying the built environment for social meanings and postcolonial cultural studies' geographical or spatial turn (Yeoh 1996; D. Gregory 1994; Duncan 1990; Holdsworth 1993, 96–109; Nast 1994, 1996).

Timothy Mitchell (1988, 45–62) identifies three broad, everyday spatial strategies for the enframing order of colonial states, in their attempts at a " 'perfect' system of control" (Robinson 1990). The first of these involved altering African "orders without frameworks" in terms of settlement design to an order reducible to a segmented plan. Racial segregation was inherent within this orderly segmentation, but it also extended the effectiveness of routine health and sanitary inspections by colonialists, reinforcing the ordinariness of their power (Yeoh 1996). Second, colonialism in urban British Africa aimed to create a fixed distinction between inside and outside in domestic architecture and urban design, thereby codifying neighborhood, family, and gender relations in a manner distinct from African systems of domestic order. This fixity between inside and out extended the segmentation of strategy number one down to various microscales. Third, the segmented plan of settlement forms under colonial rule provided a place from which the individual could observe or survey the city, as a means of abstracting and objectifying the built environment. The often well-surveilled central spaces of observation served to distance traditionally rural Africans from the communal, "fused" conceptions of space with which they approached the city, seemingly making the rational, Western planning approach to urban space normalized in their eyes (Sack 1980; Cooper 1987). These central spaces also served as reminders of the might of colonial power to the general population. Each of these strategies, to Mitchell, became part of colonialism's effort to separate "container" (the colonizing power) and "contained" (the African community). In later chapters, I demonstrate the presence of these tactics in colonial Nairobi, Lusaka, and Zanzibar, as well as in the postcolonial revolutionary government's reconstruction of Zanzibar, and the postcolonial Malawian government's construction of Lilongwe.

Like the planning mechanisms of most African states today, the enframing system of control that colonial states developed in Africa was anything but "perfect," as the question mark in the title of Robinson's article, " 'A Perfect System of Control'?" suggests (1990). As Michael Watts argues, the power of the state all across Africa has nearly always been "far from overdetermined" (1987, 216). Analysis of colonial and postcolonial states generally brings to light the inability of the apparatus to accomplish its goals, even some of the most mundane legal and juridical components of them. African states, whether colonial or postcolonial, have consistently been undone in trying to use planning and building control to implant their ideological maps onto cities, or to combat what Robinson (1990, 148) calls "the persistence of disorder." Why does the enframing so often come unframed, or get reframed? Why do the Houses of Wonder become so unwonderful? It is useful to start by tackling the question of why states in Africa do what they do in spatial terms in articulating their power.

The central tasks that Bruce Berman claims for the colonial state in Kenya are pertinent (1990, 161–66). The first of these Berman calls "accumulation": "to secure the conditions for the extraction of commodities." Colonial states, like the British occupiers of the Zanzibar House of Wonders, wanted to be geographically and economically "at the customs house." Berman labels the second task "legitimation:" "to provide . . . a framework of stable political order and effective control over the indigenous population" with their "active consent." Berman's third task, which bridges accumulation and legitimation functions, is domination, through security, order, and control.

Berman's terms are similar to the three "ideologies" that Robert Home sees in the colonial urban landscape and the practice of urban planning in the British Empire (1997, 3–4). In place of domination, Home speaks of "the ideology of state control." His second ideology, termed "capitalist ideology," is identical to Berman's "accumulation." Rather than speak of legitimation, Home refers to a third, "utopian" ideology of colonial urban planning that experimented with new "forms of social organization." Since the ultimate aim of this utopian experimentation was, in effect, the legitimation of colonialism, Home's third term fits well with Berman's use of the term legitimation.

These tasks and ideologies are essential administrative elements of Mitchell's enframing idea. However, Berman adds to this an empirical appreciation that colonial states did not always accomplish the tasks assigned. A colonial state had "definite limitations as an instrument of capital . . . beset by periodic crises and struggles that [led] to the destruction or transformation of its structures." Rather than a "finely tuned structure of domination," the colonial state was more a "diverse and ambiguous collection of parts . . . partially integrated and partially in conflict with each other." The bureaucracy "mediated" between these diverse and ambiguous parts as best it could (see also Berman 1984, 7–23).

Colonial governments were "both strong and weak," with overlapping or ambiguous agendas (Berman 1990, 162; Phillips 1989). Both "centralization" and "fragmentation" existed side by side in colonial states attempting to control African territories (Robinson 1996, 28). Colonial administrators struggled to find "the way to act as the agent of a coercive system of exploitation and at the same time gain African compliance" (Berman 1990, 182)—to *rule* with *goodwill*, in Dutton's words. These roles were often conflictual, helping to ensure the state's ineffectiveness. Postcolonial states have inherited this centralized/fragmented contradiction. This conflict is not the only reason enframing tactics come undone, though;

the urban majorities also have active agency within each city's evolving dynamic of urban spatial creation. Therefore, our understanding of why colonial and postcolonial African states so often have failed in their planning agendas must incorporate more from below, of "the ways in which ordinary people . . . struggled against and sought to cope with the hardships of city life" (Maylam and Edwards 1996, xi).

Verandahs of Power

Studying the actual planning processes that colonialism produced, looking at architecture and urban planning and pairing them with the responses of those whose spaces were being planned means getting more of a sense of the people involved in these evolving dynamics, including the people in those urban majorities. There is a burgeoning literature in geography that recognizes the importance of people's capacity to "make a difference" (Porter 1995, 84; Blunt 1994; Crush 1995, 1996). A thorough grounding in the actual urban landscapes and in the biographies of those who helped shape them, paired with those who lived in them and gave them meaning, can remind us just where and how colonialism lingers. It also can provide a picture of the ambivalence, conflict, and contradiction in the expression of administrative power or urban-planning ideology, as well as local responses to these, a picture necessary to seeing the "entanglements" in the operation of power (Sharp, et al. 2000).

The first layer in this book is that of the colonial elite and the postcolonial elite who replaced them. It needs little explanation to show that if we are to understand the tactics of enframing that colonial rule utilized in African cities, it is helpful to know what the developers of those tactics themselves articulated about the plans. By adding a personal dimension, we can also see the ways in which this elite related to the colonized middle and the urban majority in the implementation of their plans. It is important not to overlook the significance of personal power within colonial and later postcolonial bureaucracies in Africa. Personal power was of profound import to many precolonial African regimes (such as the Sultanate of Zanzibar), and early British regimes were likewise reliant on individual personalities. Even later regimes had bureaucratic structures within them that relied on the cultivation of friendships with the colonized as a means of facilitating the local adoption of social programs (Robinson 2000, 67–92). It is essential to pay attention to the interests and personal character of planners, politicians, and bureaucrats in order to "examine the kind of worldview that professional planners and the bureaucrats they advise bring to the resolution of the problems" of city life (Mabogunje 1990, 123). If colonial and postcolonial states have been done in by internal contradictions and fragmentations, it helps a great deal to know more about the exact people in conflict, and their internal contradictions. Eric Dutton proves a valuable personality to follow in the book, as a means toward understanding the worldviews of the colonial elite, the legacies of those worldviews in African cities, and the contradictions and fragmentations within them.

Negotiation and contestation engaged two broad constituencies resident in British Africa—those who worked for the regimes in positions of modest importance and those who did not. I categorize the former constituency as *the colonized middle*. The colonized middle comprised the non-European functionaries in British colonial Africa, the African or Asian portions of the "middle and higher echelons of the bureaucracy" directly engaged with colonialism's intellectual elite in the construction and maintenance of colonial urban order, and, later, in the decolonization process (Gramsci 1971, 13; Johnson 1992).

Analysis of this colonized middle demands that we "look more closely at the kinds of institutional and intellectual linkages which developed between ruler and ruled" (Arnold 1994, 133). In Britain's colonies, "it was the Western-educated intelligentsia whose loyalty to the empire was linked to the progress-oriented discursive formations," like urban planning or modern architecture (Engels and Marks 1994, 10). Ajit Singh, for instance, came from Punjab, the archetypal case of a constructed organic intellectual milieu in the early-twentieth-century British Empire (Engels 1994, 88–91).

European colonial systems in Africa only functioned because of African and other non-European agents of colonial rule. British indirect rule, through which parallel governmental structures ("native" and "European") coexisted in a "decentralized despotism," was a particularly influential system for the operation of colonialism in Africa (Mamdani 1996, 18). Although much is often made of the difference between French and British colonial systems in Africa in cultural terms, both systems came to rely on a class of colonized people judged by their "ability to function as balanced intermediaries" (Stoler and Cooper 1997, 7; see also Celik 1997; Mamdani 1996; Wright 1991). The other European colonial powers created and relied on a similar class of in-betweeners in Africa. Yet they remain an underexamined middle.

In part, the colonized middle has receded from the picture of colonial Africa for reasons related to race and identity politics. In Britain's eastern and southern African colonies, people with non-European and non-African backgrounds occupied a fairly significant segment of this middle. Works continue to come out on South Africa's Indian communities (Freund 1995; Robinson 1994, 197–226), but studies of Asians in East and Central Africa have virtually disappeared after a spate of books, mostly by East African Asians, in the 1960s and 1970s (for instance Ghai and Ghai 1970; Mangat 1969; R. Gregory 1971; although see R. Gregory 1992 and 1993). It is too extreme to say that Asians have been "written out of East African history" by colonialists, nationalists, and revisionists alike for racially or politically motivated reasons (R. Gregory 1993, 4). However, the massive out-migration of Indians from East and Central Africa since 1970 has inevitably shifted research toward those who are "twice migrants"—African Indians in Europe or North America—and away from the Indians' histories in Africa (Bhachu 1985; Barrier and Dusenbery 1989; Helweg 1986). Still, the "degree of empirical care and historical empathy" afforded to the Asian part of the colonized middle has been underwhelming, especially considering Asians' importance to the development of capitalism or of social welfare and civil society institutions (Hopkins 1987, 136; Himbara 1994; R. Gregory 1992; Iliffe 1987). My focus on Ajit Singh helps to write Asian middle agents back into the region's historical geography.

Certainly, space was ideologically charged in the colonial city. But what about how the people being planned, the urban majority, responded to colonial planning and enframing? Frederick Cooper writes that "the continued tension over squatting and prostitution, slum clearance and police raids reminds us that an elite's idea of hegemonic urban culture exists in a close, uneasy relationship to other, quite viable patterns of social relations and values" (1983, 34).

As yet in the literature of African urbanization, there have been few attempts at problematizing the local frame of awareness informing these viable patterns of social relations and values in such a way as to create useful analytical concepts. A number of analyses of Western bias in African urban studies have effectively critiqued the adoption of inappropriate Euro-American legal structures or administrative practices in the city. Although such critiques typically focus on an insensitivity to "local experience" and "local culture," they make little attempt to get behind the actions of grassroots planners or builders, or to systematize them (Kironde 1992,

1278). Getting behind the local ways means problematizing "local experience" and "local culture."

In modern Africa, as Anthony O'Connor argues, "the physical form or spatial structure of each city is . . . being influenced to a very large extent by the planning decisions of a few foreign firms and thousands of local individuals and families, rather than by officials of any town planning department" (1983, 237). The "aggregate impact" of the planning decisions of these local individuals and families in African cities may be "less discernible" than the decisions of rulers or foreign firms. Yet it has in many cases been "ultimately more significant, and affected the lives of more people directly" (Hakim 1986, 18–19; Mabogunje 1990, 160). The decisions of ordinary, low-income citizens are the creative heart of African urban form.

In each chapter, addressing the urban majority "verandah" through examples from places like Pumwani in Nairobi, George in Lusaka, Ng'ambo in Zanzibar, and Chinsapo in Lilongwe, I argue that at least three strategic concepts repeatedly inform those decisions: highly unequal individual power, local customary practices, and religious faith. I utilize the Swahili terms *uwezo* (power), *desturi* (custom), and *imani* (faith) as labels for the three cornerstones by which the urban majorities of these cities in essence reframe the urban form. Although I argue that in an adjusted fashion these terms account for many of the informal planning systems of the marginal urban majorities in Nairobi, Lusaka, and Lilongwe, these cornerstones first emerged for me in the 114 interviews I conducted in Ng'ambo areas of Zanzibar during 1991–92. Hence it makes sense to explain them by visiting Ng'ambo (literally, the city's "Other Side") briefly at this point.

Ng'ambo residents often use the term *uwezo* to express relative power. *Uwezo* has its basis in a number of spheres of social life. Material wealth is a major sphere of *uwezo*—attainment. Land or plot control is the most tangible daily reminder to Ng'ambo residents of their general lack of *uwezo*; agitation for land rights became the central defining feature of anticolonial movements. Gradually weakened as land barons, descendants of the Zanzibar sultanate's Omani elite still retained large holdings on the city's Other Side through the 1964 Zanzibar Revolution. What is more, only tiny parcels of Ng'ambo ever were owned by its African majority prior to the unevenly implemented nationalization of land by the revolutionary government in 1964. The crucial role of fundamentally uneven and varying degrees of *uwezo*, particularly as expressed in plot access and control, appears across the urban landscapes of much of eastern and southern Africa, and in each of my other cities, as a fundamental determinant of the shape of the urban majority's lifeworld.

Much spatial planning in Ng'ambo was and continues to be based on socially accepted customs (*desturi*). Customs influenced the initial spatial organization of *mitaa* (wards) around houses sharing a communal identity, as Ng'ambo grew between 1870 and 1920 (Hino 1971, 10). Neighborhood consciousness had and has real consequences in the landscape. Pathways and passages comprising the street plan were produced primarily through it and still are vigorously maintained through daily sweeping and continual negotiation (Allen 1979, 4; 1993, 227; Horton 1984). Much of this negotiation occurs on the verandahs, known as *baraza*, of Swahili houses. As a particular example of customary manifestations in the street plan, many paths were designed to avoid *mizimu*, the haunted places of spirits (Zanzibar National Archives [hereafter ZNA] files AE 8/11, AE 8/19, AW 2/26, AW 2/100, and AW 2/113).

Work places for fisherfolk and craftspeople, shops, small markets, dancing squares, or recreational areas were common on the Other Side from an early date, but their pattern was not random (T. Wilson 1982). Many workspaces or dance areas had origins specific to the African cultures that slavery and trading brought together there; Manyema, Yao, Nyamwezi, Zanzibar islander, Comorian, and Zaramo dance squares all existed into the 1960s. The evidence of borrowing and sharing among these peoples in forging the Other Side's unique Swahili character is strong. *Mitaa* in Ng'ambo formed through the "coming together of a number of diverse groups, giving each group some participation in the affairs of the settlement" (Allen 1993, 223). Ng'ambo's melange of cultures manifested this coming together.

The implementation of *desturi* as a cornerstone of spatial planning for the urban majority appears repeatedly in African cities. Abdoulmaliq Simone notes that "in most African societies, the capacity to treat people well—your neighbors, kin . . . friends—is the organizing ethos of social networks" (1994, 19), and across urban Africa communities are "doing their best to maintain good neighborliness." That neighborliness should not be romanticized, etherealized, or left in stasis, most of all because it is itself built around the *uwezo* of particular residents, in mutually reinforcing codes. As Simone put it, "access to material well being always must go through channels, must be channeled through a nexus of social relations" and a vibrant, yet highly stratified associational life (1994, 17).

Faith-based associations commonly form the center of customary practices within local awareness and understanding in African cities. In keeping with older Swahili cities, the Other Side of Zanzibar historically had few prominent public buildings (Allen 1993, 227). The most obvious exceptions to this dearth of public structures were mosques—although not even these were grandiose. Sunni Shafi'i Islam (practiced by 95 percent of Ng'ambo's residents) is distinguishable from other schools of Islamic thought mainly by its stronger emphasis on forging the consensus of the entire mosque community in debates or discussions of social affairs (Hakim 1986; Schacht 1965; Anderson 1953). These modes of religious practice fit well with the diversity of African cultures in Ng'ambo during the creation of neighborhood consciousness. *Imani* helped Ng'ambo to be relatively free of neighborhood conflicts and ideally helped create workable solutions to physical planning problems, albeit solutions reliant on potentially coercive religious authorities. Religion provides a key connective—and coercive— power within each of the similar urban majority neighborhoods examined in the book, as in much of urban Africa.

It is through recourse to faith and customary practice, within the variegated constraints of power, that African cities are so frequently reframed by their urban majorities. Not only colonial states but the states inheriting power from them have attempted to impose some variety of enframing urban order. However, their failure to do so is only rarely some kind of victory for the people who walk in the "people's parks"; the urban majorities often remain marginalized and must struggle with conditions of overcrowding, poverty, unemployment, hunger, and endemic disease. Nevertheless, cities in Africa, as lived environments and social systems, often display an order much more akin to the lifeworld of the majority than to the enframing order of the upper verandahs in those "Houses of Wonder."

Conclusion

Colonial cities have long been a subject for geographic research. Recent work has stressed the importance of geography and space to the establishment of a framework of understanding and controlling colonies and colonial subjects. In this book, I use Timothy Mitchell's analytical construct of enframing, and three of its central strategies, to draw attention to the spatial tactics of British colonial rule in building programs. I link these to the deeply flawed territorial tactics of both colonial and postcolonial states in

Africa. I trace the operation, impact, and responses to enframing on three different metaphorical verandahs of power: the colonial elite, the colonized middle, and the urban majority.

The colonial legacy in Africa's geography continues to expand as an important academic theme, and many phenomena remind us of just how long-lived, and how spatial, the legacy of colonialism is. Urban planning is one of those phenomena. The creators of urban spatial plans under British colonialism and under its successor states in Africa conceived of their plans as a means of generating consent from, and "goodwill" among, the governed, as well as of articulating their "rule." They failed from the outset to achieve these goals largely because of contradictions within the aims of the states their plans served, and because they could not "secure the collaboration and goodwill of the colonial [or postcolonial] peoples themselves" (Jones 1946). Instead, African urban majorities commonly have reframed colonial cities within cornerstones of circumscribed power, coercive faith, and customary practices.

Chapter Two

The Interstitiality of Colonial Lives

> "Our position in East Africa is most uncertain and anything can happen at any time, and therefore we remain ever-ready for all times. With the political storm in a teacup the position of a foreign civil servant is ever drastic. . . . I take life as a big battle and to win it. . . . requires a courageous soul and a great perseverance."
> —Ajit Singh Hoogan to Eric Dutton; Singh papers, Major Dutton file, 1962

In this chapter, I introduce the individuals whose experiences, perspectives, and interrelationships are explored along with the narrative of planning and development in the four cities. The first section focuses on how my representative of British colonial power, Eric Dutton, speaks for at least a good part of what it meant to be on the metaphorical verandah of the colonial elite. The second section introduces Ajit Singh Hoogan as a character of the colonized middle verandah and assesses his position in the colony of Zanzibar relative to Asian and other intermediate positionalities in the four cities. The third section begins with Juma Maalim Kombo as a representative of the urban majority verandah, but here I expand outward to a biography of Juma's place, that part of Zanzibar city known as Ng'ambo, the Other Side. This third section is an introduction to the experiences and ideas of Ng'ambo residents as representative of the similar urban majorities of the other cities.

Eric Dutton and the Colonial Elite

Eric Dutton was not really a glory-bound exploration geographer "whose adventures are ripe for biographical treatment" (Carter 1988, 83). Indeed, at first glance, Dutton is rather more like the "marginal men" that John Mc-Cracken (1989, 538) uses to "gain some insight into the shifting character of colonial relationships" in British Africa. Between 1918 and 1952, Dutton served in five African colonies (today's Lesotho, Uganda, Kenya, Zambia, and Zanzibar) as a clerk, private secretary, assistant chief secretary, and chief secretary. He wrote four books with geographical themes (Dutton 1925, 1929, 1935, and 1944a), but only one (Dutton 1929) enjoyed much popularity. He therefore remained, in his own words, "in the shadow of power" (Dutton 1983, 104). Yet in that shadow, Dutton "gave a gentle shove" to "the wheels of government" and to colonial efforts to remake African urban landscapes (Huxley 1983, ix).

Throughout his career, Dutton corresponded intimately with Britain's most powerful colonial administrators and analysts of African affairs, in friendships that literally helped articulate colonialism. This group included Herbert Baker, Cecil Rhodes's architect, and Robert Coryndon, who had been Rhodes's private secretary and went on to serve as a governor in four colonies. Dutton's lifelong friend, the widely known Kenya settler and writer Elspeth Huxley, wrote the introduction to his memoirs, and her parents lived quite close to him in his retirement in Portugal (Huxley 1983). The writer Hilaire Belloc wrote the introduction to Dutton's one major work, *Kenya Mountain* (Belloc 1929). Although Dutton called himself a "Conservative Progressive," he corresponded regularly and amicably with Arthur Creech Jones, Britain's secretary of state for the colonies under the Labour Party in the 1940s and 1950s (Jones Papers). Frederick Lugard, often considered the creator of indirect rule, relied on Dutton for intellectual critiques and field reports on colonialism during their two decades of correspondence (Lugard Papers). Dutton and Joseph Oldham, head of the International Missionary Council and cofounder of the International Institute of African Languages and Cultures, corresponded so feverishly and at such length that, said Dutton, "they might almost be love letters, I read them so many times" (Oldham Papers, Box 6, 1929). For his part, Oldham replied: "I am to blame for not having discovered sooner that I was enjoying the friendship of so great a master of English style" (Oldham Papers, Box 6, 1930).

Through his connections with this intellectual elite and his love of architecture, rather than through high position or formal training, Dutton became an influential urban planner and power broker wherever he went. His correspondences and actions give evidence of a pervasive conceptualization of British colonialism in Africa by its functionaries and intellectuals as a highly geographical project of consensual persuasion paired with domi-

Fig. 1. Eric Dutton in Zanzibar, 1946. From Papers of Ajit Singh Hoogan. Courtesy of Parmukh Singh Hoogan, MP.

native force—in Dutton's terms (from the quotation beginning this book's preface), *goodwill* and *rule.* This "cultivation of public opinion on the spot" was, as Dutton wrote to Oldham, to be built with "concrete and bricks." In later chapters I demonstrate that the urban development projects with which Dutton was associated in Nairobi, Lusaka, and Zanzibar were in Mitchell's terms (1988), projects of enframing, but ones meant to "win the hearts and minds" of Africans (Carruthers 1995, 12). Geographical space became the physical language of both control and legitimation, most forthrightly in urban areas and most cogently later in the colonial period.

Dutton's story provides an opportunity for seeing commonalties of urban planning and the exercise of power across British colonial Africa while at the same time assessing the importance of local differences between colonies. Although a form of indirect rule operated in all the territories in which he served, substantial differences existed among them. For instance, Kenya in the 1920s was one of the centers of contention in the British Empire, pitting those aiming to make it an elite white settler colony against those favoring the introduction of greater rights and powers for Africans. Dutton lived for the role of a tinkerer between these two camps. Northern Rhodesia functioned as a copper-mining colony where Africans comprised a labor reserve army, but within the idea of a future settler colony. In the 1930s, its new capital, Lusaka, was built in the rural, sparsely populated midsection of the territory. It was planned as a city by, of, and for the intended settler populace, with Dutton as its overconfident chief booster. By contrast, the project Dutton led in Zanzibar after World War II took place in a densely populated, closely built-up city (Sheriff and Ferguson 1991).

Dutton's career is also suggestive of what kept "the machinery from working properly" as he himself put it, and kept most—but not all—of the empire's subjects from believing, from what they saw with their own eyes, that the British were "there to help." Hence, attention to his work highlights the ambivalence and imperfection in urban planning that both largely prohibited the achievement of enframing and persisted in the postcolonial societies, physically and socially. The ambiguous and contradictory tasks assigned to colonial states that Dutton served by devising a "perfect" system of control—accumulation, legitimation, and domination—also remained behind after colonialism ended.

Dutton's early life and young adulthood clearly engendered both his skill with words and his indefatigable character. He was born in 1895 in Lothersdale on the moors of Yorkshire, the eighth of nine children in a deeply religious, middle-class parson's family. When Dutton was sixteen, his father passed away, leaving the family in a financially precarious position. Still, Dutton attended Hurstpierpoint College Officers Training Corps and, briefly, Keble College in Oxford, under the tutelage of A. S. Owen. Like his four brothers, Dutton aspired to a career in the civil service after a stint in the military. Dutton's parents, and particularly his mother, nurtured what Jonathan Smith (1996) identifies as "gentlemanly" English qualities in all five sons and stressed to all the children the importance of status, appearance, character, bearing, and education far in excess of interest in finance or wealth. It was, by all appearances, a very male-dominated family, at least until his father's passing: in all of Dutton's available writings, including books and letters, there is only one mention of one sister, and that for having introduced him to Gilbert and Sullivan (Dutton 1944a, 277). Still, his was a relatively broad-minded masculinity. Dutton developed an abiding love of English literature (particularly Dickens and George Eliot), Greek and Roman imperial history, natural science, geography, and the propriety of dress codes, becoming a "master of English style" in more ways than one.

World War I ended Dutton's formal education before graduation and nearly ended his life. Dutton served as a major in the West Yorkshire Regiment sent in with the New Army to the Gallipoli Peninsula in early August 1915 (Steel and Hart 1994, 247–98). He suffered crippling shrapnel and bullet injuries and compound fractures in both legs near Suvla on September 21, 1915, a month after most of the horrific fighting had ended and after most of his regiment's other officers had been killed (Walker 1985, 25–30). Operated on more than a dozen times over the next seven years, he experienced acute neuralgic pains in both legs and in the spine for the rest of his life (Coryndon Papers 1918; Dutton 1983; Singh Papers). After repeated surgery, hospitalization, and rehabilitation, Dutton gained the ability to walk with crutches. He remained on crutches, in padded iron leg braces, or even in a chair for most of his career.

Dutton rarely walked without a cane or braces even on good days. During bad days during his colonial service, he often had to be transported in a carrying chair (in Swahili, *machila*) by African porters. He found this necessity quite humiliating, a very different twist on imagery that shows white colonialists being carried by African porters to demonstrate colonial power (see the cover of Godlewska and Smith 1994). For Dutton, such porterage meant only vulnerability. He fought any impression of incapacity whenever he encountered it. Incredibly, he led several expeditions on Mount Kenya in the 1920s, very nearly becoming the second European expedition leader to reach the summit (in the footsteps of the first, the geographer Halford Mackinder, in 1899), only to be carried back down in a makeshift *machila* (Dutton 1929). His model of the ideal colonial officer was someone who was energetic and, above all, present in the lives of those he served and ruled (Dutton 1944a). This meant he had to be exceedingly mobile to be good at what he did. For Dutton, this proved the greatest frustration of his career: "My infirmity resulted in there being yawning gaps in my knowledge" of colonial development programs, political intrigue, and popular attitudes (Dutton 1983, 85). It is my contention that his infirmity and the bitterness that came with it was a crucial factor in his reputation for being "damned difficult" to his superiors and underlings throughout his career (Dutton 1983, 126). Yet it also helped to make him more empathetic than most in the male elite toward those he viewed as powerless or in need, on lower verandahs of power.

Dutton was the intellectual stepchild of a generation of "muscular Christian" men (Bale and Sang 1996) and "soldier heroes" of adventure (Dawson 1994) who had established the structures and codes through which Britain attempted to control its African territories. He went to extraordinary lengths to prove his "vigor" and his muscularity in spite of the agony of his shattered legs. He knew he would never be like his acknowledged heroes, Governor Robert Coryndon and the adventurous district officer of Kenya's Northern Frontier, A. T. Miles, the kind of men who decorated a colony's government house with taxidermic evidence of their "gusto" (Huxley 1983; Dutton 1944a). Yet he doggedly pursued acceptance into the colonial community's masculine pantheon. In the same manner, while Dutton mentored some members of the African communities where he served and gained the admiration of others, he never shook the racial dogma of these muscular Christian mentors, either.

This exasperating and complex man is thus not only quite literally well situated to help narrate the development of enframing tactics in colonial Nairobi, Lusaka, and Zanzibar. By his contradictory combination of chilling meanness and yet charming compassion he helps unsettle any easy categorization of colonial elites as merely dominant and bloodless, breathing life into abstract ideas such as that of simultaneously centralized and fragmented colonial states.

Ajit Singh and the Colonized Middle

By the time of Ajit Singh's arrival in Zanzibar in 1937, the Indian presence was substantial in political-economic terms. The British had declared a protectorate over the Omani Sultanate of Zanzibar in 1890, formalizing a controlling influence in local affairs that had been expanding from the 1840s onward in this center originally built on the trade in slaves, cloves, and ivory. Britain's initial commercial and strategic interests in the islands waned with the growth in importance of its other East African colonies. The protectorate remained a valued possession nonetheless—at the very least for symbolic reasons, evocative as it was of the beginnings of Britain's geographical projects in eastern and central Africa. The ease of transport between the western provinces of British India and the East African coast, coupled with the promise of economic opportunity that East Africa offered to enterprising Indians, led to a steady rise in the Indian population of Zanzibar in concert with the rise of British control. This was a migration stream that did not peak until the 1940s (Sheriff 1987; Sheriff and Ferguson 1991).

Indians constituted an important component of urban colonial Zanzibar. Zanzibar's 1948 census estimated that while Indians accounted for only 5.8 percent of the population of the protectorate as a whole, almost 85 percent of those Indians lived in Zanzibar city, where they accounted for more than 25 percent of its residents. Moreover, 95 percent of the urban Indian population lived in the city's Stone Town section, which was its commercial and governmental center, underscoring the key role that Indians played in the financial life of the protectorate (Zanzibar Protectorate 1962). The proportion and position of colonial Zanzibar's Indians were very similar to those pertaining in most of the British colonies of eastern and southern Africa, where by the 1940s these generally urban Indian communities played vital mid-level roles in colonial economies and bureaucracies.

However, the roles of wealthy Indian merchants, landlords, or financiers in these colonies are far better known than those of the middle-class Indian civil servants like Ajit Singh, or even Indian peasants or Indian working poor. More than half the Indian population in Zanzibar, for instance, belonged in what was termed the "middle class," and 35 percent were placed in the "lower middle" or "lower" class by the 1948 social survey (Zanzibar Protectorate 1962; de Saissy 1979; Lofchie 1965). Many Muslims, Hindus, and, in a few cases, Christians and Sikhs of Indian origin labored right alongside the town's majority of working poor. Still others served the protectorate directly in various low- and mid-level capacities (for example, as clerks, surveyors, accountants, carpenters, and gardeners) from its inception until independence in 1963. The Indian middle and lower classes formed similar majorities within small but vital urban Indian populations across the region.

In a few ways, Ajit Singh, a Sikh who lived in the overwhelmingly African section of Zanzibar city known as Ng'ambo, is atypical of the experience of the Indian civil servant in that protectorate or in any other eastern or southern African British colony. Fully 98 percent of all Zanzibari Indians in the colonial era were Muslim or Hindu, as were most migrants to Africa from the subcontinent of India. Most of Zanzibar's Indians lived in Stone Town, and Indian communities generally in British Africa did not congregate—indeed, often were not allowed to congregate—in African residential areas. Zanzibar never has had more than a handful of Sikh families (Zanzibar Protectorate 1962). While Sikhs were much more significant in number in Kenya, Uganda, and Tanganyika, their populations everywhere in British Africa were much smaller than those of Indian Muslims and Hindus.

Yet in most other ways, Ajit Singh's career embodies the issues and challenges faced by those who were both "insiders and outsiders" to the colonial regimes of the region (Freund 1995)—those who were, metaphorically speaking, standing rather tenuously on the second verandahs. Even the path of family ties and opportunity seeking that led him to East Africa is a story reflected in the lives of a large number of Indians who came to eastern and southern Africa in great numbers between 1885 and 1945 as free migrants (R. Gregory 1993).

By the time of his appointment in the civil service of the Zanzibar Protectorate, Ajit Singh was part of "a growing number of Indians" all around the empire "who were enthusiastic disseminators" of Western ideas (Arnold 1994, 135). He honed his craft under Dutton's tutelage, thereby solidifying his functionary engagement with colonialism's intellectual elite. Through his link with Dutton, Singh came to embrace many of colonialism's architectural and intellectual ideas and forms.

Fig. 2. Ajit Singh in Malawi, 1967. From Papers of Ajit Singh Hoogan. Courtesy of Parmukh Singh Hoogan, MP.

However influential Western ideas may have been on Ajit Singh's development as an architect, though, his earliest environment for the creation of artistic sensibilities was far from fully Westernized. He was born in 1910 in Ferozepore to a family of modest means. He earned his first degree at Khalsa College in Amritsar in 1932. Although he studied math and engineering, he found a second home from 1930 to 1932 at the Indian Arts Institute, subsequently renamed the Thakar Singh School of Art for its founder (S. Singh, n.d.). Ajit developed deep friendships and correspondences with Punjabi artists like Thakar Singh and his associates, Sohan Singh and Shamseer Singh, whose works still adorn his former home in Zanzibar. Through them, he came in contact with a world of Indian artists and intellectuals, including the Nobel Prize-winning Bengali poet Rabindranath Tagore. During his fifty years in Africa, Ajit would try to replicate in his own home the cosmopolitan, diverse, and open-minded intellectual milieu to which Thakar Singh and his colleagues introduced him. This meant drawing on the arts and crafts traditions of Punjab, the Swahili coast, and the African mainland, as well as the West, by both appropriating elements of those traditions and maintaining friendships with people who practiced them.

Ajit's first career in India, in photography and film, foundered in the mid-1930s. In 1936, when Ajit's younger sister married a Sikh mechanic who had migrated to Zanzibar, the new husband invited Ajit to come and work with him, and he agreed. He was not there long before happenstance swept him into the colonial service, when his artistic abilities gained the attention of a mechanical superintendent, Reginald Wheatley, who promptly made Ajit the draftsman in a Public Works Department short on skilled labor. Even though Ajit was not formally appointed as the protectorate's architectural superintendent until 1951, he served as the de facto chief of building design after 1941, since Zanzibar had no official architect during that time. His real training was almost entirely on the job, particularly after Dutton came to the islands as chief secretary in 1942. Dutton gave Ajit wide latitude in building design, helping him to continue as a force in shaping Zanzibari building projects well after his mentor's 1952 departure.

The relationship between Dutton and Singh encapsulated something of what Ann Stoler and Fred Cooper (1997, 7) mean by "the interstitiality of colonial lives." Dutton is the only European for whom Ajit created a separate file in his meticulous archive. The two were close friends from 1942 until the early 1970s. Dutton admired Ajit for being "wholeheartedly devoted to his work," while Ajit found Dutton a "wise and patient" friend. Dutton long recalled the day when Ajit dressed him as a Sikh and sent him out on the town, where he apparently went unnoticed (Singh Papers). The two shared many traits. They also shared an immense respect for the indigenous building and design styles of Africa, Indo-Saracenic styles, and the monumental architecture of Herbert Baker. Ajit, however, had the advantage of being a truly fine draftsman and of being steeped in a Punjabi art and design background. The results for architecture in Zanzibar (and later in Malawi) were surprising and subtle buildings with a resilient capacity for blending in well with the host culture's cityscapes.

The walls in Ajit Singh's family room in Zanzibar are still covered with his artwork. The first time I sat in this room, in 1991, I noticed a careful portrait (done from a photograph) of Eric Dutton. Dutton had signed the portrait, "To the Clever Artist." Next to Dutton's portrait was a large blank square where a picture had recently been removed. "That was where we had his portrait of Banda," Ajit's grandson explained. "We just presented it to him as a gift during his state visit." Hastings Kamuzu Banda's final state visit to Tanzania as life president of Malawi the week before had included an awkward stop in Zanzibar, where, after receiving Ajit's portrait with a good grace, he had told the crowd how much at home he felt there. "After all," the aged doctor said in pointed reference to the uncomfortable past of slavery and contract labor, "most of you came from Malawi."

Out in the hallway of the home, Ajit's grandchildren have another portrait more prominently displayed. This is Ajit's portrait of Abeid Amani Karume, revolutionary Zanzibar's first president and the father of its current one. Artistically, it is not as accomplished as his portrait of Dutton (since Banda took his portrait home to Malawi, I've never seen it). Yet the choice of a subject was and is one of the wisest in Ajit's artistic career. Indeed, the portraiture in the Singh house is symptomatic of the juggling act those of the colonized middle—and especially Asians—had to play, and continue to play, politically. One of Ajit's Punjabi friends in Lilongwe explained how dumbstruck he became when actually granted the opportunity to vote in Malawi's 1994 election, an opportunity Ajit himself never took. "I spread it around, voted for someone from each party for something," he said. This man's business displayed a photograph of Bakili Muluzi, the president who won that election. His home contained a portrait of Banda, the one who lost it.

Ajit Singh's life and work in colonial and postcolonial Zanzibar and in postcolonial Malawi provide an appreciation from the middle level of several variations on enframing tactics in urban Africa. He regularly cozied up to colonial and postcolonial elites. Yet he consistently chose to live amongst, work with, and associate with the African urban majority residents in both cities. This very personal in-betweenness makes of him a vivid reminder of what ambivalent mid-level subject positions meant, and continue to mean, in urban Africa.

Bwana Juma and the Urban Majorities

Juma Maalim Kombo was born in 1906 in the *shamba* (farmland or countryside) near Kiembe Samaki, just outside Zanzibar city. As a teenager in 1921, he moved with his family to the Kikwajuni section of the city, where he lived until his death in 1993. His connection with the sea began at age eight, when he started fishing. By the 1990s, Juma was the last living member of the crew of Africans who had rowed the royal yacht of the Omani Sultan of Zanzibar in the 1910s. He also worked as a caddie for the European Golf Club, which was at that time adjacent to Kikwajuni in Mnazi Mmoja Park, but Bwana Juma worked at the port or on the seas for most of his nearly nine decades. For ten of those years, he worked for the store ship of the Cable and Wireless Company placing cables in the Indian Ocean. For a time, his bunkmate on that ship was a brash young tough named

Abeid Amani Karume, later the leader of revolutionary Zanzibar, from just up the road in Miembeni (Usi 1966). They remained friends until Karume's assassination in 1972.

Conscripted into military service in World War II, Bwana Juma was one of thousands of Africans who helped build the Burma Road in the war against the Japanese. Although he was not injured in the conflict, Juma held other scars close to his heart, from the hard labor, the diseases, the humiliation at the hands of British officers. He remembered when Princess Margaret visited Zanzibar in 1956. Before an assembly of Zanzibari war veterans she planted a plaque in front of a beautiful peltophorum tree at the Zanzibar Archives building designed by Ajit Singh. "She thanked us. The Princess thanked us, that's it [*basi*]. I thought we would at least get a medal or a present. But instead she said thank you, *basi*."

Jobless on his return from the war, Juma was one of the veterans rounded up on Eric Dutton's initiative to help Reginald Wheatley, by then promoted to supervisor of native housing, in the heavy tasks of the postwar reconstruction of the city. After going through the training at Wheatley's makeshift trade school for construction skills, Juma resigned and again went looking for work at the port. Eventually, he became a ship pilot in the port itself, working at that post for more than twenty years. In his sixties, Juma stepped down as his eyesight began to fade. His last eighteen years were spent as a customs inspector, working shorter and shorter hours as he got more infirm.

Juma had to move around to various parts of the ward of Kikwajuni over the years, mostly renting rooms. When we first met, he and his wife of forty years were renting a room in a three-room house, sharing the place with two younger households—a divorced man and his son in one room, and a divorced woman and her daughter in another. One of his chief goals was maintaining the mobility to pray five times daily in Mskiti Duara, the Circle Mosque, in the center of Kikwajuni. He did so until the end, all the time with an ear on the lively debates on a multitude of topics always taking place on his *baraza* (verandah). Juma did not debate matters of religion— they were beyond debate to him. He would break into English—he was fond of doing so with young people around—to remind me that the very word Islam means "submit to God."

Politics was one of Juma's abiding passions. He was a strong supporter of Zanzibar's ruling Chama cha Mapinduzi (CCM, or Revolutionary Party). He had been active in the neighborhood political organization of the Afro-Shirazi Party (ASP), Abeid Amani Karume's political movement that merged with the mainland's Tanganyika African National Union in 1977 to form the CCM. Even if Juma's rhetorical swords were sharpened by the postcolonial "struggle for ideological hegemony" waged by the ASP/CCM against its opponents (Shivji 1991, 67–85), his vision of colonial rule and the Omani sultanate it protected was personal, deeply felt, and not flashy ideological armor. Zanzibar, even today when it is a city with more than 200,000 residents, can be a very small town: people know each other, from the top of the power structure to the bottom. Bwana Juma knew the people who ran the colonial state. He knew people who worked for the sultan's household, and many of his "middle-class" neighbors (like Ajit Singh) worked for the regime as something more than coolies or gardeners: they were teachers, town planners, agricultural extension workers, or architects. Juma called Ajit Singh a man of "many jests" (*masihara mengi*), and he remembered Ajit especially on the day they opened Raha Leo, the Civic Center for Ng'ambo that Ajit had played a key role in designing. This state was not a distant or arbitrary power, but a "diverse and ambiguous collection of parts. . . . partially integrated and partially in conflict with each other," one that unsuccessfully "mediated" the social relations of Zanzibaris in the interest of its own legitimation (Berman 1984, 7–23).

When Juma talked about colonialism or the sultanate, he told stories about people, like Eric Dutton, or Reginald Wheatley. "If you wanted a driver's license you went for a test drive with Mr. Wheatley. Oh, he was something. He used to recruit people during the driver's test to play for his [football] team, PWD [Public Works Department]." One day in the 1940s, Juma had to go to Dutton's office in the House of Wonders, to help a colored South African woman. The woman was the wife of one of Juma's bunkmates, but his friend had left her when he went out to sea:

> You know, he was my mate, so it was my responsibility to look out for her, make sure she had a place to stay, food, and so forth. Well, one day she realized her husband wasn't coming back, and she told me she wanted to go back to Cape Town. She said, "Take me to the chief secretary," because, you know, the British flag had status in her country like in ours. Well, we went to his office. There I was, me, Chickie-Boy [his nickname], saying *"Hodi!"* [the announcement of arrival in Kiswahili, meaning roughly, "Anyone home?"] This voice—and. . . . his voice was deep in the throat and surprising—said, *"Karibu"* [welcome]. He was so polite to her. He got

out the shipping schedule for the next ship to South Africa. "You sit tight and when the time comes, come right to me so I can get you your ticket," he said. . . . Oh, that one, Dutton, very clever. An expert with words. But if you were with him [literally, "if you were his,"] he did right by you.

Juma's life story and his very personalized perspective on colonialism are in many ways quite typical of Zanzibar's older residents. The cornerstones of Juma's experience of living in Ng'ambo were *uwezo, desturi,* and *imani*—his relative lack of power in the urban political economy, the customary bonds he developed and reinforced with neighbors, and his Islamic beliefs that helped shape how he felt space ought to be created and enlivened in the city.

There is no one single voice to speak for the urban majorities of four rather different cities. But figuratively, voices like Juma's reverberate in my own research, experience, and interviews in places like Pumwani, George, or Chinsapo, just some of the "squatter" and "traditional housing" areas of Nairobi, Lusaka, and Lilongwe where the urban majorities reside. These commonalties lead me to suggest that Ng'ambo is in some ways the historic forerunner and archetype for the "other sides" of many cities that developed later under British colonialism in eastern and southern Africa.

Like the other urban majority areas I will examine in the book, these older parts of Ng'ambo as a whole experience a high renter population, severe overcrowding, crushing poverty, unemployment and underemployment, a poor service infrastructure, and greater incidences of endemic, epidemic, and now pandemic disease. However, Zanzibar's Other Side is several decades older than the urban majority areas of the other cities.

Mitaa in Ng'ambo began to be settled in the 1850s, largely by African and Swahili slaves, servants, and peasants (Myers 1995, 30–45; Guillain 1856). In most cases, Ng'ambo's earliest residents settled on lands of their owners, employers, or patrons. The earliest settlers included large numbers of Manyema, Yao, Nyamwezi, Gogo, and Zaramo mainlanders, as well as Zanzibar islanders (Swahili peoples). This agglomeration of cultures included both peasants, like Bwana Juma, and slaves.

Most land on the Other Side prior to its urbanization belonged to the Omani royal clan, to its allies and rivals, or to Indian merchants (ZNA, AE 8/10, HD 3/5, and HD 6/155; Myers 1995). During Ng'ambo's first seventy years of settlement (c. 1850–1920), though, residents were "allowed to do just as they liked" in most matters of architecture, design, and develop-

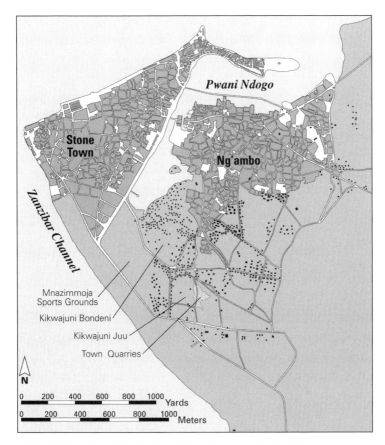

Fig. 3. Zanzibar City in the 1890s. Courtesy of the Kansas
Cartographic Services Office, Geography Department,
University of Kansas.

ment (Christie 1876, 281). The first Omani sultans in Zanzibar left matters
in the hands of trusted overseers and slaves or locally chosen imams of the
Other Side's mosques (ZNA, HD 6/155). British colonial rule, which began
formally in 1890, involved only gradual intervention into old Ng'ambo's
spatial form until Dutton's reconstruction efforts in the 1940s and 1950s
(Andriananjanirana-Ruphin 1995). Oskar Baumann (1897) called old
Ng'ambo an "attractive part of the city," and an early guidebook called it
"a study in African town architecture unequaled by anything to be seen" in
East Africa (Zanzibar Protectorate 1912, 18).

By "do[ing] as they liked" (Christie 1876, 281), Ng'ambo residents articulated and manifested their own system of planning and design. This highly informal and unregulated system was based around the concepts I articulated in chapter 1: unevenly distributed individual power (*uwezo*), customs (*desturi*) that often evolved to meet contemporary demands, and strong faith (*imani*). In the fifty-eight years since Eric Dutton began his program of reconstruction with new roads that sliced through their *mitaa*, ordinary residents of Ng'ambo like Bwana Juma have struggled against the draconian tendencies of those who have ruled and attempted to enframe them, negotiating with those rulers as they sought to win consent among the governed. The residents' struggles and their reframing of city life run parallel to planning narratives in similar neighborhoods in Nairobi, Lusaka, and Lilongwe, as we will see.

Conclusion

I have argued in this chapter for the importance of grounding the study of colonial urban planning in the actual experiences of people at three levels of analysis. These levels consist of the colonial elite, the colonized middle, and the urban majority. I utilize the careers and life stories of Eric Dutton and Ajit Singh to personify the first two of these levels. At the level of the local community, I have expanded the idea of the larger "other sides" of the cities, albeit beginning here with Juma Maalim Kombo and Ng'ambo. Only in hearing the panoply of perspectives and in analyzing their views can we come to understand the extent to which colonial or postcolonial enframing has (or has not) become infused into community life and memory.

Zanzibar is a microcosm of many of academia's and the world's most pressing cultural concerns. But this is not the only place I am examining. Just as my narrative utilizes different levels in biographical analysis, so too are different places important to it. For this reason, in chapters 3 and 4, I turn the analysis to the development of first Nairobi and then Lusaka as colonial cities. In each of these chapters, I seek to situate the development of these cities within the wider colonial space that they were meant to serve as capitals and to interrogate the development of African space in these capitals.

Chapter Three

Colonial Nairobi

> "Colonial towns have ever been fated to a ramshackle adolescence. . . .
> A town plan ambitious enough to turn Nairobi into a thing of beauty
> has been slowly worked out, and much has already been done. But
> until that plan has borne fruit Nairobi must remain what she was then,
> a slatternly creature, unfit to queen it over so lovely a country."
>
> —Dutton 1929

Introduction

Even though Eric Dutton's main legacies in urban design lie in Lusaka and Zanzibar, his long-held beliefs in colonialism's urban mission first developed in Kenya. The later enframing urban projects in Northern Rhodesia and Zanzibar with which Dutton is most associated take their cues from the colonial conceptions of space and power that Dutton witnessed and to a limited extent participated in constructing in Kenya in the early part of his career. Also, the responses of Africans to the enframing of Nairobi offer a suggestion of what was to come in those other projects, as we see the emergence of a different urban order than that sought by the colonial regime in the first of its planned African native locations for the city.

If we consider how significant a city Nairobi has become, it is perhaps surprising to recall that Kenya had actually been incorporated into the British Empire more or less as an afterthought. The space between Uganda and a small British zone of control along the East African coast had been claimed by the Imperial British East Africa Company (IBEAC) in 1886, but the company could conceive of no viable means of exploiting it. This area's economic future was taken to be "dismal and hopeless" (Wolff 1974, 47). Only 20 percent of its land surface was arable, it had no known mineral deposits, and its people appeared hostile to the IBEAC. The IBEAC collapsed and sold its interests to the Crown in 1895. The only use for this land then, from the British perspective, appeared to be as a railroad bed to Uganda (over which the IBEAC's lead negotiator and military commander, Dutton's future friend Frederick Lugard, had secured British protectorate status in 1893).

Colonial administrators planned to develop a settler agricultural economy in the East Africa Protectorate (renamed Kenya Colony only in 1920) to defray the costs of the Uganda railway and a road running roughly parallel to it. After much debate, the local colonial leadership promoted the creation of a "white man's country" in the Kenya Highlands. This phrase, attributed variously to Charles Eliot or Harry Johnston, the protectorate's governors at the turn of the century, was later used by Dutton's confidant Elspeth Huxley as the title of her well-known apologist book for colonialism in Kenya. The qualities of the Highlands' soils were at the root of their usurpation, but the aesthetic qualities of the landscape and its apparent appeal to English sensibilities were not far behind. Early colonial administrators proclaimed that vast tracts in the Highlands and the Rift Valley were "empty," though this emptiness of the bush was a comfortable illusion based on ignorance of African land practices and political geography in the area (Mackenzie 1998).

The East Africa Protectorate's leaders had decided early on to replace the Imperial British East Africa Company's seat of European administration, the Indian Ocean port of Mombasa, with a new capital city. This new capital, roughly halfway up the railway line to Uganda, eventually became Nairobi. It started as a mere campsite, given the name Caldbeck, but by the time the railway reached Kisumu on Lake Victoria in 1901, most administrative functions in the protectorate had been transferred there (Obudho 1981; Morgan 1967). Nairobi grew to become what is often seen as a quintessential example of a British colonial city in Africa (Brunn and Williams 1993). Earlier characterizations of Nairobi as one of the "key taproots of colonial exploitation" (Soja and Weaver 1976, 252) largely withstand the test of historical reflection. Its geographical situation had much to do with the development of Kenya's Highlands as a white settler agricultural zone, and its internal spatial form demonstrated the intentions of its builders that it be a segmented city where European settler interests came first. It was a city where the colonial elite and settler interests made defining "inside" and "outside" for that segmentation a central tenet of planning, legal structures, and politics. The third component of Nairobi's enframing entailed construction of central sites of observation and surveillance, epitomized in the

1920s by a new Government House on Nairobi Hill, designed by Herbert Baker.

Some of the enframing tactics of urban control in Nairobi were well in place by Dutton's arrival in 1922. However, his period of service in Kenya (1922–30) offers us a valuable opportunity to examine the formalization of this version of enframing through the words and experiences of that frame's architects.

Compartmentalizing Nairobi

In the 1920s, Kenya Colony became a flashpoint for Britain, in searching analyses and debates over questions of race, colonial authority, and imperialist objectives; it was the "acid test of Empire" for a few short years (Youe 1986). In this acid test, the main matter for debate—a multiyear debate in the British parliament in the 1920s—concerned what kind of colony Kenya ought to become. For many participants in this debate, the subject of Kenya brought up the deepest questions concerning the purposes British colonialism served in Africa.

The debate catapulted to a high level of attention in the empire with the duke of Devonshire's 1923 White Paper on the Kenya Colony. The 1923 White Paper actually declared "African paramountcy" the prevailing policy of governance in Kenya (Kamoche 1981; Parkinson 1947). This meant that African interests were taken to be the paramount purpose of the colony, which would thus continue to be ruled through a Colonial Office administration (as a trusteeship for Africans) rather than through white settler self-governance. The Devonshire White Paper, on paper at least, also declared an end to racial segregation of Asians and Europeans in Nairobi.

Particularly via debates over land control and the very landscape itself, geographical space was a prominent element in this crucial window of time in Kenya (Mackenzie 1998). The city of Nairobi was a central fulcrum on which this issue of space arose. In 1922, the colonial regime installed Pumwani, its first planned Native Location within Nairobi, with several more being built in that decade. The regime constructed many key government buildings and architectural symbols of state in Nairobi during Dutton's time there, including Baker's Government House. In 1926, the first urban plan for the city was written, and the remaining years of the decade witnessed attempts to implement it.

The enframing of Nairobi involved several substantial steps, some of which were deeply embedded in the city already by 1922. The first step of this colonial spatial order was racial compartmentalization, the formation of a segmented plan. In this plan, the best lands were reserved for whites, the worst for Africans, and a middle-value buffer zone between became Asian residential land, parkland, the Central Business District (CBD), or industrial estates (Obudho 1994, 198–212; 1997, 292–335; Kobiah 1984–85). In many ways, both for the city and for the colony at large, the first order of business in the process of compartmentalization in the 1920s was something termed the Indian Question: what to do with the colonized middle verandah.

The Indian Question

The Indian Question was, for the British administration in the 1920s, a question of whether to allow the expansion of Indian migration and how to shape it should it be permitted. The first wave of Indian migration to the East Africa Protectorate had occurred between 1890 and 1914. Most of these migrants were indentured servants, though, and less than 20 percent remained in the future Kenya Colony when their contracts ended (R. Gregory 1993, 12). After 1918, almost all migrants came of their own free will and in substantial numbers. By 1921, Kenya had twice the Indian population of Zanzibar, with 25,253 Indians listed in the census that year. Nearly 20,000 new Asian migrants arrived in Kenya during the 1920s alone, with the overwhelming majority settling in towns and Nairobi as the main recipient town (R. Gregory 1993, 12–13). Even in 1906, there were 3,582 Asians in Nairobi, then a town of only 11,000. By 1926, nearly 10,000 of the city's 30,000 residents were of South Asian origin (Kobiah 1984–85, 18).

Winston Churchill, secretary of state for the colonies in the early 1920s, appointed Robert Coryndon as Kenya's governor specifically to "solve" the Indian question. Churchill supported productive white settlement but without creating a self-governing colony; he saw the necessity of at least some Indian settlement as well, in his mind to provide middle-class merchants. Indeed, white settlers vilified Churchill as pro-Indian (E. Smith 1984).

Eric Dutton, as Governor Coryndon's private secretary, played a crucial role behind the scenes as a defender of white settler interests within the debate over the White Paper's Indian Question (as well as its African policy directives). Both before and after its publication, Coryndon used his private secretary to drum up anti-Indian sentiment in the form of letters from regional leaders decrying Indian greediness; one such was the sultan of Zanzibar, with whom Dutton would later work quite closely. When, as was his custom with Dutton, Governor Coryndon asked him to offer an analysis of how to deal with Indian demands for land in Nairobi, Dutton responded, "I believe nobody wants an Indian to come and live next to him. . . . If we can prevent an Indian from living next to us, without treating him with injustice, then we should do it" (Coryndon papers, Box 3, 1923).

The bluntly racial and spatial character of this expression of Dutton's early perspective on the Indian Question was made manifest in the broader scheme of Nairobi's space economy. Even by 1923, when Dutton scribbled this note to his boss, Indians comprised a large share of Nairobi's economically influential population. Many of the small town's shopkeepers, small-scale industry owners, railway workers, and government clerks were of South Asian origin. After the 1923 White Paper, whites initiated an exodus from areas just north of Nairobi's Central Business District that left Indians literally occupying the middle of the city. The broad northern ring around the CBD became overwhelmingly Asian, directly between the Upper Nairobi western suburbs of the white elite and the African settlements growing in the lowlands of the Nairobi River east of the city center. Indians eventually would become the main landholders in African areas of the city, too.

Despite this and other ways in which Indians acted in an ambivalent middle zone of colonial exploitation, Robert Gregory (1993, 36) is at pains to remind us of several facts. Most Indians, he writes, "did not come consciously to exploit nor were they willing . . . participants in any British imperial design. . . . On the whole the Asians were wanted in East Africa neither by the British officials, settlers, traders, and missionaries there nor by the Colonial Office in the metropolis." Dutton's sentiments in his note to Coryndon certainly evidence this view. Yet, as Dutton's later friendship with Ajit Singh in Zanzibar would prove (see chapter 5), colonialists were not averse to using Indians toward colonial ends. The strategy Dutton and Coryndon embarked upon in the early 1920s appeared to be one of mollifying settler concerns by making Indians look the guilty party. This meant balancing the contending possible directions of the colony without a decisive break from the status quo. It would be Europeans, not Indians, who really dominated the economy and power hierarchy of the colony, but with Indians as a protective buffer between whites and blacks, literally in the highly segmented form of Nairobi and figuratively in its urban functions.

African Paramountcy

George Kingoriah (1983, 252) argues that as far as Nairobi is concerned the 1923 Devonshire White Paper basically "ignored the African race except to set [for] them 'locations' in the town periphery." Really, though, the establishment of these Native Locations in the 1920s did not reflect a regime that ignored urban Africans—far from it. The 1920s saw the initial rise of *national* African anticolonial consciousness, and Nairobi was the center of its rise. Indeed, the racial compartmentalization embodied in the planned townships of the 1920s was a deliberate means of enframing that African consciousness. In the language of the time, the creation of locations belonged within the second central racial question of 1920s Kenya, the "Trusteeship" or "Paramountcy" Question.

The White Paper's declaration of African paramountcy was certainly farcical as far as Nairobi is concerned. Africans were from the beginning highly restricted in terms of their rights of residency, types of structures, and even capacity for employment in the city. Since the East Africa Protectorate had its emphasis in export enclave settler agriculture, the city received little attention and little in the way of industrial investment that might have provided for significant African employment, until at least the 1950s.

Africans were not even supposed to be in Nairobi. Frederick Cooper (1983, 7) uses an apt illustration: "In 1920, the Municipality of Nairobi declared that anyone "lodging in any verandah, outhouse or shed, or unoccupied building, or in a cart, [or] vehicle" without a visible means of support, was a vagrant, subject to prosecution. Having helped to build a society in which Africans might choose to live in an outhouse or a shed, the colonial state forbade them to do so" (see also van Zwanenberg 1977, 196).

The 1926 city plan, created by Walton Jameson, ignored the issue of African paramountcy's relevance to the city. Instead, Jameson "enforced the existing racial city structure" that "froze" Africans out of the picture (Kingoriah 1983, 252). Squatting, although illegal, represented "the only way Africans could even live in the city" (Kobiah 1984–85, 17). Even so, squatting prompted a vociferous outcry from white settlers driven by, it is often argued, "self-preservation" (E. Smith 1984, 100). Squatter settlements that developed at various times in the early colonial period were frequently simply eliminated, without any sufficient planning of a new settlement zone.

Nevertheless, the most significant experience in urban Kenya from

1922 to 1930 was unquestionably the growth of African communities in Nairobi, both in size and in political consciousness. This was the decade when Africans became the urban majority, albeit consigned to the metaphorical lower verandahs of colonial segmentation. In 1921, Nairobi had 23,000 residents, of whom more than 12,000 were Africans. By the time Eric Dutton departed, the city's population had nearly doubled, to 45,540, with 26,781 Africans comprising nearly 60 percent of the total in 1931 (E. Smith 1984, 79). Controlling growth in African urban conscious-ness went hand in hand with urban planning and political control.

Political control was intrinsic to the creation of a racially segmented plan. Earlier urban geography studies of Nairobi (e.g., Morgan 1967; Barnow et al. 1983) detach themselves from the political developments that were and are inseparable from the spatial ones on which the geographers focus. Many studies of Kenya's political development similarly ignore the spatiality of that development. But space and politics were inseparable, as Luise White's (1990) study of prostitution in colonial Nairobi makes plain. It is no accident that the creation of the first planned Native Location (Pumwani) occurred immediately following the 1921 rise of the East African Association of Harry Thuku, Kenya's first real "urban protest movement" (E. Smith 1984, 111). Thuku's determination, organizing skill, and real po-tential to develop an anticolonial alliance beyond his own Kikuyu peoples with Luo, Maasai, and even Indian residents in Nairobi terrified the colonial regime and its settler cohort (Furedi 1977, 228). Even if Thuku gathered strength from rural land issues, it was when his movement drew massive, multiracial rallies in Nairobi that the colonial regime moved in and arrested Thuku. In March 1922, twenty-five Africans were killed when government troops opened fire on a crowd demanding Thuku's release from prison, and yet the Colonial Office blamed the "Thuku affair" on "unruly elements in the town" (E. Smith 1984, 121). Scarcely three months later, the colonial regime opened its planned and controlled Native Location to those "unruly elements." The planned location system was seen as the way to differentiate between who could be inside the city and who had to remain outside it, while at the same time dictating just how someone inside it should live in it.

White City

The enframing tactic of racial segmentation, however, cannot be effectively understood without a critical examination of whiteness, too. For instance, in Kenya, the racial attitudes of those who served in the colonial state were often less clear-cut than those of the white settlers. On the surface, Dutton espoused throughout his life a "guiding principle," which he laid down explicitly long after his service in Kenya had ended, in a letter to Lugard (papers, 1941). Dutton held out for "absolute equality in the paths of knowledge and culture, [and] equal opportunity for those who strive." Behind this point a demand for prestige revolving around whiteness surfaced: "in matters social and racial a separate path, each pursuing his own inherited traditions, preserving his own race purity and race-pride; equality in things spiritual, agreed divergence in the physical and material." Carolyn Shaw (1995, 7–8) has recently picked apart white colonial society in Kenya in the interwar years for its fractures along ethnic, class, and gender lines. Shaw highlights how the theme of "white prestige," so central to Eric Dutton's worldview at the time, was an "imperative for the British middle class," rather than the all-pervasive view held to uniformly by all whites. Poorer whites threatened white privilege and prestige, and yet at the same time some of the aristocrats looked down their noses at the strivers like Dutton (Hetherington 1978; see also Stoler 1992, 319–52).

Dutton appears, from his memoir, to have stayed on the fringes of white Kenya's social scene, but he saw enough to give an appreciation of the fissures within it. He decried the "camp followers" and "night flowers" of distinguished visitors, of whom Kenya saw a great deal in the interwar years (Dutton 1983, 94–98). For their part, most of Shaw's "socialite settlers" in the city took little notice of the governor's secretary, who was after all lower than a civil servant—a financially underdressed and physically unprepossessing gofer. Many in the intelligentsia of the metropole with regard to Kenya affairs felt similarly. Margery Perham had little to say about him other than to express disdain (Perham 1970; Smith and Bull 1991). The well-known Kenya historian Reginald Coupland (1938) wrote Joseph Oldham (papers, 1929) in March of 1929: "I am reluctant to see Dutton because his talk will irritate me so much that I shall probably lose my temper. . . . His influence is, no doubt, considerable but it cannot be too deep or too lasting. People at the top are not going to commit themselves to a policy because a young private secretary upholds it." Divisions like these within the white community remind us that no completely, uniformly united elite existed to impose colonial rule from above. Contradictions and fragmentations continually manifested themselves in undoing the enframing goals of colonialism.

Eric Dutton's presence in Nairobi, his published writings about it, and his works about Kenya more broadly offer valuable opportunities to examine fissures in the colonial power structure, and to see the broader mindset behind colonial spatial planning in Nairobi and other cities on the continent.

Colonial Space in Eric Dutton's Kenya

Buried among the key themes of Eric Dutton's books one finds the single consistent policy ideal he upheld from the late 1920s until the 1950s: urban order. And unlike some of the policies Coupland had felt would be rejected if left in the hands of a private secretary, the quest for order in the sphere of urban planning brought Dutton reach and influence beyond his position. Specifically within this ideal, Dutton separated what belongs inside a city from what is, or should be, outside it. The very idea of a city, and particularly its domestic space, was, to Dutton, the centerpiece of what colonial rule should be. In addition to replacing orders without frameworks with racially segmented plans, Dutton's ideas of a city contain several other essential themes. Among these are the intrinsic nature of a separation between inside and outside at various spatial scales, the importance of highly visible central places of objectification and observation, and the role of a city not only in establishing colonial rule (domination) but in fostering goodwill (legitimation). The well-planned city was Dutton's inner diagram of what a colony ought to look like, down to the scale of individual houses. Tellingly, he cites Lord Byron in his book, *Lillibullero* (Dutton 1944a, 181): "Survey our Empire, and behold our home": homes were the very model of the imperial order in his mind.

The setting of all of Eric Dutton's actual residences in Africa was a colonial city, Frantz Fanon's "world divided into compartments" (1979, 29). In *Kenya Mountain* (1929) and *Lillibullero* (1944a), Nairobi is an image not only of what colonialism could be, but also of what it should not become. Dutton's relationship to Nairobi's urban form shows the urgency with which he sought to maintain divisions between his "prestige" and the position of Indian and African city-dwellers. On the one hand, he upheld Nairobi as a European city and dreamt of its emergence as a modern town, a city like Mitchell's colonial city that was "dependent upon maintaining the barrier that keeps the other out" (1988, 165). In *Kenya Mountain* (1929,

1–2), Dutton gives a clear picture of what he thought of "unlovely Nairobi," and of what he thought it ought to be:

> There may one day arise a citizen who will proclaim to the world his pride in Nairobi. It is possible. What is not? But in 1926 . . . it had the look of a mining camp . . . littered with refuse; the streets were cumbered with a jumble of architectural abuses. . . . The roads were execrable. It was, indeed, a very young town. . . . Colonial towns have ever been fated to a ramshackle adolescence. Maybe one day Nairobi will be laid out with tarred roads, with avenues of flowering trees, flanked by noble spaces and stately squares; a cathedral worthy of faith and country; museums and galleries of art, theaters and public offices. A town plan ambitious enough to turn Nairobi into a thing of beauty has been slowly worked out, and much has already been done. But until that plan has borne fruit Nairobi must remain what she was then, a slatternly creature, unfit to queen it over so lovely a country.

He was slightly more forgiving by the time of *Lillibullero,* and he had moved beyond a simple segmented plan. In departing the capital city on an adventure in Kenya's Northern Frontier, he admitted that he once "wrote her down as unkempt." But at least one avenue there, then known as Delemere Avenue, "was laid out with a thought or two, and some of the buildings which flank it have a pleasing design" (Dutton 1944a, 10). Still, he seemed astounded that the colonial regime thought so little about architecture and design, and their connection not simply to domination but—in his mind— to winning the Africans over with a highly gendered idea of a "queenly" city. He told Joseph Oldham of his pleasure at seeing the town-planning scheme for Nairobi, which had been a "pet project" of Governor Coryndon, get under way, because of "the necessity for cleaning up this horrible town." The Native Locations in particular made manifest the problem of "detribalized natives" (Oldham papers, February 12, 1931). "A wise governor," he wrote, would "preach the gospel of more homes, and still more homes; and he would not rest until he had seen them built and built well. I mean homes for all" (1944a, 231). This is precisely the "gospel" Dutton preached in Northern Rhodesia and Zanzibar from 1930 until 1952, and variations on this theme dominated British colonial urban policies in Africa from the 1930s through to independence.

Dutton and Coryndon: The Colonial Order

It is important to note that Eric Dutton only came to this illusive "empty land" of Kenya in 1922. Before his arrival in Kenya, he served in Basutoland (1918–19) and Uganda (1920–22). Neither colony seems to have played the formative role that Kenya played in the emergence of Dutton's spatial sense of colonialism. Yet the development of his idea of colonial space and order would never have occurred as it did without the influence upon him of the man he served first in Uganda and then in Kenya, Robert Coryndon.

Dutton's deep connections to Coryndon, whom he idolized, self-consciously placed him in the "Rhodesian" lineage. Coryndon, a veteran of the Pioneer Column by which Rhodes claimed Rhodesia, had the deepest and most profound effect on Dutton as a colonialist and as a man. There are at least seven references in Dutton's memoirs and his later letters to Joseph Oldham and Frederick Lugard in which he lovingly recalls Coryndon's main strategies of governance. Among these are Coryndon's biblically aware aphorism that "in a young country there should be faith, hope, and continuity, and the greatest of these is continuity," and his policy approach of traveling the country for six months upon appointment as governor, then writing down six things to accomplish during his tenure. Coryndon learned the value of these tactics as one of Cecil Rhodes's "twelve apostles."

Coryndon was, said Dutton (1983, 78), a "simple man with simple ideas." Dutton was a complicated man with complicated thoughts who longed for just the clarity of vision and purpose that glares out at the viewer from every photograph of Robert Coryndon. According to Dutton, Coryndon's idea of indirect rule was to "build up a more modern society on the traditions of the people" (Dutton 1983, 19). Coryndon was a masterful "handler of men" who also "understood and liked the African" (Dutton 1983, 56). Even if he understood and liked Africans, though (and that is by no means certain), he was at best ambivalent toward improving African lives. Christopher Youe says Coryndon's policies in Uganda were driven by "pragmatism, commonsense and Lancashire cotton capitalism" (1986). The hitch in this was the "shamelessly racial" ideology underpinning all his plans (Kiwanuka 1974, 318). African agriculture was often held back to placate European coffee planters, and Coryndon's distrust of Indian industrialists did much to hold back the development of milling and weaving in the territory.

Fig. 4. E. A. T. Dutton, *right,* with Palmer Kerrison, *left,* and
Governor Robert Thorne Coryndon, Nairobi, 1923. From
Coryndon's papers in MSS AFR. s. 633 Box 14/1 fol. 1, by
permission of the Bodleian Library, University of Oxford.

Coryndon influenced the development of Dutton's thinking about
colonial political economy, and also its spatiality. The issue, at least in
Uganda, was not urban space. Kampala in 1920 was a very small settlement, and even in 1948, when it was Uganda's largest town, it had a population of twenty-two thousand (Gugler 1970, 1–27)—one-third that of
Nairobi and half that of Zanzibar at that time (Hutton 1970). When
Coryndon and Dutton moved to Nairobi in 1922, urban questions became
much more central to their activities. But even in Kenya, Governor Coryndon himself more or less followed a roving capital system: he was always on
the move, mostly camping in each district for a time. He had followed a similar strategy in Basutoland, arguing that it gave him "first hand knowledge"
of the land and its people, and he could "make sure that the chiefs and people knew he was in command" (Youe 1986, 108).

For his frequently paralyzed personal secretary, Coryndon's constant
movement was exasperating, yet instructional. While everybody else on
staff walked, Dutton (1983, 3) "was carried, like a minor mandarin of the
eighth grade, in a swaying palanquin." Yet this constant motion taught
Dutton one key principle of governance during his African career, a princi-

ple broadly applicable to the operation of colonial power in urban areas: to be present in the lives of the African "subjects," because such a strategy proffered both intimacy and the appearance of control. Dutton boasted in his memoirs that "no one visited so many district officers and their outbacks in East and Central Africa as I" (1983, 6). Such tours of the roving administrator served the purpose of surveillance, and they underlined the importance of the representation of power to its actual operability. Geographically, the colonial state—territorially constituted and acting through everyday practices of territoriality—went nowhere if it didn't go everywhere (Robinson 1990).

Coryndon's death in 1924 left Dutton completely at a loss. He was disabled, broke, and out of work. After some traveling and several more rounds of surgery on his legs, he took up his new crutches, gathered his nerve, and went about convincing the newly appointed replacement for Coryndon, Edward Grigg (who was still in London), to take him on as a private secretary. Grigg grudgingly agreed to retain Dutton. The two men did not like each other, and seldom agreed with each other. In contrast with what Dutton felt about Coryndon's views, he thought the somewhat fascistic Grigg had utter disdain for local African peoples. When it came to enforcing order on Africans "there were no bouts of fantasy in Grigg's administration" (Dutton 1983, 112).

Ironically, it was during his time of service to Grigg that Dutton began to see more immediately the applications of Coryndon's ideas of colonial space to the colonial city of Nairobi, through the passage and implementation of the Jameson plan of 1926 and the completion of Government House. And it was largely about post-Coryndon Kenya that Dutton wrote in his publications and his unpublished memoir.

One Coryndon-inspired theme that we see in the two books that Dutton wrote about Kenya is that identifying colonialism as a utopian fantasy of escape. "Escape," writes Dutton, "it is a fine word. It smacks bravely of adventure and romance. It brings trooping to the mind . . . above all the great escape of all of us to the spaces of Africa"(1929, 24). This fits very well into the operation of colonial regimes in urban areas. This is Home's (1997, 4) "utopian ideology" of colonial urban planning, where "a colonist was escaping to a new society," an idealized isotropic plain on which to work the magic of modern Western aesthetics.

The second Coryndon-inspired theme in Dutton's writings about Kenya is that of making order out of the wilderness. Mitchell focuses in on the urban dimensions of this theme, as in the creation of segmented plans out of orders without frameworks. Cartography, more than any other science, served the cause of "an appearance of order" (Mitchell 1988, 163), since "putting regions on a map . . . exercised power in a pure subtle form—as the power to name, to describe, to classify" (Fabian 1986, 24). Dutton, whose mentor Coryndon had been the chief cartographer of the first Rhodesian white government, played his part, too. Mapmaking had an "overwhelming fascination" for him throughout his career, and he named many features on Mount Kenya and in Northern Kenya more generally.

In *Lillibullero* (Dutton 1944a, 93), we read a third key theme that Dutton learned under Coryndon's wing: that legitimation and domination go hand-in-hand in colonial space. He reveals that he has "for many years now . . . kept a manuscript" of what he would do if appointed governor in Kenya, inspired by Coryndon's strategy of writing down his goals: "proposals for constitutional development, the application of sound common sense (my common sense) to social services, to the schooling of colonial architecture, town planning, and local government, the creation of new forests and the maintenance of the old, the cherishing of streams, the building of dams, and many another—a prodigal accumulation of castles in Spain (Dutton 1944a, 27).

Underlying all of his thoughts about "castles in Spain" one finds a set of basic principles that he puts into the mouth of Vincent Glenday in *Lillibullero* (1944a, 33), but which clearly evokes the spirit of Robert Coryndon. "Come down to earth," said that practical man, "and see things as they are today. [Colonial Kenya] is the victim of romance. . . . Cut all that out and what is left: my job; and that is as clear as the day—*to maintain law and order, to keep the wells open, and to improve the conditions of the people*" (emphasis mine).

This answer Glenday gives is "clear as the day" and might have been written for Bruce Berman or Robert Home. Their job, as leaders of the colonial state, had three aims. One of these was domination (they maintained law and order because that was fundamental to the territoriality of state power). Domination, or its appearance, was necessitated by the second goal of accumulation (they kept the wells open to keep cheap northern feeder stock flowing to white ranches in the south). And, third, they sought legitimation (they improved the conditions of the people to get them to "see with their own eyes that we are there to help").

The Coryndon-born themes and principles found in Dutton's writings about Kenya—a sense of escape into wilderness; a drive to make order out

Fig. 5. Nairobi, 1928. From *Kenya Mountain* by Eric Dutton
(London: Jonathan Cape, 1929).

of that nature; as well as the importance of domination, legitimation, and accumulation—appear straightforwardly in his later urban-planning work in Northern Rhodesia and Zanzibar. Before he got to Lusaka, however, he also had eight years of practical experience behind the scenes administering Kenya. For instance, his time as Grigg's private secretary coincided with the completion of Herbert Baker's Government House for Nairobi, the most evocative structure for the third of Mitchell's tenets of colonial enframing, that of objectifying central spaces of surveillance.

Dutton and Baker: Spaces of Observation

If Dutton is ever noticed in accounts of Kenya in the 1920s, it is for his backroom politicking on the "Indian Question" and the "Trusteeship Question," or, for his exceptional achievements in mountaineering. For himself, his "passion" during that decade ran completely in a different direction, toward thinking about remaking Nairobi, and some of Kenya's smaller settlements, into his idea of "a thing of beauty":

> [W]hat could be more enthralling than taking a hand in the building of a young country, and in particular the practical task of building in brick and mortar? . . . When research students have come with their notebooks and well-sharpened pencils, I have noticed that their thoughts seem to revolve

around constitutions, always constitutions; and after a while they would look at me with a touch of reproof, as though I had said "For forms of government let fools contest/whate'er is best administered is best." I daresay I gave them reason. I talked as though I believed that bricks and mortar, that is to say hospitals and schools, railways and harbors, public buildings and aerodromes, were the more urgent. (Dutton 1983, 120)

In Kenya, Dutton had little of the significance in these matters of "bricks and mortar" that he came to enjoy later in Lusaka and Zanzibar. He was on hand to cut ribbons for new post offices, to help lay the new deep-water pier foundation in Mombasa, and to consult with the governors in matters of policy. It seems likely that he wrote many of Coryndon's speeches, and he probably wrote most of Grigg's: he at least compiled and edited the volume of Grigg's speeches deposited at Rhodes House Library in Oxford. It was in these speeches, as much as in his hands-on work, that Dutton may have influenced the urban form of Nairobi. There were times, with these preoccupations, when Grigg insulted him by suggesting that his abilities were "more suited to the PWD, perhaps as a Clerk of Works" (1983, 108). It was probably Herbert Baker, among others, who rescued him from such a fate.

When Baker first came to town, Dutton disapproved of his grandiose plans for Government House in Nairobi and drew up plans of his own to show the knighted architect. Baker wasted no time in declaring Dutton's version "botched up and inconvenient, skimpy and overcrowded" (1983, 109). Perhaps surprisingly, this marked the beginning of a friendship and correspondence that lasted until 1946. Part of their correspondence concerned the development of a history of colonial architecture, to be coauthored between them, but the project was cut short by Baker's death. Dutton (1983, 110) described Baker's letters to him as "educative and admonitory" and praised him as a "practical visionary" whose "constant theme was a belief in the influence of architecture on the people of young countries." Baker (1944, 3) drew upon Christopher Wren's proclamation of the "political uses" of architecture ("it establishes a Nation . . . and makes the people love their native Country") during his long service to the empire. Baker (1944, 103) called Dutton a "devout student" of Cecil Rhodes and said he was "understanding and sympathetic in all things pertaining to architecture in its widest implications as affecting the establishment of our civilization in the new, untamed countries."

If Baker's Government House in Nairobi is what taught Dutton about

Fig. 6. Government House, Nairobi. From *Architecture and Personalities* by Herbert Baker (London: Country Life, Ltd., 1944).

"establishing our civilization in the new, untamed countries," then several lessons must have related directly to the third of Mitchell's tenets of enframing, the establishment of central spaces for observation and surveillance. For Thomas Metcalf (1989, 247), "Baker's architectural ideals spanned, as they were meant to join together, a far-flung empire that would forever secure Britain's position in the world." Baker used ideas from classical Greek and Roman architecture for the deliberate purpose of linking Britain's imperial buildings symbolically to those ancient empires. Huge, indeed "monumental" government buildings Baker designed all over the world were placed high on hills, in bright sunlight, for all to see the "ideals of law, order, and government" at the heart of his vision of British imperial power (Metcalf 1989, 247). "The Nairobi Government House, with its colonnaded patio, tiled roof, and loggias giving vistas across the city below" from the slopes of Nairobi Hill "incorporated the central features" of Baker's ideals (Metcalf 1989, 248). These lessons Baker taught to Dutton are certainly evident in the colonial Lusaka and Zanzibar programs, and even in the postcolonial Zanzibar and Lilongwe project in which Dutton's protégé Ajit Singh participated.

Yet I believe that Dutton's understanding of the political uses of architecture and design went farther than the surface appreciation of symbolism and national iconography Baker instilled in all his pupils. Dutton was conscious throughout his career of the centrality of "giving the natives a square deal" (Oldham papers, Box 7, 1931) in any attempt at earning their "goodwill." He often expressed the belief that the only way to do so was "to build up on the natives' own traditions" (Lugard papers, Box 10, 1931) in building matters. This took him into the realms of colonial spatial planning that dealt more palpably with the creation of goodwill among Africans, potentially to territories beyond the making of a grand government house or fancy monuments. Although Dutton had no formal hand in the colonial regime's plans in Nairobi, one particular project drew his attention again and again in his correspondences and day-to-day preoccupations. This was the creation of the first planned Native Location in the city, Pumwani. As Pumwani was and continues to be one of Nairobi's main African neighborhoods, by examining its creation and African responses to colonial plans there, we can gain a picture of how Nairobi's Africans came to transcend the enframing strategies of the colonial state.

Nairobi as an African City

Pumwani was populated in 1922 as "the first attempt by British officials to plan a settlement for Africans in Nairobi" (McVicar 1968, 106). The siting of this Location was aimed at increasing the spatial efficiency of the African labor force in the city while at the same time protecting European areas from racial or health-related "contamination." It grew out of a gradually emerging enframing strategy where "the control of urban space became more than the control of infection: it became control over African social and sexual relations" (White 1990, 46). Pumwani is about a twenty-minute walk from downtown to the east, and it is downwind and downstream from European areas to the west. The project included construction of roads, drains, public toilets, and washing blocks, along with a layout of plots in a regular, rectangular grid. Pumwani's original residents were Africans forcibly relocated from squatter areas that had cropped up further westward in the city, nearer the downtown, and nearer the white areas.

This new Native Location was planned to be the only legal area of residence for Africans in the city, and its form on paper was very much a tool of dominative control. It had clearly defined natural and political borders marking it off from the rest of the city—pointedly, in its position well across the Nairobi River from downtown. Pumwani to this day has a distinct inside and outside as a neighborhood unit, with limited entrance into and exit from it on the road grid.

In practice, obviously, Pumwani did not become the only African area of the city, and its form did not remain completely under the state's control. People were responsible for building their own homes, albeit technically they were to do so according to the guidelines of the newly introduced municipal building codes. In practice, few of the codes were ever followed or enforced in Dutton's years in Nairobi. For instance, Kenneth McVicar (1968, 108) notes that almost all houses exceeded the tiny maximum sizes called for in Pumwani's original terms, ensuring plot coverages in the neighborhood of 80–90 percent when 50 percent was the original upper limit. The reason for the increased plot coverage lies in the fact that most houses had sublet rooms, when subletting was technically illegal. And most Pumwani residents did their best to improve their houses and make the most of an oppressive system. "We put everything in ox carts provided by the City Council, and then we came here," one of the original residents told McVicar (1968, 110):

> The City Council cut down all the grass and nothing grew after that. Nobody refused to have trees planted, but who bothered to plant them? It was up to the City Council and they didn't care. If you have seen any trees growing around here they were not planted by the City Council: Pumwani people did it. I would have planted one but I was afraid the City Council would cut it down. These plots are so small, you know, even when we were building our houses they didn't want us to make them bigger. There just wasn't room for trees.

As McVicar notes, Pumwani did not conform to "the rigidly organized workers' housing estates" of the late colonial era (1968, 263). Still, it was "the first attempt by colonial officials to impose some degree of order on the random patterns of occupance" found in the first African communities in Nairobi. It was, to put it in Mitchell's terms, the first urban attempt that Eric Dutton witnessed to explicitly make a segmented plan from an order without framework.

Eric Dutton saw very directly the inseparability of spatial and political control, and he was not at all convinced that the city council's work in Pumwani was even close to sufficient. He chastised Lugard for neglecting settlements like Pumwani in the latter's series of lectures at the London School of Economics in the early 1930s:

> [T]he growing towns you have left out of the scope. . . . In a location on the outskirts of Nairobi [Pumwani] . . . as you may imagine most of the discontent and agitation and misunderstanding is fermented and I think

that anybody who visited it would admit that it is only natural that these manifestations of unrest should ferment there. . . . It is difficult to visit these places without feeling some sense of shame that so little has been done; one would not imagine it would cost much to give them their small post office, a dispensary, a reading room, their playing fields, and above all a hospital among their own people. . . . In the material comforts and necessities of life we should give enough, and more than enough, especially in towns and locations, to make the native think it worthwhile to follow his own path, to advance with credit on his own plane and achieve the admiration of us all. (Lugard papers, Box 10, March 19, 1932)

What we see here, in addition to overbearing paternalism, is the development of ideas Dutton would try to put into practice, first in Northern Rhodesia, and then in Zanzibar. The "towns and locations" matter most of all, as the places to prevent unrest by practical manifestations of colonialism's attempt at legitimation. This legitimation brings gendered containerization—"follow his own path, on his own plane, among their own people"—and ultimately domination, after the quelling of discontent.

In spite of the rhetoric and the legal structure created with the formation of Pumwani and the new town plan to which Dutton refers, though, it is evident that Nairobi in the 1920s was a city where the production of space was quite contested. African conceptions of space and utilization of the containerized new neighborhoods ultimately transcended the enframing tactics of the colonial state. Prostitutes, landlords, and a budding urban proletariat "demanded an obedience to rules and codes of which the state had little or no knowledge" (White 1990, 223). Among these rules and codes, White cites loyalty to one's community, "coastal Islamic values of hierarchy and respect" (because so many of Pumwani's landlords—ironically, it was not state-owned land—were coastal Muslims), and an understanding of "how to manage space and diversity for profit." In other words, Pumwani had its own version of *uwezo, imani,* and *desturi* (power, faith and custom) cornerstones to guide its development more than anything the colonial state imposed.

The elaborate workings of custom and faith within varied constraints on power are evidenced in the creation of community in Nairobi's squatter areas and marginal neighborhoods into more recent years as well. Hotly conflictual landlord and tenant associations, sports and dance clubs, ethnic associations, and most strongly, religious organizations strengthened the "community development" that both David Clark (1978–79, 43) and Diane Kayongo-Male (1980; 1988) studied in Nairobi's African neighborhoods. Clark (1978–79, 43) found, into the 1970s, that a "formidable array of associations" made a deep "sense of community" pervasive in Nairobi's informal settlements, but that the effectiveness of these associations and community groups depended upon the "economic position" of their leaders. Kayongo-Male (1980, 33) evidenced "very strong patterns of social organization" based on "socio-economic status, religion" and customary practices in many African areas of eastern Nairobi. She speculated that for some of these urban settlements, "it is doubtful whether the term 'uncontrolled' makes any sense" because of the degree of internally regulated control in them (Kayongo-Male 1988, 137).

In African urban majority neighborhoods like Pumwani, the colonial state, and in many ways its postcolonial inheritor state in Kenya "could build walls and drains, but no lasting bonds" as White (1990, 223) put it. A very basic "difference in the conceptualization of space" separated the colonial elite like Eric Dutton from the African communities (Kamau 1978–79, 105). The colonial regime proved unwilling and unable to secure its legitimacy by developing a spatial order built from African understandings and in African residents' interests.

Conclusion

If Kenya in the 1920s was something of an "acid test" for the British Empire in Africa, then it also provides us with a window onto colonial conceptions of space. Many of the commonly held beliefs about space and urbanism in British colonial Africa appear in the letters and published writings of Eric Dutton about this time and place. Dutton encapsulated the ideological and practical perspectives of many on British colonialism's elite verandah during the interwar years. In fact he actively pursued association with this elite, however divided the white community may have been at times. His writings and experiences therefore speak for and to a broader mindset in the empire.

For those of this colonial elite verandah, Africa in the 1920s was at some level a clean slate, a wilderness to escape to and remake. In this remaking one finds an enframing. Colonial spatial planning in urban areas can be seen therefore as an expression of a broader colonial conception of space, perhaps its most explicit manifestation. The colonial city would be compartmentalized into a segmented plan, where the appearance of order and domination, coupled with the self-proclaimed "strength, courage and fairmindedness" (Dutton 1929, 96) of the colonialist, would produce legitimation, through contrived intimacy and protected prestige. Nairobi is often seen as a city that encapsulates colonial expressions of urban order. It was highly compartmentalized in racial terms, and that compartmentalization was formalized into laws and plans in the 1920s. That compartmentalization involved making a separation between inside and outside at various spatial scales, including in the planning of Native Locations. With Herbert Baker's Government House, Nairobi also gained its first significant central space of observation and gleaming symbol of colonial power.

Tellingly, though, we see from the beginning of the efforts to plan where and how Africans would live in this colonial city, in the construction of Pumwani Native Location, that the colonial state in effect watched Africans transcend the enframing tactics of this order right and left. As I show in the next two chapters, colonial Lusaka and Zanzibar are cities in which very similar colonial enframing tactics were both implemented and transcended.

Chapter Four

Colonial Lusaka

> "In Zambia, Eric left a mark that has not been erased . . . in the lay-
> out of Lusaka. To a large extent Zambia's capital was Eric Dutton's
> brain-child."
>
> —Elspeth Huxley, Introduction to
> "The Night of the Hyena," 1983

Introduction

The transfer of urban-planning ideologies and practices from colonizing powers to the colonies is an important recent theme in planning and urban geography. As Home points out, though, the actual "process of transfer" and the precise agencies and pathways of that process have received surprisingly little attention (1990, 23). Lusaka is "frequently cited as the first planned garden city" in Africa (Simon 1992, 147). Its history has been well excavated from its origins in the ideas of famous British consultants through the story of how "the imported values of the colonial power were translated into the physical form of a city" (Collins 1977, 227).

Yet even in this case, where attention to the process of transfer of the garden city concept has been very considerable, one crucial agent has yet to be examined. In published accounts of Lusaka's origins, the original planners and consultants are said to have had only a limited influence on the plans. A town planning engineer in the Public Works Department, P. J. Bowling, is credited with creating the actual layout of the city, and the government is said to have been forced "to rely instead on [the] Secretariat" to oversee the building (Gann 1964, 259; Rakodi 1986; Collins 1977, 227–41). The chief secretary position (the top job in the secretariat) was vacant for a significant stretch during the planning and construction. When Charles Dundas came to fill it in late 1934, in his words "construction was so far advanced . . . that I did not occupy myself much with the business, leaving it to those who had handled it before my time" (Dundas 1955, 169). The missing element in all of these accounts is Eric Dutton, the assistant chief secretary who was, according to the governor, "responsible for the actual carrying out of the program" (Public Record Office 1936).

Lusaka's construction as the capital, I argue, exhibits each of the three characteristics of colonial enframing in urban Africa (Mitchell 1988). Its planners sought to replace an order without framework with a segmented plan, to develop and articulate separations between inside and outside at various spatial scales, and to create central sites of observation and surveillance as object manifestations of their power. Even as the colonial regime seemed to try and make Lusaka readable like a book, though, the poetry of that book was being rewritten from underneath. The enframing strategies proved unsustainable, and the city gradually became reframed within African idioms of urban life, dependent largely on uneven and unequal deployment of power by individual householders, on religious institutions or ideas of space, and on customary neighborly understandings.

To understand the program of Lusaka's construction or how Elspeth Huxley might ever have come to see it as Eric Dutton's brainchild, though, we must have some sense of what the British were doing there in the first place. The colony of Northern Rhodesia had its origins in the grandest spatial plan of British colonialism in Africa. That plan was Cecil Rhodes's dream of turning the map of Africa pink from Cape to Cairo. The main street of Lusaka makes this dream plain in its name, Cairo Road. In 1888, Rhodes's British South Africa Company claimed effective governance over Northeast Rhodesia, half of the area that would become Zambia. In 1911, the BSAC amalgamated Northeast Rhodesia with the Barotseland Protectorate, Northwest Rhodesia, to form the distinctly two-eared shape of Northern Rhodesia. It was more than twenty years, however, before Lusaka was chosen as the site of this consolidated colony's capital.

The BSAC had two main aims in the future Zambia, beyond the projection of British imperial power and the prevention of German or Afrikaner incursions north of the Zambezi River. First, Rhodes intended to expand white settlement into what was perceived as a sparsely populated territory, as part of his general strategy for what he saw as the "social problem" of Great Britain's "surplus population" (Heisler 1974, 2). Second, and ultimately more importantly, the BSAC sought to extend the base of its mining wealth. Northern Rhodesia never really approached the Rhodesian ideal of a white settler colony, but the BSAC rapidly discovered what would become the raison d'être of this territory for the entire twentieth century, its metals. Although the BSAC lost a bitter negotiated campaign for rights to the Katanga (Congo) finger of the Copperbelt, copper turned out to be hardly in short supply on its side of the border. The first mine in the territory, initially for lead and zinc but eventually for copper, opened at Kabwe (Broken Hill) in 1902. The BSAC began to explore the Copperbelt to the north of Kabwe by 1909, but its explosive growth as a mining center came between 1924 and 1930.

The BSAC relinquished political control over the territory in 1924, paving the way for its development as a colony distinct from Rhodesia itself to the south (even as the BSAC retained substantial shares in the copper mines). In contrast to Kenya, Northern Rhodesia, from early in its development, had a pronounced trend toward urbanization and industrial production, mainly because of the mines. Its first territorial capital, Northeast Rhodesia's Fort Jameson (now Chipata), was, said Eric Dutton, "the kind of place where you want to write love letters" (Oldham papers, August 1, 1934). Like neighboring Nyasaland's capital at Zomba, it was sited deliberately for what Europeans perceived as its natural beauty. Livingstone, which became the second capital at the 1911 unification of Northeast and Northwest Rhodesia, was more of a working town (although it was not far from Victoria Falls). With the rise of the copper mines, industrial centers like Kabwe, Ndola, and Mufulira established an urban character quite different from Fort Jameson's "love letter" quaintness, too.

The colonial administration gradually saw the need to address the spatial disjuncture and unevenness between the settler-dominated capital at Livingstone on the far southern border and the economic lifeblood at the Copperbelt on the far northern border. At almost the exact point in time when Eric Dutton arrived in Northern Rhodesia, its government set about the tasks of locating the best site for a new administrative capital and lining up expertise to plan it. They eventually settled, not unlike the East Africa Protectorate before them, on a railway watering station about halfway up the line, a place known by the name of a local Lenje headman, Lusaakas (Sampson 1959).

"A Tree-Lined and Well-Planned City"

Northern Rhodesia's colonial government chose the capital site with the assistance of British planning consultant S. D. Adshead. Its location roughly halfway between Livingstone and the Copperbelt made it convenient both geographically and politically. Settler or mining interests in either area would not automatically control its development (Public Record Office 1934; Jules-Rosette 1981). The capital's physical site itself was chosen via aerial reconnaissance flights and cadastral analysis in which Dutton played an important role alongside the architect Jan Hoogterp, another student of Herbert Baker. This site had the distinct advantage of being on nonalienated Crown lands, meaning that, unlike the Pumwani scheme in Nairobi, it was owned by the state and unoccupied. It sat adjacent to the existing railway stop of Lusaka Township, but this was still a rather small settlement. The capital did not require large-scale removal, demolition, or reconstruction of African properties (Collins 1977, 227–41).

Still, as Dutton himself said, it was surely "a strange idea" to build a new capital city in the midst of a severe, worldwide depression (1983, 132). He found the first two governors who worked on the plan, James Maxwell (1930–32) and Ronald Storrs (1933–34), to be "odd choices" for the governorship. Where Maxwell "ruled the country with a rod of iron"—a strategy the consent-conscious Dutton never accepted—Storrs "was assuredly lost in Central Africa. He was not there. He did not look as if he were there" (Dutton 1983, 131 and 137). Yet these two governors were responsible for Dutton's extensive involvement in the project from the outset. Dutton wrote a sixty-three-page memo to Maxwell strategizing how to build and fund the city project in March 1932, but the plan died only a few months later owing to the depression. In 1932 Dutton headed the government financial commission charged with cutting back government expenditures, and once it was clear that Colonial Office funds were not forthcoming for the Lusaka project, local funds became subject to these cutbacks. Northern Rhodesia, like independent Zambia, rose and fell on its copper mines, and the local colonial state's chief weakness was dependency on either the Colonial Office or mining companies for its financial security (Schuster 1979, 19).

When Storrs assumed the governorship in 1933, though, he left Dutton "full freedom . . . to deal with public affairs" (Dutton 1983, 142). Lusaka's construction was the main public affair for which he wanted this full freedom (Dutton 1983, 137). He had become obsessed with what he saw as the

urgent task of "building up decent native towns," but he found only dis-
couragement when the Colonial Office corresponded with him about the
new capital. "We seem to have lost our nerve halfway across the stream;
nowadays to every proposal about the new capital, there is always a 'but.'
The reply to that is," wrote Dutton, " 'there are no blinkin' 'buts' " (Oldham papers, Box 7, 1934). On six weeks' leave in London, Dutton lobbied
heavily and successfully with friends at the Colonial Office to produce loans
to get the project under way again (Dutton 1983; Public Record Office
1934).

The third governor of Dutton's time in Northern Rhodesia, Hubert
Young, sent him from Livingstone to supervise Lusaka's construction in late
1934, telling him to have it done by the king's birthday (late May 1935).
Young proved to be the first boss since Governor Coryndon for whom Dutton had deep admiration and respect. The new chief secretary, Charles
Dundas, showed potential to rein in the grip of his assistant on the colony's
affairs. But Dundas was considered unsympathetic to the white settler and
mining concerns that saw themselves as the ultimate purpose of the colony
(Tait 1997, 167), while Dutton had earned a reputation for supporting settler interests in Kenya (Oldham papers, Box 3, 1930). The white "business-
men and shopkeepers" of the colony's old capital and the Copperbelt cities
opposed the plan to build Lusaka (Dutton 1983, 132). Young told the Colonial Office that Livingstone's whites took to calling it "Deadstone," in their
bitterness over the loss of revenues and customers brought by the capital relocation (Public Record Office 1935). Dutton was a wise choice politically
for Young to use in fronting the operation since he could and did assuage
settler anger about Lusaka, even while he managed the colony's correspondence with his contacts in the Colonial Office to satisfy the scheme's
bankrollers (Public Record Office 1934).

In his memoir, Dutton describes his relationships with Young and Dundas as "a kind of administrative *menage a trois*" (1983, 159). It is apparent,
not only from Dutton's memoir but also from each of theirs, that the governor and his chief secretary were "as different as a nettle and a pink carna-
tion" (Dutton 1983, 159). Dundas resented the authority granted to his
assistant, telling him, "sometimes I think you confuse our positions and believe our roles reversed" (Dutton 1983, 159). Dundas had thrived under
Donald Cameron in Tanganyika, one of British Africa's most left-leaning
governors and one who attempted more than most to actually implement
his idea of "African Paramountcy" (see Neumann 1998). Dundas disliked

Northern Rhodesia and the gruff, "nettlesome" regime of Young. He left a
note on Dutton's desk one day that said:"Land of cursed rocks and stones,
land where many leave their bones, land of rascals, rogues and peddlers,
busy, scandalizing meddlers, land of poverty and want, where pride is
plenty, money scant. Take this, my very heartiest curse. And if I could, I'd
give you worse: for all your natives, I know well, love me as I love hell. That
is Northern Rhodesia" (Dutton 1983, 159). It is no surprise, then, that
Dundas was happy to leave the capital project in his underling's hands.

Lusaka Enframed

Dutton recognized, reluctantly, that he was neither architect nor governor—he wasn't even the chief secretary. Instead, he played the role of facil-
itator and, building on his contact with intellectuals and professional
advisers alike, he kept the project rolling while leaving other technical aspects to those with more training. He conducted the aerial surveys of the
site with Hoogterp, but admitted Hoogterp scoffed at his claims to architectural expertise (Dutton 1983, 144). Beyond his overall supervisory role,
there were three specific portions of the Lusaka plan with which Dutton became directly involved from the design stage onward. These were the layout
of trees and gardens in this "garden city," the siting and spatial planning of
the colony's first African secondary school, and the construction of its
model African compounds (Dutton 1935).

These three portions of the plan display both the hybrid nature of
Dutton's ideas of urban landscape and the basic flaws that undermined any
attempt to build a long-lasting and consensual sort of enframing from
them. "Africa is a queer continent," Dutton told Lugard, "once you get it
into your blood, you can never get it out" (Lugard papers, Box 10, 1942).
Africa clearly became enmeshed in his sense of self and in his practice of
urban design. At the same time, saying he was "bound by our conscience
and not theirs" (Oldham papers, Box 7, 1936), Dutton deliberately dis-
tanced his identity and life from those of Africans, shooting through with
racial and gender bias any work he did "on behalf of" African interests.

Dutton was a keen observer of African society, almost in spite of his
background. The special place for silviculture, and particularly avenue
trees, found to this day in the cities in which he served, in large degree
began with him because of what he saw and learned in Africa, and not entirely because he sought to recreate an English landscape for white settlers.

Part of his being "a master of English style" (as Joseph Oldham wrote of him) lay in knowing just what he had to know of gentlemanly professions, including landscape gardening. He expressed an emotional attachment to English moors and likened some of Mount Kenya's heath to those "at home" (Dutton 1929, 29). But in actuality most of what he learned about plants he learned in Africa, about African plants (Dutton 1929, 1935, and 1949). Although nearly the whole world can be found in its original street trees, about half of the plants not native to Northern Rhodesia imported for plantation in Lusaka came from other African colonies, especially Kenya (Dutton 1935). What is more, Dutton appreciated the meanings imparted to trees in African societies at a deeper level than most outsiders did. This was especially so by his last years of service in Zanzibar (Dutton 1949, 5–32), but even in Lusaka he was cognizant of the complexity and importance of trees in African conceptions of the natural world: "[I]n Africa, trees hide a multitude of sins" (Dutton 1935, 43).

Ideological messages figured even in the planting of trees and shrubs in Lusaka. Ilsa Schuster (1979, 23) noted even in the late 1970s that, on the drive into the city center from the airport, the African compound areas were "carefully hidden from the traveler's eye by a grass-backed fence of magenta bougainvillea kept in splendid condition by municipal gardeners." Dutton planted such "sin-hiding" plants throughout the city (Dutton 1935), including mulberry hedges on the lines separating compounds from one another in the African areas addressed below. Yet Schuster betrayed how clever Dutton was with trees when she remarked that "only the rows of flame trees" that this unashamed colonialist and his chief gardener Chillika planted on Cairo Road reminded her "that one might be in Africa" (1979, 24).

Construction of the new secondary school at Munali, just outside the capital, followed a decade of debate in the 1930s on placement and design in which Dutton was an important influence. Governor Young's 1935 memorandum to the secretary of state for the colonies, evidently (according to other memoranda in this National Archives of Zambia file) prepared by Dutton, articulated the reasons for placing the school in or near the new capital, and the guidelines for its spatiality. "The glamour of the capital would probably appeal to Natives throughout the country, who would regard the siting of the Centre [originally planned with a high school and trade school combined] at Lusaka rather than elsewhere as an earnest of the sincerity of Government interest in Native development." There was also a need, this memo claimed, for "attractive buildings suitably arranged." With phrases that Dutton later utilized in Zanzibar—phrases that seem to have clear origins with Herbert Baker (see chapter 3)—the memo argued for the political importance of architecture: "The influence, unconscious perhaps, but still strong, that good buildings exercise in promoting the sense of dignity of education and in forming a standard of taste, is a factor that should not be lost sight of" (National Archives of Zambia, file Sec B1/474, November 18, 1935). Governor Young (via Dutton) concluded that in the buildings of the school "it was their duty to show the natives the way in which they should live" with just the right emphasis on subservience.

By contrast, Dutton had little liking for the design features of Lusaka's Native Trades School as it had originally been planned, because it was built on "European lines" and thus was "apt to create the wrong values" in "natives" (Oldham papers, Box 7, 1931). The right values would emerge with a design that aimed at "preserving his traditions" while at the same time "giving him our ideals and our prestige" (Oldham papers, Box 7, 1931).

Munali School ultimately opened just outside the capital two years after Dutton's departure. Its most famous graduate, Kenneth Kaunda (independent Zambia's first president), came in the second year. Kaunda's autobiography suggests that the goals Dutton and his cohort had for Munali as a social and spatial instrument of rule and goodwill in some ways came to fruition. "Once at Munali," Kaunda wrote, "I found myself in a new and wonderful world. For the first time I saw a laboratory and we started to learn some real science. We lived a full and interesting life at Munali" (1962, 14–15). That life clearly involved learning the ideals and prestige of the British, engaging in the life and "glamour" of the new capital, and yet all the while not entirely losing sight of African traditions.

In both the main compound for Africans and the governor's model village in Lusaka, Dutton actively worked to put these same notions into the plants, bricks, and mortar. The plans for African areas in the new Lusaka, such as they were, vividly demonstrate each of Mitchell's three themes of enframing. First, the plans transformed the spatial character of Zambian settlements that had an "order without framework" into defined portions of a segmented plan. Northern Rhodesia was a very diverse place ethnically, like most British African colonies, so it is dangerous to generalize about the spatiality of African settlements. Nonetheless, it can be said that Zambian settlements typically appeared to outsiders as "disorganized" (Jules-Rosette

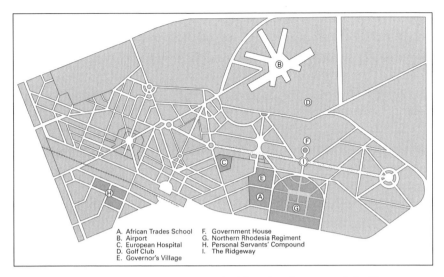

A. African Trades School   F. Government House
B. Airport   G. Northern Rhodesia Regiment
C. European Hospital   H. Personal Servants' Compound
D. Golf Club   I. The Ridgeway
E. Governor's Village

Fig. 7. The 1930s plan for the new capital of Lusaka. Courtesy of the Kansas Cartographic Services Office, Geography Department, University of Kansas.

1981, 11). For instance, the already existing township of Lusaka, dominated by Africans in population and in design, was typically described as a collection of "ramshackle buildings" (Copeman, in Hansen 1997, 23). The shifting-cultivation agricultural systems common in the region had caused mobility to be a key component of settlement geography, and there were traditions of temporary or seasonal housing even before the development of male mine-labor migration made transience and circular migration common (Moore and Vaughan 1994, 113–15). Furthermore, female-headed households, matrilineality, matrilocality, and households with extremely fluid boundaries of inclusion were commonplace phenomena on the settlement landscape (Hansen 1997). In place of these fluid indigenous orders, the new British Lusaka was meant to be a highly ordered city segmented by race, class, and gender.

To the colonial administration, the new African layouts were considered an attempt to preserve "what is best in the traditional plan of the African village" (Bradley 1935, 47). Yet these "African villages" were carefully placed within the larger plan of Lusaka. Racial segregation permeated the map, where, for instance, the poorest-quality lands were set aside for Africans. The plan even wedged in the one higher-quality African area, the Governor's Village, right next to the military barracks. The plan subdivided Africans by class into "senior and better-educated people" in the

Governor's Village, "personal servants" in a separate African compound, and "others," who were left out of any planned compound and instead consigned to the unplanned "old Lusaka." By so doing, this map also assumed that African residents of the planned areas would be more or less temporary urbanites whose only purpose in town was service to the administration's personnel (Hansen 1997).

Since most servants were male, this fed into the plan's gender segmentation as well. Dutton saw what was best in African village planning as its reliance on "the family unit." Kenneth Bradley's commemorative volume on Lusaka's construction leaves little room to wonder at how that family unit was gendered in British minds on the Native Side: "The compounds consist of several units of four huts, each unit, so to speak, looking into itself and divided by an appreciable space from its neighbour to preserve for each house-holder that sense of intimacy which he had . . . [and to preserve the] feeling that, however large the village, he was living in one clearly defined section of it and was concerned only with that section" (1935, 47–48).

Dutton consistently spoke of the need to rely on existing architectural and design traditions, and he did stay somewhat true to this in the Governor's Village and African compounds by utilizing local materials and local craftsmanship to construct houses designed to follow Zambian house styles (Public Record Office 1934). Yet in the process these house designs were placed in the neighborhood units of a containerized village structured within a masculine British worldview. In seeking to be "educative in the designing of the huts themselves," Dutton and those working with or under him spatially remodeled the family units of Zambian villages into a form much more recognizable as an English nuclear family revolving around patriarchy (Bradley 1935, 49; McClintock 1995). The householder was conspicuously male, the unit was designed to protect *his* sense of intimacy. The outdoor kitchens were built to please the "modern housewife" (Bradley 1935, 47–48; Hansen 1997). What made this misstep so extraordinary are two facts of the local context. First, most Zambian culture groups were and are matrilineal (Schuster 1979, 13). Second, the whole social structure of the colony was built around male labor migration that militated against the idealized stability of a patriarchal nuclear family (Schuster 1979, 15).

Furthermore, if we examine the order within these villages of Dutton's, we see very clearly Mitchell's theorized enframing strategy of creating a fixed distinction between inside and outside. The units of the personal servants' compound had "each unit looking into itself." The "intimacy" af-

forded by this inward orientation implies a patriarchal dominance not unlike that which Heidi Nast (1996) has identified in the practices of female
seclusion of the medieval palace of Kano, Nigeria, but one that was certainly uncommon in precolonial Zambia. The hedges Dutton planted between units spatially cut off even the man of the house from the formation
of any sort of politically improper and more broadly based urban consciousness. The ordinary compound was built with no central gathering
places. The fixed notion of an inside and an outside to each compound unit
"preserved the feeling that, however large the village," the residents were
"living in one clearly defined section of it" and were "concerned only with
that section."

The Governor's Village did have a central gathering place beyond the
hedges of each four-unit compound. This becomes a part of Mitchell's
third enframing strategy of providing an observation point. The village layout was a series of crosses, with "a well controlled beer hall" at its center, because "a modicum of beer" was deemed to be as essential to the African as
to "the British working man" (Bradley 1935, 49). The beer hall was to be so
well controlled that it served only watered-down beer, and thus these more
privileged Africans would still be sober while under observation (Hansen
1997, 40). Moreover, most of the Governor's Village provided views of the
adjacent Ridgeway (a wide boulevard along the crest of a ridge) on which
the main government center was built. It was deemed essential for Africans
to be able to see the Government House as frequently as possible: "Northern Rhodesia is a Protectorate in which the Africans outnumber the Europeans by a hundred and twenty to one. To them, this House and its great
occasions will be the outward and visible sign at all times of the dignity of
the Crown" (Bradley 1935, 44).

This observation was made by Dutton's associate, Kenneth Bradley.
From Dutton's expressed admiration for Bradley's book, though, there is no
doubt that he shared Bradley's understanding of how the Governor's Village open spaces were positioned to preserve the "prestige" Dutton saw as
so essential to the maintenance of the empire (1983, 152). The Ridgeway
thus provided the idealized third tenet of enframing.

Lusaka's Legacy

From the point of view of the African urban majority verandah, Lusaka's
planning can be criticized on a number of fundamental grounds. On a

practical level, colonial planners from the 1930s onward failed to plan adequately for the large urban population of Africans—far larger than that of European settlers—that the new city eventually attracted. The low-density land use framework established in Lusaka from its beginnings also created far higher transport costs and inefficiencies than befit a city of its size and import (Collins 1977, 227–41). Moreover, "the underlying ideologies of separate development . . . debased" whatever high-minded conceptualization of a "garden city" for Africa that may have been in the plan at its origin (Rakodi 1986, 213). "The associated and parallel development of European and native" was a basic premise of Lusaka's spatiality from the beginning (Jellicoe 1950, 8), with native interests clearly coming second. Dutton was a crucial party to the city's development, and thus many of the "structures, attitudes and feelings" that Rakodi (1986) identifies as central to colonialism's detrimental legacy in the postcolonial urban-planning apparatus of Lusaka began, at least in part, with him.

Nonetheless, Dutton felt that the Governor's Village and the Personal Servants' Compound met with African approval. He told the secretary of state that "for the first time in Northern Rhodesia I have found natives enthusiastic about the accommodation which Government is supplying them" (Public Record Office 1934). He based this conviction on his belief that the house plans followed Zambian designs, but also on the beauty of trees and gardens available for residents' enjoyment within a short distance of these homes. His claim seems somewhat unlikely, given that these were remarkably small one- and two-room huts with communal cooking and bathing sites looking up from floodable land onto the shining Ridgeway of government offices. Still, in his memoir, Dutton spoke with pleasure of his own return visits to the city particularly for the sight of the tall and mature avenue trees he had planted as young saplings (Dutton 1983, 133). The beer hall indeed remained popular, and the other gathering areas became centers for the government to show educational films and propaganda, or for people to stage dances, so there is a certain degree of legitimation subtly attributable to his work (Hansen 1997, 36–42).

Dutton insightfully responded to a 1935 strike and wave of rioting on the Copperbelt—about which he wrote the government report and testified for the Colonial Office—by saying that "both the Administration and the Police are sadly out of touch with the natives" (Oldham papers, Box 7, 1935). They were even more out of touch in Lusaka, for there a city was built with little regard for Africans beyond the showpiece compounds Dutton designed. Dutton himself betrayed the sentiments characterizing this project from the beginning, in his admission to Oldham regarding his "doubts about the paramountcy of native interests: I simply do not believe in it. I believe in the paramountcy of the interests of my own people" (Oldham Papers, Box 7, 1936). In spite of his stated belief that colonialists needed to show the "natives" that their interests mattered by building up a spatial and social order for them, that order for Dutton began with a fundamental assignment of the "natives" to a lower rung of opportunity and consciousness, the bottom verandah. Hence, there is a distinct ambivalence in his own claim that the British were "there to help": underneath the legitimating principles, the British were there to help themselves. This prefigured structuration of inequality in his thinking, and its pervasiveness in British colonial circles from Northern Rhodesia to London in the 1930s, shows through clearly in how Lusaka was built.

Still, Lusaka as planned by Dutton and the other colonialists was eventually overcome by an African city they had neither planned nor desired. Ultimately, part of one model area Dutton created was torn down to make way for a "state run department store" in independent Zambia in 1965, and the model homes were nearly all replaced by contemporary cement-block houses (Hansen 1997, 43). A handful remained in use in 2000—in a wonderful irony, as part of a government-sponsored "cultural crafts village." In the next segment of the chapter, I examine African constructions of space in Lusaka as a reframing order for the program in which Dutton was involved.

Lusaka as an African City

To appreciate Lusaka as an African city, we must begin before the creation of the capital in the 1930s. From its establishment as a railway siding in 1905, cold winds, sparse vegetation, and dust storms made Lusaka a less than desirable location for many Africans. The setting is also prone to flooding in many areas, and poor surface drainage has contributed to recurring malaria and typhoid fever. Its undesirability as a place helped perpetuate labor shortages for early white residents; this struggle to secure African labor led to a generally more lax application of colonial regulations on African urban living, even after the capital project (Tait 1997, 195). The white-run village management board created an African compound in 1914 west of their white township, but did little to control building in it (Tait

Fig. 8. Rondavels of the cultural village. Author's photograph.

1997, 192). This compound, like much of the city, came to be characterized by an irregular and fairly generously spread settlement form. Other African areas that arose before 1935 were scattered throughout the city. While they remained segregated from white areas, with the exception of servants' quarters on white properties, their scattered character meant that Lusaka came to confound the stereotypical areal distinctions of the colonial city model (Tait 1997, 195). As John Tait points out, "the colonial urbanization of Africans was a far less straightforward, even haphazard process," than that of European urban settlement on the continent (1997, 152).

It is important to note that this was a very small town before 1935. The 1921 census lists 1280 African males in employment (Hansen 1997, 32). Tait gives an estimated 1928 population of 282 Europeans and 1596 Africans spread over a relatively vast township of thirty-six square kilometers (1997, 197). In contrast to Nairobi and Zanzibar, Lusaka experienced very little Asian immigration during the colonial era. Even at independence Lusaka's colonized middle included fewer than a thousand Asians, however influential they may have been economically. Asians were confined largely to the neighborhoods known today as Luburma and Madras, situated just southeast of the Cairo Road Central Business District. In colonial times, these areas, like Indian areas in Nairobi, formed a geographical buffer between the CBD and white areas, on the one hand, and the planned African residential areas of Kamwala and Kabwata on the other.

African migration to the city continued to expand throughout the en-

Fig. 9. Government House of colonial Lusaka. Author's photograph.

tire colonial era. By 1946, the number of African males employed in town
had grown to 7485, with an additional 59 African women legally employed.
These figures of course mask the real numbers for the African population
of Lusaka. As in Nairobi, in Lusaka Africans were required by law to carry
passes with an employer's endorsement when in town, and influx control
ordinances based on those for Southern Rhodesia and South Africa restricted legal African rural-to-urban migration (Heisler 1974; Seymour
1976, 45). Africans were technically not allowed to retire in cities either
(Seymour 1976, 63). We can gauge from 1944 government estimates of the
African population of Lusaka as 50 percent adult male, 27 percent child,
and 23 percent adult female, that the 1946 African population had to be at
least 15,000, with probably many more uncounted women and children,
compared to 2615 Europeans (Hansen 1997, 32).

Be that as it may, the city really took off demographically only after
World War II. There were 64,754 Africans in Lusaka by 1957, evidence of
the extraordinary postwar growth that most scholars of Lusaka emphasize
in their accounts. Tait shows that, after independence in 1964, the abolition
of colonial influx control gave rise to one of Africa's highest rates of urbanization in the postcolonial period (1997, xviii). By 2000, Lusaka was estimated to have nearly 2 million people, almost all of them African.

Housing and living conditions for Africans varied in the colonial period. As Karen Hansen writes, by the 1940s "the majority of Lusaka's pop-

ulation, namely its African residents, was either tucked away in compounds beyond the varying splendors of the European first-, second-, and third-class residential areas or lived in these residential areas as domestic servants on the premises of their employers" (1997, 27). Domestic service and government work were the main job sectors, but colonial Lusaka provided a more diverse and complicated socioeconomic setting than the Copperbelt. From its inception, it had more squatters and a greater diversity of house types. Culturally, Zambia's main ethnic groups, languages (Ngoni, Nsenga, Tonga, Nyanja, Lozi, and Bemba, for example), and home regions of the country were represented in Lusaka from an early date.

Fearing "detribalization" meant that British colonial development policies tended to be "anti-urban" (Tait 1997, 153). Although Africans were viewed as only temporary residents, the Northern Rhodesia administration "did not have sufficient resources either to repatriate men who remained in the cities once they completed work or were laid off and lost their housing, or to send the women and children who kept arriving back to the villages" (Hansen 1997, 27). There were also unauthorized squatter compounds, as in Nairobi, but to a greater degree. Africans either rented plots from Indian or European landlords amenable to their presence, or they occupied vacant Crown lands. These settlements were unlawful, but they were tolerated because even the British administrators recognized that insufficient housing was available, and labor demand was high in many urban areas. Eight main squatter camps existed by the 1950s. Most, but not all, arose in the outskirts. At least six planned or semiplanned African neighborhoods came into existence between 1936 and 1963 (i.e., roughly during the last quarter-century of colonial rule). Many of these—including the earliest one, Maploto, initiated partly by Dutton in 1936—were just self-help housing or bare-bones site-and-service schemes (Hansen 1997; Tait 1997).

Attention lavished on European areas left the local authority with little time or money for doing anything about African land and housing needs (Bates 1974). The "informal planning of African settlers" thus came to dominate the production of space in the city. Large stretches of Lusaka are often said to have grown "without any plan or guidance concerning land use" in a formal sense (Tait 1997, 194). What took the place of formal guiding structures from the colonial state? Within the confines of quite circumscribed and highly gendered individual power for most of the residents, faith- and custom-based precepts for community organization played critical roles.

Despite colonial fears of detribalization, interethnic relations became far more common and sophisticated than colonialists ever gave Africans credit for (Tait 1997, 186). The African communities in colonial Lusaka had a rich associational life: funeral groups, hometown clubs, ballroom-dancing groups, charismatic churches, drinking societies, and drumming clubs had formed by the 1940s, and by no means all of these were organized along ethnic lines. Among the churches, the Watchtower movement (Jehovah's Witnesses) had perhaps the strongest base. Hansen estimates that as many as 75 percent of Lusaka's Africans in the 1930s belonged to it (1997, 43). Eric Dutton commented at length on the Watchtower movement as a grave concern for colonialism, because of its followers' nonparticipation in tax payment and its generally anticolonial tone. These very aspects, no doubt, fueled its growth in Lusaka.

New migrants found places to stay with the help of relations or other people from their region of Northern Rhodesia who were already in Lusaka. They built houses according to the design principles they brought with them from Lozi, Bemba, Chewa, Ngoni, or other traditions, even into the 1950s (Tait 1997, 207). The city's still-plentiful open areas often became the sites for market gardens.

What did Africans think of the colonial city as it evolved in the early years? Little, if any, record exists of these views, but a few recent anthropological accounts give us at least some idea. Hansen's study of "place as a lived experience" brings many aspects of African society in colonial Lusaka to life (1997, 31). Hansen takes the approach of contrasting two very different recollections of early Lusaka, one male and one female, culled from her several decades of research in the city. Her "Mr. Zulu" thought the city was "nice in those days" of colonial rule. He came to Lusaka as a boy with his family when his father came to work for the administrative headquarters on the Ridgeway. He grew up in the "lines," the messengers' compound not far away from Government House. Mr. Zulu resisted discussing the colonial era as restrictive when Hansen talked with him. He said that even with the pass laws, employers typically handed out night passes that let them get out and about. Even though they couldn't go to white areas, they were free to go all over the African areas, and there were plenty of these. He enjoyed the Dutton-planned beer hall and the dance hall, and went ballroom dancing up until "politics took over" in the late 1950s (Hansen 1997, 36).

By contrast, Hansen's "Mrs. Mubanga" was born in Lusaka right around the grand "opening" of the capital. She worked her whole life in the informal sector and lived in more "fringe" compounds than those of the likes of Mr. Zulu. Hansen suggests that a strong connection existed between the high proportion of women in the informal sector and the higher female population in the squatter areas. Beer gardens run by women were among the more popular options for getting by, along with market trading in fruits and vegetables produced right in the city. Hansen sees these two brief synopses of sense of place as opening up onto two broad categories of African life in Lusaka. Her dichotomies are perhaps a bit simplified by the presence of just these two examples. Yet further research by Hansen and others provides evidence that the experiences of the African urban majority in colonial Lusaka were conditioned by gender divisions, differences between formal- and informal-sector employment, and distinctions between municipal (planned or semiplanned) housing areas and unplanned squatter areas.

Ann Schlyter's many works detailing the development of George, a squatter area northwest of Lusaka's city center, offer another, albeit somewhat later, picture of what it was and is like to be African in this colonial city (Schlyter 1981, 1984, 1987, 1988; Schlyter and Schlyter 1979). George had only begun to be settled at independence in 1964. In 1959 it had only two hundred dwelling units. As its name hints, George was named for a settler farmer, and its original residents were his farm workers; that is, it was "George's Compound." Residents built most of its houses themselves. The houses varied in quality, were far more widely spread than those of Pumwani in Nairobi or those in Zanzibar, and followed no regular grid pattern in layout. George's residents survived by means of informal-sector employment and were generally very poor. The neighborhood was exceedingly underserviced. In these and other ways, George represents many elements of the colonial legacy in postcolonial Lusaka.

Yet what we also see in Schlyter's portrait is an emergent African order, some of which exists outside of either the colonial legacy or the postcolonial state's capacity to control it. For instance, "Kinship ties and the habit of hospitality from pre-capitalist African society [were] still alive" in George, at least in the late 1970s (Schlyter and Schlyter 1979, 34). When asked to name the best thing about their area of the city in 1977, residents' number one response, overwhelmingly, was "good neighbors," and the Schlyters found evidence to back up the sense of neighborliness with real interdependence in five of their six study groups (Schlyter and Schlyter 1979, 50). Lively informal or independent social organizations seemed to surpass in strength the formal organs of the state in George. Uses of public space were "not random, but planned by the self-builders" (Schlyter and Schlyter 1979, 87). The overall layout of houses disclosed within its apparently chaotic form discreet clusters of houses that were "visually" and socially "connected" to one another even as people started to build in something closer to straight lines as the settlement expanded. "The colonial system of titles to land was probably foreign to many inhabitants in George" (Schlyter and Schlyter 1979, 94). Instead, residents marked the otherwise nondemarcated plots by sweeping their "yard" area out to its perceived edge, based on their morally held "right to the land on which their house stood" (Schlyter and Schlyter 1979, 95). These and many more examples give rise to highly suggestive links between the apparently disorderly order of George, and that of Ng'ambo in Zanzibar or Pumwani in Nairobi, among many examples in African cities.

Hansen's extended research with residents of the Lusaka "compound" known as Mtendere shows how fragmented social relations have become, particularly along gender lines, in the many years since Eric Dutton's "brainchild" of a city first came into being (1997). Yet even in demonstrating this, Hansen points to the ways in which Lusaka's versions of *uwezo*, *imani*, and *desturi*, as developed under colonialism, still produce much of the cityscape. Residents of Mtendere, into the 1990s, understood the city as one fundamentally divided by power between "those on the top" and the majority of residents like themselves, and this division of *uwezo* is spatially expressed: Lusaka is comprised of "Yard" people and "Compound" people (Hansen 1997, 68). Even in the years of single-party rule in Zambia, Mtendere land control and transfer operated "beyond the letter of the law" (Hansen 1997, 67). Yet "the church [was] a central influence that perhaps [was] more significant than the party in many people's lives, especially women" (Hansen 1997, 67).

In Jon Bachmann's (1991) study of Lusaka squatter areas, his central argument concerns the importance of colonialism's legacy of the individualization of urban values and the shift from an extended family to a nuclear family conception of urban living. Yet even here, the weight of his evidence shows these shifts only among the elite of these squatter areas. The majority of urban informal-settlement residents live in recognizable clusters of neighborliness, where "the houses are oriented so that the women can talk to each other while they work. The spacing of the houses is determined by shouting distance: if your neighbor can't hear you when you raise your voice, you are too far away" (Bachmann 1991, 23). Although only twenty-six of Lusaka's seventy-two officially designated residential areas are considered informal settlements, these house more than half of the city's population (Zulu 1998, 9). One must conclude that the local framework of understanding and shaping urban space, with its version of the corner-stones of *uwezo, imani,* and *desturi* within the constraints of colonial and post-colonial planning, ultimately has the most to say about what the city looks like and how it is lived in. This is not to conclude that Lusaka's urban order is unchanged from the 1930s; of course not. Nor is it to lay claim to these cornerstones of an alternative order as a genuinely liberatory reframing. Rather, I am suggesting that the failures of the Dutton-era enframing tactics of colonialism in the city gave rise to what are in essence survival mechanisms that are quite similar to the mechanisms still employed in the postcolonial city by its marginalized urban majority.

Conclusion

In Lusaka in the 1930s, British colonialism in Africa experienced the beginnings of a new kind of colonial urbanism. Yet the "garden city" in Northern Rhodesia had, at its origins, a racial compartmentalization, an objectification and containerization of space designed to both represent and foment the growth of colonial power. Unlike Nairobi's and Zanzibar's, Lusaka's racial compartmentalization at that early date had only a tiny "compartment" for an Asian colonized middle, in terms of either sheer numbers or land control, yet found a way to make a spatial buffer out of it. In the ideal, the city made manifest in spatial form and social function the key tasks of the colonial state, namely domination, accumulation, and legitimation. Eric Dutton played a central role in the attempted spatial construction of Lusaka. In this city as in many colonial cities, however, colonial planning and enframing was largely undone before it began. Instead, the emergent spatiality, within certain constraints, had within its key propulsive engines the conceptions of space of the majority of African residents generally excluded from the planning process.

By the time of Zanzibar's Ten-Year Development Plan of 1946–55, both Dutton and the British Empire in Africa had reached a "turning point" toward the gradual Africanization of power and eventual decolonization (Pearce 1982). As elsewhere in British Africa in the 1950s, the rise of "politics" among Africans in both Zanzibar and Zambia was a largely urban phenomenon (Bates 1974, 16). The functionaries of urban spatial planning by this time would seem to have been more conscious of moving beyond showcases, in order to build the structures of a civil society supportive of maintaining some form of an alliance with Britain and the West. This was certainly true in Zambia, where the 1948 Ordinance on urban areas began the process of deracializing and democratizing urban decision making. The case of Zanzibar holds many similarities with that of Lusaka, both in terms of the urban plan with which Eric Dutton is associated and in terms of African conceptions of space and urban order that ultimately transcended that plan. Hence, it is to Zanzibar that I now move.

Chapter Five

Colonial Zanzibar

"I often think, such is the vanity of man, that if I could have been
another five years in Zanzibar we could have transformed the place.
We did alter it a lot, didn't we?"
—Eric Dutton to Ajit Singh, Singh papers, May 15, 1965

Introduction

When Eric Dutton first came to Zanzibar in the 1920s (as private secretary to the governor of Kenya and high commissioner for East Africa), its political economy was in the middle of a long wave of slow decline in wealth and significance. R. H. Crofton, who held the top post of British Resident, wrote in his memoir of the cable store ship that "always seems to be coming but never arrives" (1953, 110–11). Some still tried to claim this small port as the "metropolis of Eastern Africa" (Pearce 1920). In truth its main importance to the British had been undermined by Britain's acquisition of Tanganyika from the Germans at the end of World War I and the rise of white settlement in Kenya.

By the time Dutton returned to Zanzibar in early 1942, this time as the protectorate's chief secretary, the place was decidedly ensconced in the backwaters of the British colonial imagination. Dutton told Lugard late in 1942 what "a great joy" he felt after returning to what "I suppose I have come to regard as my other home." At the same time, he feared that in matters of colonial politics and development "the voice of little Zanzibar may fail to attract a hearing" (Lugard Papers, November 26, 1942). He may have accepted that the empire saw this as a small and unimportant colony, but his ambitions for it clearly became very large.

Joseph Oldham had counseled Dutton at an early stage in his service in Northern Rhodesia, writing, "you have power and like power, and this means that you can do Africa a world of good or no end of harm" (Oldham Papers 1931). Dutton had a lot of power in Zanzibar, more than he ever attained elsewhere, and he clearly liked having it. Under Zanzibar's protectorate status, the Omani sultan was head of state, but this amounted to little more than a figurehead role. Zanzibar had no governor; instead, a British Resident headed the colony, leaving most day-to-day affairs of the bureaucracy in the hands of his second-in-command, the chief secretary. That role was renamed chief minister in the last years of colonial rule and remains as such even under the current Revolutionary Government of Zanzibar. Eric Dutton's eleven-year tenure as de facto second-in-command was longer than that of any chief secretary or chief minister before or since. He frequently acted as British Resident owing to the ill health and war responsibilities of his superiors, and he often had far more of a grip on policy and local social relations than the Resident he served (Jones papers, Box 7, 1946–50).

The propitious political changes and urban development measures that he, more than any other single individual, helped to create and enact, have left indelible marks on Zanzibar—indeed, marks that resurfaced with a vengeance upon Zanzibar's return to multiparty politics in the 1990s. If Dutton was still in the shadow of power even in Zanzibar, then he himself has cast a much longer shadow. When Julian Asquith assumed an administrative post in the islands at the close of Dutton's tenure, he recalled in an undated interview by I. L. Phillips that his general feeling "was one of dismay. . . . I felt like a cog—not in a wheel but in a very small watch" (Mss Brit Emp s 529, RHL). Dutton was the mainspring of that watch.

This was a watch that was set to an enframing time zone. Postwar Zanzibar became the setting for an ambitious program of urban development that explicitly sought to remake an order without framework—Zanzibar's Ng'ambo area—into a segmented plan. The neighborhoods and individual houses within the segmented plan of the colonial order would have had clearly demarcated boundaries of inside and outside, the containerization of colonialism on a grand scale. New central sites of observation and surveillance—a civic center and several prominent schools—clearly aimed at providing Zanzibaris with constant reminders of the dignity and prestige of the Crown and its control over their political lives. Yet Zanzibar's urban majority gradually reframed this enframing order within cornerstones of power, faith, and customary practices, and ul-

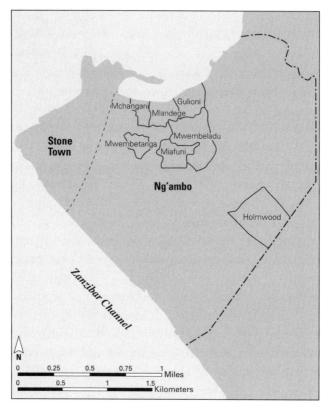

Fig. 10. Colonial Zanzibar, showing areas of the
reconstruction. Courtesy of the Kansas Cartographic
Services Office, Geography Department, University
of Kansas.

timately in the most overt way possible, by a revolution against the colonial
order.

"A Very Small Watch"

The population of colonial Zanzibar city grew slowly, if at all, during the
first half of the twentieth century. As of 1910, Zanzibar was easily the
largest of the four settlements studied in this book (35,362); over the next
forty years, however, the population inside the official town boundary crept
upward only slightly, to 38,713 in 1924, and 45,276 in 1931. By the time of
the next head count in 1948, the official population had grown by a mere 8
persons, to 45,284. To be sure, some of the same undercounting discussed

in chapter 4 for colonial Lusaka occurred here. These numbers also hide the densification of settlements outside the official town boundary but under the jurisdiction of the Town Mudir (the Native Commissioner within indirect rule) in suburban West District. Nonetheless, Zanzibar would appear to have been a city where managed growth and the effective provision of shelter, employment, urban services, and amenities would hardly seem to have been impossible. Hence, it would seem at first glance that Dutton's plans for the city, devised in the mid-1940s, ought to have made great headway in improving the quality of life for urban Zanzibaris.

Dutton's "innermost" dream was to be allowed by his connections to powerful people to "have the responsibility placed on me to build in East Africa" (Oldham papers, Box 7, 1933). It was in supervising the Zanzibar postwar development plan that he had his closest brush with that responsibility. This plan, which Dutton drafted in 1943–44 before the war ended, was the most ambitious program of state intervention ever produced in Zanzibar before its 1964 revolution. Most of the program involved remaking the city of Zanzibar, wherein about a third of the colony's residents lived regardless of the slow population growth discussed above. With substantial funding from the Colonial Office, the Central Development Authority (or CDA), which Dutton created and ran, built schools, hospitals, clinics, and roads, mostly in or near the city's elite Stone Town district. The buildings, which in 2000 still served as the city's only public hospital and its two main high schools, are among the most obvious legacies of the program. However, the plan's centerpiece was meant to be a massive redevelopment of the city's African neighborhoods in Ng'ambo (literally the "Other Side"), replete with a civic center, civic management institutions, and a council of representatives. "There is a ten years job waiting to be done here," wrote Dutton, "a job after my own heart. Provided that it is done in a sympathetic and practical fashion, it will be well worth doing" (1944b). Dutton clearly viewed his regime's legitimation as inseparable from the physical structure of the plan.

Dutton's overall program in Ng'ambo had three aspects. All of them bespoke of his goal of "improving the lot of the native in small practical ways." The first was a program to rebuild all African neighborhoods, ward by ward, with standardized house sizes and spaces between them. This program began with the construction of a model neighborhood on the edge of town. Ever conscious of the power of toponymy, Dutton chose the name Holmwood for the new area, in honor of Frederick Holmwood, an antislavery crusader who died in Zanzibar in the nineteenth century. The British often justified their rule in Zanzibar, as in other parts of Africa, by placing reminders everywhere on the landscape of their role in ending slavery. Holmwood was designed to house most residents from the first area to be reconstructed, the neighborhood of Mwembetanga. Once the residents there had moved to Holmwood, the administration demolished Mwembetanga and rebuilt its houses to mirror Holmwood's model layout. After they had moved back in, the original plan called for removing a second neighborhood out to Holmwood, demolishing it, rebuilding it, and so on, until all of Ng'ambo had been remade.

The second aspect of the redevelopment was the program of social and educational development through construction of hospitals, clinics, and schools. Although most were constructed in Stone Town, the actual sites were right on the edge between that historically Arab, Indian, and European zone and the African zone of the Other Side. This not only made them accessible to Ng'ambo residents; it made them visible and prominent on the landscape, since sites in the interior of the closely built Stone Town would have been hidden from view. Several important projects were placed in Ng'ambo itself. One of these was the Ng'ambo Girls School. This was linked to the housing improvement plan through a concentration on home economics and health in its curriculum, including an on-site model home (Pilling 1943). Other segments of this second aspect of the redevelopment had their sites on either side of the Holmwood estates. The plan called for rebuilding the Police Lines, a manorial barracks campus just west of Holmwood, and Dutton's regime constructed Zanzibar's first and only mental hospital adjoining Holmwood to its east.

The third aspect of Dutton's plan revolved around the construction of a civic center for the Other Side. The civic center was built on government-controlled residential land in the neighborhood known as Miafuni. As with the Lusaka project's central area, government land control was perceived to speed the process of construction. Unlike Lusaka, Miafuni required demolition of more than a hundred homes to clear the site of the civic center and the vehicular approach to it. Prior to the demolition, Dutton's CDA built Miafuni's displaced residents a separate model neighborhood, this time on the western side of the Police Lines, named Mji Mpya (New City).

The homes in the three settings were laid out ten feet from one another on all sides, in even rows and arcs around a "village green." The new areas were intended to "provide better examples of modern layout and housing"

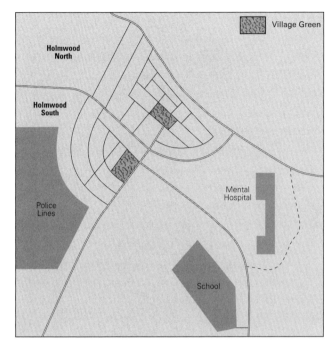

Fig. 11. Layout of Holmwood. Courtesy of the Kansas
Cartographic Services Office, Geography Department,
University of Kansas.

and "a real incentive to natives throughout the town to build on better
lines" (Pilling 1943), but, Dutton claimed, without destroying Zanzibar's
customary domestic life. The example of good construction and alignment
begun there was meant to be replicated in the rebuilding of Ng'ambo as a
whole, making for a more directly transformative agenda than Dutton had
been capable of enacting in Lusaka.

Zanzibar Enframed

This project, like the one in Lusaka and the plans for Nairobi in the 1920s,
evidences the three broad spatial tactics of enframing. Ng'ambo had been
built from the 1850s onward as a disorderly order that manifested the
power relations, religious faith, and social customs of its residents. Originally populated by the African slaves and servants of Stone Town's Arab-
Indian elite, the Other Side's crossword puzzle of alleyways represented an
"order without framework" if ever there was one. Although colonial Zanz-

ibar town had been the subject of one earlier planning effort by the planner H. V. Lanchester (1923), that plan had had little or nothing to say about Ng'ambo (Myers 1994, 212–27). Dutton's project represented the first time Ng'ambo had been fully planned. Segmentation along lines of race and class appeared prominently in this project. Ng'ambo was cut up into a set of forty "Native Locations" based on aerial photographs and carved away from Stone Town, with the exception that the two predominantly black portions of Stone Town were placed in the "Ng'ambo Area Folder" of the Town Planning Board Dutton ran. This board created in laws and codes a clear line on the map, where no official distinction had previously existed, between African working-class and Arab-Indian elite neighborhoods.

The orderly layouts of the new Mwembetanga, Holmwood, and Mji Mpya tracts had within them the second spatial strategy of enframing, that of a fixed distinction between outside and inside. Customarily, Ng'ambo house design entailed a rectangular, one-story, three- to six-room house. Most houses had outbuildings with kitchen, toilet, and store, connected to the main structure by fencing that delimited small courtyards open to the sky. Although the houses themselves had something of an "intimacy gradient" between mostly female inner and mostly male outer rooms (Allen 1979, 11; Donley-Reid 1982, 63–73), in practice gender distinctions in domestic space were more flexible than any rigid typology of the gradient would imply. Further, the spaces between Ng'ambo houses historically were small and irregular, but vibrant with both male and female residents' activities. "You never feel the limit between the street and the house as something definite" in an old Ng'ambo neighborhood (Nilsson et al. 1969, 11). By contrast, the new neighborhoods of the postwar plan had regular spacing between homes, and also "party fences" similar to the hedges of Lusaka's Governor's Village, separating each line of houses from the row behind it. This defined a separation between streets on the new road grid, principally and explicitly as a means of ensuring more effective health department and police access to the newly remade areas (ZNA file AB 39/36). Fences also marked off Holmwood's borders with the mental hospital and the Police Lines.

Although Dutton expressed a desire to rid Zanzibar of its "slum conditions," the actual areas targeted were far from slumlike in character. By the Building Authority inspector's own records, the worst "hut" areas of Ng'ambo were in the neighborhoods of Mchangani, Mlandege, Mwembeladu, and Gulioni, untouched in the reconstruction (Taylor 1943). The

Dutton administration attempted to achieve "goodwill" by proclaiming a project to improve housing and neighborhood health in Ng'ambo and attacking the housing and health issues exactly where it was least necessary to do so. But the two sites of Mwembetanga and Miafuni were important for another reason: they were on Ng'ambo's main rise and at its population center. Hence, the third spatial strategy of colonial enframing comes into view, that of creating places for observation of the city and objectification of its plan. The civic center in Miafuni, which Dutton renamed Raha Leo (Happiness Today, the name the area retains even now), had a movie theater that was intended as a place for educational and propaganda films, not unlike the central hall of the Governor's Village in Lusaka.

The control and surveillance of everyday community life was, in the Dutton years, an indispensable part of the social and political development plan for Zanzibar. Nowhere is this clearer than in the construction of the civic center for the Other Side of the city. Since Zanzibar's first revolutionary president, high court judge, and mayor all served on one of the civic bodies during the Dutton years as their first experiences of political office, whatever "policy" he demonstrated in their meetings at the civic center must inevitably be seen as influential in the postcolonial era. The civic center, though, was also clearly meant to bring "betterment, enjoyment and recreation" (as Dutton claimed at its opening) under the watchful eye of the British administration, at a time when sports and recreation associations were Ng'ambo residents' only legal arenas for political organization.

"A Tree Goes Nowhere Without a Dolly"

Although similarities exist among the projects in Nairobi, Lusaka, and Zanzibar in terms of their spatial and social enframing, the Zanzibar project is distinct in one key respect: this reconstruction faced direct African opposition, especially from women. This was manifested in each area of the project, beginning in Mwembetanga and Miafuni. Under the weight of local complaints and financial shortages, the whole scheme seemed ready to unravel by March 1947, when the British Resident thanked Dutton for his work and asked him "to find a way out" so they could "cut [their] losses and drop the whole scheme" (Glenday 1947). Construction of public buildings (a new airport, a national archive, and other structures) from the plan continued into the 1950s. But by Dutton's retirement in 1952, the broad agenda that had been begun with great fanfare and enthusiasm as a program to radically change the city both socially and spatially had virtually disappeared from view. No other neighborhoods besides Mwembetanga, Miafuni, Holmwood, and Mji Mpya were ever built or rebuilt.

Part of the problem stemmed from the project's implementation at the heart of urban-majority neighborhoods amid their self-generated political awakening. In the late 1940s, Zanzibar, like other African cities, was convulsed in a wave of work stoppages and strikes. Many people from the neighborhoods to be demolished were labor activists or homemakers sympathetic to their interests (Pakenham 1949). But the immediate concerns of residents about the reconstruction project were not overtly political, nor did they link the strikes to the project in any of my interviews. People were simply anxious about the size and quality of the new houses, and very uncertain about their postreconstruction land tenure and title status. Women were frustrated with what they saw as the poor standards of sanitation and construction in the courtyard and outbuilding areas of the project homes, especially as they'd been led to believe that their new houses would be improvements on their previous accommodations. Their bitterest complaints concerned so-called party fences, since these cut them off from their backside neighbors, and neighborliness was a crucial feature of their lives (Ladies Committee 1949; Davies Papers 1947, 1948, Mss Afr s 956, RHL). Residents outside of the reconstruction area seemed especially uncertain about the future of their homes. Pertinently, none of the grand spatial planning was accompanied by a rise in economic opportunities for the ordinary city dwellers. The most "well-off" Africans on salary or with consistent day-labor status in the port or the government still received a grossly insufficient salary for even basic needs (Davies Papers 1947, 1948, Mss Afr s 956, RHL).

From the outset, Dutton's main means of responding to residents' concerns about the ten-year plan, and indeed to their reluctance to accept colonial authority, was through development of civil society institutions along lines that he saw as appropriate. He suggested that "some measures should be taken as soon as possible which would convince the native population that the government is not gratuitously interfering with their long-established mode of living in accordance with the passing fancies of the authorities concerned, but is endeavouring to promote permanently their hygienic welfare and general enjoyment of life" (Dutton 1944c; AB 39/24, ZNA). He called for the formation of educational groups led by Vera Davies, the women's welfare officer, who would teach women why the new houses were an improvement and how to maintain sanitary controls. He also asked Sheikh Juma Aley, a local pro-British politician, to go on the radio to "counter misconceptions with truth" (Dutton 1944c; AB 39/24, ZNA). In a Kiswahili broadcast coauthored by Dutton and Juma Aley entitled "Why Ng'ambo Was Demolished To Be Built Again," Aley explained Dutton's project in ways that translated it into local sayings readily understood by Zanzibaris: "As many of you know, the government has made it its true intention to repair the state of many things in Unguja [Zanzibar] over the next ten years. . . . It is work that will take a long time and will cost a lot of money, but the costs of this work are outweighed by its benefits. Like the elders say, 'a tree goes nowhere without a dolly to carry it' " (AB 39/21–22, ZNA; author's translation).

Dutton hoped that the "tree" of the proverb, the neighborhood consciousness of Zanzibaris, would be moved by the clever "dolly" of words, spoken as they were by one of the tree's own leaves, Juma Aley. But this was only one small measure intended to addresss the immediate need to calm residents' fears of demolition. The more important response had to come within the civic center and the associations developed to use it.

Dutton wanted the civic center to serve as a focal point for the "demonstration of Government's policy . . . a big stride towards winning the confidence of the extremely conservative-minded population" (AB 39/24, ZNA). At its opening ceremony on New Year's Day 1947, Dutton said of the center that "this building—in fact the whole of this little scheme here—is an earnest of what we are trying to do in Ng'ambo. . . . Here is not only betterment, but recreation and enjoyment as well" (Samachar 1947, 1). But little went right for the center from opening day onward. The power failed on the first night at its movie theater, and persistent electrical problems led to a five-year legal fight with the operator of the projector. The roof leaked for two years, every time in different places.

The center was not simply a structural failure. Its main public goal of fostering civic responsibility was enframed within a segmented policy that doled out use-time for the facilities to ethnic organizations only (AB 9/47–9/49, ZNA). The local government structures Dutton helped establish with the civic center displayed his calculated and contained notion of what civic responsibility meant. A town board had been in place for Zanzibar's elite Stone Town section since the 1930s. It was only in 1944 that separate town councils were established for the two "sides" of the city: the Zanzibar Town Council for Stone Town and the Ng'ambo Town Council for the Other Side. "Town" meant Arab, Indian, and European;

"Ng'ambo" meant African. Ng'ambo was overwhelmingly comprised of mainlanders and Zanzibari Africans. Yet the councilors Dutton appointed for Ng'ambo were never representative of the racial or ethnic community that lived there. His original Ng'ambo Town Council was comprised of two Africans (one of whom was Christian, while Ng'ambo was 95 percent Muslim), two Arabs, an Indian, and a Comorian, in addition to three official British representatives. In this way, 82 percent of the population of Ng'ambo (its African Muslims) were represented by just 11 percent of its council. When the two sides' councils were eventually united in 1950, two more African representatives were added to the Ng'ambo delegation. This meant that four hand-picked Africans sat on a fifteen-member council at a time when Africans (excluding Comorians) constituted more than half of the city population (Zanzibar Protectorate 1962).

Dutton divided appointments to the councils among the various communities of the city to solidify the alliances of interests between the British and their closest associates in power, the Arab, Comorian, and Indian communities. African appointments to council, such as they were, went to those most amenable to British interests, whether Christians, landlords, or Western-trained scholars. Dutton's stated goal for the town council was that Zanzibar would eventually become a self-governing, self-financing municipality. Actually, the town council, as well as smaller civil entities (three ward advisory committees in Ng'ambo, the Ng'ambo Town Improvement Advisory Committee, and the Civic Center Management Committee), had political utility but little autonomy or legitimacy in the neighborhoods. The public only elected any members in the last years of colonial rule, and even then constituency boundaries were carefully manipulated to maintain a council allied with British and Arab interests (Omari 1985; Mapuri 1996).

Dutton was an awesome presence in Zanzibar; even fifty years later, older residents remember him well, with a mixture of sentiments. In a 1962 letter to his mentor, Ajit Singh looked back with longing on Dutton's "wise administration of ten years ago," and Singh was hardly alone among Ng'ambo or Stone Town residents in his admiration for the chief secretary. Several residents recounted to me Dutton's clear empathy with their financial struggles, and his efforts on numerous occasions to go out of his way to help the misfortunate. However, Dutton was widely disliked in Zanzibar, too, especially among the African employees of the Public Works Department whose work he so carefully scrutinized, because, as one put it, "he always had to have everything in order" (Dawaharo 1991). Dutton walked the streets of areas under development every weekend with his wife and inspected details of construction and sanitation (Kapyongo 1992). He arranged offices at the CDA and the Public Works Department so that there was never a "native" out of the sight of a European (Dutton to Glenday, January 9, 1948, AB 76/72, ZNA).

"We Did Alter It A Lot, Didn't We?"

In the quotation that opens this chapter, from Dutton's letter to Ajit Singh about Zanzibar's urban development, Dutton asks, in a wistful tone, "We did alter [Zanzibar] a lot, didn't we?" He seemed puzzled that all those hospitals, schools, roads, and houses culminated, albeit indirectly, in a bloody revolution and not a cosmopolitan consensus. How could British "rule" have been so far from creating the "goodwill" Dutton sought?

Dutton's manner of thinking was pervasive in the ideological self-construction of British colonialists' purposes and intentions in Africa. To his dying day, Dutton, like many British colonial servants, genuinely believed in colonialism as a morally and economically right system for Africa: "The rule of those days bestowed on all a greater measure of happiness and security than had ever before been known" (Dutton 1983, 129). But "the rule of those days" rested on a fundamental misplacement of what Dutton considered the "will of providence," which subjugated and exploited the very people it claimed to have primary interest in advancing.

Dutton claimed that he was "always . . . concerned about the means of living of the town population" more than about any other group or issue (1983, 129). The social (and physical) construction of space and place in African urban areas served as his primary focus for more than thirty years. Dutton, like many colonialists, professed belief at some level in the validation of local, African knowledge, such as local planning and building knowledge. From Nairobi, Lusaka, and Zanzibar, he wrote variations on this sentiment: "I am convinced that the best and surest way . . . of making a real and permanent advance is to make improvement after improvement on the native design. If our model houses appeal to the native we have won half the battle" (Dutton 1944c). Colonialism, to Dutton, mixed rule with goodwill. Showing respect to local customs or tradition in matters like house style was an obvious means of demonstrating goodwill.

Dutton himself acknowledged, though, that the urban improvements to which he dedicated his life in Africa had not accomplished their key moral and political-economic objectives: "More might have been done for these friendly people. . . . But to me far the greatest of all was the failure to prevent the growth of slums. Then was the chance to strangle them at birth" (Dutton 1983, 129). He went on to say that this "was all the more of a fault since the Africans' own villages were often spotless" (Dutton 1983, 129). He and others like him on the metaphorical colonial elite verandah in British Africa professed admiration for the "order without framework" of African villages and recognized the importance of cultivating "public opinion on the spot." If this was so, then what created such a consistent pattern of failure to achieve legitimacy or to implement what the British saw as effective planning measures, particularly in this city that was expanding ever so slowly?

The reasons for this failure are complex and broad, but there are some pervasive causative factors that Dutton's example encapsulates. The most central was of course the intrinsic racism of colonial space. In his memoirs Dutton recalled long talks in Lugard and Oldham's homes in the United Kingdom, saying "we thought of segregation as a system, not necessarily permanent, designed for social convenience, and certainly as one free from objectionable discrimination. As far as I remember, we never debated it for and against, or examined it in depth: we accepted it" (Dutton 1983, 194–95). But segregation was indeed examined in depth; it was a carefully constructed discourse of colonial culture.

For instance, Dutton and Frederick Lugard corresponded for over a decade, with the main focus of their exchange centered on racial segregation. Dutton several times wrote of his regard for Lugard's assertion that "repugnance to miscegenation" is "a natural and purely physical instinct" (Lugard Papers, Box 10, 1932). Lugard for his part enjoyed Dutton's deployment of "my formula about the colour bar." In a letter to Dutton dated October 9, 1941, he explained, "I intended in it to emphasize that there seems to be much confusion of ideas between antagonisms due to psychological and racial differences wisely implanted by Nature . . . and antagonisms due to inferiority and superiority complexes" (Lugard Papers). In another letter dated May 2, 1932, Lugard argued for "making Native Councils attractive" to ambitious Africans, precisely and explicitly because this would keep them from desiring "the magnet of the Legislative Councils" that held the real power (Lugard Papers). For these and many other explicitly segregationist tactics, Dutton gratefully acknowledged his debt to the elder Lugard, writing, on March 21, 1932, "Unless we who are growing up in the service now can take our foundations from those who did all the building in the first days there can be little hope of continuity" (Lugard Papers). Achievement of goodwill consequently depended upon convincing Africans to see segregation and attendant inequalities of urban services as the natural and commonsense outgrowth of the prestige of the colonizer. What they "saw with their own eyes" was more often that the British, like Eric Dutton, "had power and liked power" (as Oldham said of Dutton in their correspondence), while the Africans lacked what others had as a direct result of the colonial system.

Yet in spite of—or perhaps because of—the stupendous schemes, orders without frameworks continue to be the primary planning engines in much of Zanzibar, Lusaka, and Nairobi, whether in the sprawling squatter areas that surround them or embedded inside them. In the sections below, I look at the Zanzibar project from the verandah of the colonized middle, and then from that of the urban majority, the creators of the orders without frameworks that have survived colonialism's enframing tactics.

Ajit Singh in Colonial Zanzibar

Ajit Singh served as the main architect and draftsman of Dutton's reconstruction program. I concentrate here on reading some of the cityscape of the postwar reconstruction for which Singh is responsible as a means of articulating his part in colonialism's spatial tactics. I focus on two of Ajit Singh's building designs from the era—the "utility house" style of the neighborhood reconstruction, and the Ng'ambo civic center. I then examine Ajit Singh's own views on the reconstruction effort.

The Utility House

All the houses in the postwar reconstruction's model areas—Holmwood, Mwembetanga, and Mji Mpya—had the same design, called a utility house because of its function in the redevelopment. The original architectural drawings from 1944 are marked simply as having been drawn by Ajit Singh, with no name in the space for "architect." Dutton revealed in his "semi-official" correspondence with the Colonial Office that the core design concepts of what is variously called a Lee House (after the medical officer of health), a Pilling House (after the British Resident), or a Wheatley House (after the supervisor of native housing), actually belonged to Ajit

Singh (AB 39/24, ZNA). Throughout his career, Ajit believed in "team-work, close cooperation and mutual open opinion" in the building process (Singh Papers). As a result of his philosophy, but also of the European bias of colonial rule, here and in numerous other cases designs dominated by his ideas are known by white people's names.

Ajit based his house design on "native huts." He came to believe an ar-chitect had to be "tuned to the local sensibility" to design properly (Singh Papers). The houses were constructed to improve durability; the usual pole frame was replaced with a set of twelve reinforced concrete pillars, while the walls incorporated both larger stones and a greater quantity of coral lime in the mud-lime wall mix. The main materials and room layouts re-mained quite in keeping with Zanzibari *mtomo* (daub) construction tradi-tion: a rectangular, one-story, three- to six-room house with a kitchen, a toilet, and a store room as outbuildings. Several aspects of site planning were, however, new ideas with connections to social engineering. Ajit Singh widened the traditional *ua* (courtyard) at the back of the main home. The *ua* is conventionally a space open to the sky between the outbuildings and the main house, in which most household chores, such as cooking and laundry, are done. On the basis of the gender patterns of housework and space in Zanzibar, the *ua* is the central arena of most women's lives. Hence its widening was seen by the colonial regime as an enhancement of women's domestic space, bound to be popular and to improve neighborhood health and the circulation of air.

For this latter reason, Ajit's original design also did not include walls for the sides of the *ua*. In spite of this original absence of *ua* walls, the orderly layouts of the new Holmwood, Mwembetanga, and Mji Mpya tracts had within them a different form of fixed distinction between outside and in-side, the "party fence." Both women and men rejected the lack of a fence or wall to demarcate the sides of their *ua* so forcefully that Singh and Wheat-ley relented and sided with them. This caused the Dutton administration to allow utility-house residents to build their own *ua* walls or fences over the fierce objections of the medical officer of health and the police commis-sioner (AS 1/77 and AB 40/13a, ZNA). Residents' complaints concerning the party fences eventually brought them down; where they were put in place in the model neighborhoods, most had been broken down by the mid-1950s. The only fencing that remains now is that separating the former Holmwood estate from the police barracks.

On one level, then, this particular spatial enframing tactic appears to have foundered in the face of internal resistance. On other levels, though, the house design created by Ajit Singh subtly transformed domestic architecture in the city over the next twenty years. Uppermost in his mind, Ajit strove consistently to "kick the ball rolling toward good taste with the man in the street" (Singh Papers). Indeed, several elements of Ajit Singh's utility-house style spread throughout Zanzibar's new and old areas. Local builders gravitated toward reinforced concrete pillars, increased the stone and lime content of ordinary walls, and widened the *ua*. Although many of these improvements might have happened over time without the redevelopment's incentive, the reconstruction clearly set something bigger in motion. The movement to recreate utility houses in older neighborhoods became widespread, even playing a role in events leading up to Zanzibar's revolution through a debate on how to define—and tax—a "native hut" (see the section of this chapter entitled "The Aftermath of Reconstruction").

The utility-house design demonstrates the problems in seeing colonial spatial planning merely as alien Western imposition against indigenous resistance. Utility houses were, ultimately, negotiated spaces in between. On the one hand, they were part of a colonial tactic of control. On the other hand, they simultaneously became sites of oppositional consciousness. Ajit Singh, cooperative with both the colonial regime and the forces that would eventually topple it, resided in an uncertain and uncomfortable middle, but Ajit was not alone with his contradictions. Even the family who has owned the first utility house in Mwembetanga for the last fifty years, for instance, retains substantial pride in their part in the abortive town improvement scheme: successive wall remodeling jobs have skirted around the engraved cornerstone. Yet they hardly commemorate this as a moment of resistance—it was mainly a moment when they thought they were getting a nicer house than the ones their neighbors had.

The Civic Center

The civic center's main hall is a deceptively plain building to look at, given what it was expected to do. Part of what makes Ajit an important designer, besides the fact that many prominent buildings in this very architecturally significant city bear his touches, is that his buildings rarely stick out uncomfortably from the cityscape and its cultural fabric as many of Zanzibar's postcolonial structures so obviously do. The limited embellishments to the facade, the flat roof with ornamental protrusions, the very thick and white-

washed mud-lime-stone walls, the Islamic-style arch, and the interior courtyard all mimic the best of Stone Town's famous architecture. Indeed, the
civic center was not a building dramatically different from the recently re-
stored Sultan's Palace on Stone Town's waterfront, right next to the House
of Wonders, and this is no accident. The sultan and his Omani relatives
and allies, followers of the puritanical Ibadhi sect of Islam, not only appreciated a spare architecture; they were clearly meant, by this building's form,
to be put in a more accepting mood for the investment of time and energy
the protectorate had showered on what they saw as the African community's center. The Sultanate and the monied elite of Stone Town had ob-
jected most forcefully to the whole of Dutton's scheme—their own (Arab)
community had not had such a center built for it, after all, and many were
suspicious of Dutton's efforts to win the hearts and minds of blacks. What
better way to appease their sensibilities than to ape the architecture of the
palace?

Aside from designing the buildings of the civic center, Ajit Singh actually did his best to avoid direct involvement in the overtly political aspects of
Dutton's plans. Ajit was, as Dutton said of him, "wholeheartedly devoted to
his work": he liked to design buildings, not to play politics. Ironically, what
seemed at the time of its building to be his most important contribution to
the colonial redevelopment efforts became a meeting place of the very
community associates who would later plot the revolution that would over-
throw the sultanate Ajit's building had been designed to please.

The narrative of Ajit's buildings for the political aspects of the postwar
plan like the civic center is a cautionary tale for any tempted to apply an
easy simplification of the spatial tactics of colonialism as alien imposition
opposed by indigenous people. The eventual leaders of Zanzibar's revolution liked the civic center so much that they made use of its campus in a
number of rallies and meetings in the years leading up to the 1964 revolt.
Indeed, Raha Leo was the headquarters of the revolution itself.

Ajit Singh, architect of those headquarters, often seemed to be both for
and against the colonial order. Singh always wrote to Reginald Wheatley,
Julian Asquith, and other British superiors from the colonial period—and
particularly, of course, to Eric Dutton—with great affection tinged with
deference. In 1965 he encouraged Dutton to keep plugging away on his
memoir (the unfinished "Night of the Hyena" [1983]), praising his "digni-
fied influence" and "personal charm and power. . . . I am quite sure that

Fig. 12. The Ng'ambo Civic Center at Raha Leo, 1948.
From Papers of Ajit Singh Hoogan. Courtesy of Parmukh
Singh Hoogan, MP.

your autobiography will be most interesting and colorful" (Singh Papers).
He fawned over Dutton's children, both in letters and in their visits to Zanzibar as young adults. And Ajit always flattered his mentor's achievements:
"You would love to see the buildings you designed and supervised," he
wrote in 1962. "Zanzibar must be thankful to you. You radically changed
the topographical features of the town by your genius in architecture and
administration. I have found few people of your caliber" (Singh Papers).

Dutton, for his part, played up a mentoring role with Ajit, not in a
blandly paternalist fashion but rather as the "wise and patient friend" that
Ajit called him. In 1953, a month after leaving Zanzibar, Dutton wrote, "I
miss my morning talk with you on the broad subject of architecture. My association with you was a very happy one and I think it was productive of
some good for Zanzibar. . . . Do your very best for Trace [the new head of
the Central Development Authority]. Don't make things difficult for him
through relations with other members of your Department" (Singh Papers). A few months later, in 1954, he advised, "You must try to remember
that a chance to create such as came to Mr. Wheatley [the supervisor of native housing], you and I does not come very often." He responded to Ajit's
praise of his design genius by saying they had designed the buildings "together . . . we were a good team" (Singh Papers). When Ajit's father died in
1963, Dutton wrote a touching letter of condolence. He wrote of how he

could still remember "as if it were yesterday" the death of his own father in 1911, an event that indeed had enormous significance for the then sixteen-year-old Dutton: "[O]h, for the touch of a vanished hand" (Singh Papers).

Thus, the very same Dutton who had advised Governor Coryndon in Kenya that "no one wants an Indian to come live next to him" entrusted his Indian protégé with the private tutoring of his son in draftsmanship and with intimate details of his own life. Ajit Singh admired not only Eric Dutton, but also what he stood for. He was a proper English gentleman to Ajit, even if Dutton had trouble all his life convincing the upper class of England that he belonged with them. Dutton, and colonialism writ large, tried to teach Ajit how to behave, to teach him his place. That place was in-between, but decidedly below the colonizer-British, on a middle verandah.

Zanzibar as an African City

This colonial reconstruction of Ng'ambo that Singh and Dutton performed had only a slight impact on the urban form of most older neighborhoods, like Kikwajuni, where Bwana Juma Maalim Kombo lived. Many Kikwajuni residents did work on the reconstruction, however, or housed relatives affected by it. Many greeted favorably the opportunities for work it afforded them, even if they saw as minimal the project's ultimate impact on their families' daily struggles to get by. Bwana Juma did some work in the reconstruction project. In interviews with me in July 1992, he didn't mince words about the life of most people in Kikwajuni and Zanzibar as a whole in the 1930s and 1940s: "What were our living conditions? They were very, very, very poor. You lived in a rotten little hut, and you paid for the right to do so. For water, you depended on a water carrier. You cooked on lousy firewood. Your salary was mud if you even had one. When I came back from the war, I got a big "thank you," that's it. . . . The revolution did a lot of good. It brought us rights" (Kombo 1992).

Yet colonial power was a personalized thing. Juma Issa, a neighbor of Bwana Juma, was proud to say that he had worked as Reginald Wheatley's head of house, and later as the head servant of the next native housing officer, A. P. Cumming-Bruce. "They were men of respect. Respect mattered a great deal to Dutton, Wheatley, and Cumming-Bruce. They came from good families. . . . The whites lived here very respectfully, without any nonsense. You got trouble from them if you gave trouble; if you were peaceful and respectful, so were they" (Issa 1992).

Personal narratives and personified visions of colonialism were re-peated over and over again in different interviews with older Zanzibaris. For Salama Hussein Mohammed, like many others in the urban majority, "life was extremely hard. People went without shoes. They had dirty clothes. Many Comorians and some Africans pretended to be Arabs so they could get around the discrimination. Things got better when we woke up" (Mohammed 1992). Many Zanzibaris spoke of the 1964 Zanzibar Revolution as the time when they "woke up." But colonialism was not a simple time of bitter sleeping; here again the personal elements come into the story. Bi Salama singled out Ajit Singh's family especially, without prompt-ing, for their work in organizing charitable events for the poor in Kikwa-juni: "There were a lot of Indians who were people with power [*uwezo*] and faith [*imani*], and they cared a lot about society. Karimji Jivanjee . . . did a lot for Zanzibar. A great many people were helped by people like Singh. With the landlords, we were an investment, but we had the usual sort of human relationships, it wasn't like we were always at odds" (Mohammed 1992).

Some residents were less ambivalent, or expressed less confidence that the colonial regime had their interests at all in mind, in the reconstruction or in any matters. Bi Mkubwa Ali Saleh, who was a young child in Kikwa-juni at the time of the reconstruction, and who has since studied in Britain, put it this way: "The English are very tricky. They have many tricks. You never know what they are really up to" (Saleh interview 1992). To Anthony Thomas Mandrad, the whole project was a "show," and the underlying aim had to do with policing Ng'ambo: "In Mwembetanga *mtaa*, the British built some houses as a show. Here in Kisimamajongoo *mtaa*, they only built roads. . . . And they only built roads so their cars could get to the Police Sta-tion. They did nothing for us. We didn't have any cars" (Mandrad 1992).

Bwana Juma Maalim Kombo worked together with his friend Mo-hammed Ali Jobo for a few months on building those roads, and then Juma quit, while Mzee Mohammed became a building inspector as a result of his connection to Wheatley. One day, they invited me to share some of their recollections:

> JOBO: There was this one *mzungu* [white], do you remember, he was the chief secretary for a long time, Dutton—
> KOMBO: Oh, Dutton! He took the best door in Stone Town and made it his front door in England!

MYERS: Did he steal it?

JOBO: He was the chief secretary.

KOMBO: Do you know what that means? He was the sultan's door-keeper. You didn't get to the sultan without going through Dutton.

JOBO: He had real power.

KOMBO: Heh, if he wanted to use the sultan's yacht just to go fishing, he did it. And who's going to say he did something wrong? Me? Hah! Dutton! (Kombo and Jobo 1992)

Many others have recounted to me what seems to be an urban legend about Dutton having taken the spectacular carved doors from Mambo Msiige, the government records building in Stone Town. Since Dutton retired first to Morocco and then to Portugal (not England), and since neither he nor Ajit mention the door in their correspondences on the woodwork and carpentry of his house in Portugal, it seems unlikely that he took it. Perhaps the greatest source of genuine resentment against Dutton, though, at least in the reconstruction, was his use of six thousand pounds from the Colonial Office Fund for the construction of his own elaborate home on the southern seafront in Zanzibar city. This sum represented the potential for sixty to seventy more utility homes. Dutton was seen to be living as ostentatiously as the Omani elite, and many residents resented him accordingly (*Al Falaq* 1946, 1).

The doornapping is a fanciful tale, but the sense that Dutton "had real power" and that he often appeared to take great advantage of it—fishing on the sultan's yacht—has the weight of substantial evidence behind it. And this may be one of his most enduring legacies in Zanzibar. Within a half-mile of that house he built on the southern beachfront of the city, one can visit the sparkling villas of Abeid Amani Karume, Aboud Jumbe, Idris Abdul Wakil, Ali Hassan Mwinyi, Salmin Amour, and Amani Karume, the six presidents of revolutionary Zanzibar since 1964. There is something about that sea view that seems to do Zanzibar "no end of harm" (Oldham Papers 1932) as its leaders abscond with the country's wealth to make palaces for themselves.

Kikwajuni residents, ultimately, are of mixed minds about the reconstruction and seem to greet colonialism in general with a shrug. "We were like slaves. Their administration made the decisions and they made the maps, *basi* [that's it]," said Mzee Mandrad. "There was health control, that's true. The rat office [what residents call the health inspectors] came around, and if you wanted to build or make repairs, you had to go there, then they'd come inspect. But really, under colonial rule the citizens were not there. They had no say" (Mandrad 1992). There are aspects of colonial spatial planning and colonial culture that did sink in to Zanzibar's urban majority, such as the vigorous health inspections, but these internalized notions now sit side by side with a cool bitterness about what colonialism did not do for their lives and their neighborhoods. "You see," said Mr. Mandrad, "I cooked for Wheatley, he was a nice man, but the point is in those days you had to do for yourself" (1992). These ambivalent aspects of residents' memories of the colonial order become clear in visiting with the residents of Mwembetanga, the main reconstructed neighborhood.

The Voices of Poland

People in Mwembetanga were unhappy about having their houses demolished. They were grudgingly willing to go along with the process as long as the promise that the new homes would be better was fulfilled. Early indications were that this would not be the case. The reception houses seemed like bare-bones shells, with an enormous amount of finishing work left to the new residents and a confusing number of adjustments in domestic spatiality. The earliest complaints of residents took the form of derogatory place-names for Mwembetanga and Miafuni (the civic center area): "Poland," in reference to images they were shown in newsreels from the Second World War, and "The First Devastated Area" are those most residents remember. Complaints were even voiced, albeit timidly, on the newly formed Ng'ambo Council (Pilling to Dutton, September 25, 1945, AB 39/21, ZNA).

The issues were not overtly political, as demonstrated by one focus group interview, Yahya et al. 1992; all the following quotations are taken from the transcript of that interview with Yahya Salim Yahya, Ali Khalil Ali, Bi Mtumwa Fundi Tausir, Bi Salhina Saleh Haji, Ali Iddi Juma, Mohammed Omari Said, Ali Talib Yahya, and Hamid Mohammed Amour. These residents experienced both the first and the second reconstructions of Mwembetanga—the colonial and revolutionary versions. Clearly, not all of the gathered residents shared the same politics. Some went to great lengths in protesting the revolutionary government's actions on a number of fronts while defending certain aspects of the colonial program. But even these defenders had their "doubts" about the colonial reconstruction, and even they acknowledged the subservient position of Swahili people in the colonial order. Colonialism "was harsh," Bi Salhina said, "like a strict father." Ali Talib, to the assent of all in the room said, "that was colonialism, you were afraid to complain." The fact that Mwembetanga residents expressed their doubts or complaints by making up names like Poland for their neighborhood or by sending off respectful letters to the Ladies Committee of Mwembetanga and the women's welfare officer reveals a great deal about their consciousness of their subject position. These were the "weapons of the weak," not quite the rebellious spirit of an urban majority bent on revolution—not yet. As Yahya put it, "politics didn't start until 1957." After 1957, when what Zanzibaris literally call the Time of Politics took over all aspects of the planning agenda, that rebellious spirit rose with a vengeance. And within that spirit, the aborted Ng'ambo reconstruction was reframed within the cornerstones of power, faith, and custom held by Zanzibar's urban majority.

The Aftermath of Reconstruction

Urban planning and building control became pivotal sites for the clash of colonial-elite mental visions with Zanzibar city's urban majority. The 1964 revolution itself was largely an urban event, and many processes leading up to it were tied to urban issues. Housing and building-control politics were key arenas for generating anticolonial and anti-elite feeling at the household level, and African urban areas provided the landscape in which and on which these politics were played. The conflict-ridden relationship between colonial administrators, landlords, and tenants over rents, property rights, and building rules in the city underscores how both colonialists and the local elite transgressed the majority's community consensus in spatial strategies aimed at social control. When all "appeals to the softer side" (Zanzibar Protectorate 1928, 51) by Africans failed, then rent strikes, squatter actions, rallies, and ultimately, rebellion ensued.

Popular consciousness escaped the authority to plan claimed by colonialists and the elite alike, leaving them ineffective in shaping space to control their subjects. The spatial form of houses and neighborhoods in Ng'ambo, and efforts to remake that spatiality, ultimately became a contested terrain of colonialism's end. The failure by both the colonial state and local elites to "understand and conceive of" the customary practices of Ng'ambo's majority in their "originality and uniqueness" made attempts to "dominate and direct them" nigh on impossible (Gramsci 1971, 240).

For many of its officers, colonial Zanzibar was, as the police chief of the time, R.H.V. Biles, stated in 1971, a place "with an enormous feeling of hierarchy" where they "were up against tradition the whole time" (Mss Afr s 1446, RHL). They perceived their effort to change traditions in the domestic and neighborhood environment as a forced "change of philosophy of life and therefore a revolutionary idea" (Davies Papers 1957, Mss Afr s 956, RHL). Zanzibari resistance to this revolutionary idea was conceived of as subtle and uneven, but frustrating nonetheless. An official in 1946 argued that "opposition in Zanzibar is never very forceful and true feelings are usually not expressed. . . . They are too polite to make good politicians" (AB 39/21, ZNA). Bi Salama Hussein Mohammed responded to my question about people's resistance to colonialism similarly: "Oh, you know how people are in Zanzibar. If someone doesn't like something, they say nothing; three years later they grumble about it enough to make their point, and then it is over" (Mohammed 1992).

Communication between the popular masses and the colonial powers was often filtered through the elite or the colonized middle, especially during the 'Zanzibarization' phase of decolonization, when the favored elite and middle agents gained substantial positions in the civil service. Paternalism and bemused disdain seeped into the colonialist view of Ng'ambo housing. John O'Brian, the urban district commissioner, put it this way in explaining to Dutton why people were so opposed to the 1940s reconstruction: "[T]he townsman is touchy about his hut (his only tangible possession: heap of sticks and rubble though it may sometimes be termed); it is his all. The townsman . . . resents being moved, but all these things can be overcome" (AB 9/48, ZNA). A close reading of the urban majority's replies reveals a sense that Ng'ambo dwellers spent a half-century "grumbling about" the colonial situation, trying unsuccessfully to "make their point" that not all things could be "overcome."

Countless pieces of correspondence in the Zanzibar National Archives from Ng'ambo residents to the colonial state over a period of seventy-three years are signed by "humble and obedient servants." "Sirs" are capitalized, submissions said respectfully. Albeit occasionally with the help of professional letter-writers, Ng'ambo's crowd met the British on their own ground; but from the beginning of colonial interventions into Ng'ambo, African appeals to the British to "come forward and help" (AE 8/10, ZNA) seldom brought results.

Building control was an extremely problematic sphere of operation for colonial agents in the Time of Politics. The legal definition of a "native hut," which formed the basis of the Building Rules for "Native Locations" under Dutton's amendments from the 1940s, was fundamental to colonialism's defining of the geographical order, but it became one of its most problematic fundaments. Dutton's reconstruction project set into motion a new wave of home improvement among residents on the Other Side in the 1950s. Owners sought to improve their home values before their neighborhood came to be reconstructed. They recognized that home improvements increased the likelihood of a house being exempted from demolition, or at least increased the potential for a compensation payment (AB 40/13a, ZNA). Chief among the improvements performed in the 1950s were use of reinforced concrete pillars at six-to-nine foot intervals within the side walls and increased use of coral stone or cured lime plaster, both of which were features of Ajit Singh's model houses. These home improvements, even though the reconstruction had initiated them, confounded the racialist legal structure meant to contain them.

To the urban majority in the 1940s and 1950s, housing problems were framed in much different terms than those belonging to the realm of British building-control standards. Residents faced overcrowded conditions in western parts of the Other Side and could not afford the premium payments demanded for plot development in its eastern suburbs. They did not see a solution in dickering over the English words used to tell them what was a "hut" and what was a "house," as the colonial planning apparatus spent the 1950s debating. Their immediate solution was more direct and spatial: end the overcrowding of houses in the west by squatting in the east. For many, that was the only option their *uwezo* allowed them.

To the security-conscious protectorate government, the growth of unplanned settlements on the edge of town established a dangerous trend. This outer edge was arguably the strongest center of support on the islands for Abeid Amani Karume and the Afro-Shirazi Party (ASP). Controlling how the outer edge grew, or whether it grew at all was, said Native Housing Officer Cumming-Bruce in 1955, the "indispensable corollary" of good political policy (AE 5/3, ZNA). Colonial political policy and urban management had a decided bias toward the Zanzibar Nationalist Party (ZNP), which was dominated by the local elite and colonized middle, since the Zanzibarizing civil service consisted overwhelmingly of ZNP operatives. Yet many British officials implemented policies under the naïve assumption of their neutrality in the ZNP-ASP conflict. The Zanzibari points of view solicited and consulted in the British sphere were largely those of the local elite, as Biles, the police chief of the time, admitted in 1971 ((Mss Afr s 1446, RHL). Hence they had a limited appreciation for the motivations behind the expansion of the outer edge.

Supposedly, the Ground Rent Restriction Decree of 1928 was designed to keep land rents low in Native Locations, while the Dutton-era Building Rules were intended to foster measured and orderly urban development. In practice, however, the main landowners used the protection of the rent law to cram more houses onto their lands (Alawi 1986; Awadh 1989). With increased migration to the city in the 1950s, the clamor for new building plots grew still further. Nothing in the laws restricted premiums, which consequently soared throughout the town. Outer-area landlords were only too willing to repeat the densification pattern of the inner areas, but many people were unable to pay the premiums being demanded.

Cumming-Bruce, the housing officer who succeeded Reginald Wheatley, hoped that town planning might offer a way out of the policy conundrum on the edge of town, especially in what he called "the public relations aspect of planning." He and the more liberal officers clearly wished to avoid using the "reserve power of firm authority" and saw professional planning as the mechanism through which to "educate their masters"—and their servants—and to manufacture consent (AE 5/3, ZNA). Most of the subsequently developed 1958 Zanzibar Town Planning Scheme was abandoned soon after its publication, but the colonial state did implement the zoning principles set out by planning consultant Henry Kendall. Kendall divided residential areas into Zones A ("high class"), B ("middle class") and C ("Native-type Huts"). The high-class zone included Stone Town and extended to the north and south of town along the beachfront. The beachfront areas between Stone Town and the new Zone A farther out of town were given Zone B status, along with some buffer areas between outer Ng'ambo *mitaa* and the elite villas. The Native zone, Zone C, covered the rest of the city, comfortably contained behind the map's buffer areas (Kendall 1958; AE 5/7, ZNA).

The northern suburban beaches had long been home to the country estates of the royal clan. The beach area to the south had for a number of years been a popular residential area for colonial administrators like Dutton. Kendall reserved these areas for "first class residential development."

The 1958 plan legalized the distinction between this "villa zone" and the poor outer areas of Ng'ambo north and south of it. Some southern villas underwent a Zanzibarization of sorts. Thirty-six plots were developed in 1959 at Migombani as a Zone A community, with twenty-seven different owners. At least ten of the new plot owners were relatives of the royal clan or main city landlords. Thirteen were high-ranking Arab, Indian, or Comorian government officials (DA 1/266, ZNA). The zoning apparatus put in place with the 1958 plan thus had the effect of legalizing segregation based on both race and class. The enframing tactic of segmentation from Dutton's postwar plan resurfaced in the 1958 version.

However, far from alleviating the squatting problem on Zone C's edge, the 1958 plan exacerbated it. The outer-area landowners found the plan's requirement that they provide "essential services" (water, sewage, drainage, and roads) prior to renting out plots unacceptably expensive and left their plots undeveloped. The colonial government ordered a halt to legal plot development until essential services were provided. Thousands more people began squatting in the outer areas, "resulting," according to the senior district commissioner, "in slums being created" (Busaidy 1960). In what was seen as a worse offense than this initial "hut" construction, the people in these "slums" were actually improving their houses through customary wall conversions, making "semi-permanent slums" (Busaidy 1961). By 1962, the sprawling Zone C had reached the airport road in the south—Kendall's division between the intended A and B zones.

These "slums" of the Time of Politics were seen by the ZNP-dominated provincial administration as "a political repercussion" from the "tendency of some members of the public not to respect law and order" (Busaidy 1962). They irritated landowners, who often claimed to receive no rents from the "huts." They "bothered" the town planning office because they were "haphazard" and had poor ventilation, and no "vehicular access" (Hamilton 1961). Yet private landowners were not "in the least interested in providing land" for low-income housing: it did not pay (de Sechi 1961). Whereas the town-planning records for the 1958 Plan show that by 1961, 150 of the 371 plots in upper- and middle-class zones were already legally under development, not one of the 932 official homesites on surveyed native zone land was being legally developed (DA 1/163, ZNA). Instead, they were being invaded by Zanzibar's urban majority. Neither landowners nor the state seemed to appreciate that Ng'ambo dwellers were "speaking with space" (Constantin 1987), "making their point" that this was their city, and its form manifested their *uwezo, imani,* and *desturi.*

The official census numbers for Zanzibar city expanded only marginally between 1948 and 1958, from 45,284 to 49,502, with most of the increase recorded in the outer Ng'ambo neighborhoods along, but inside, the boundary—places like Holmwood. This hides the jumps in population recorded for the *mitaa* just outside this official boundary. Nearly 10,000 people were officially recorded in 1958 as living in the census tracts immediately beyond the town, up from fewer than 5,000 in 1948. Collectively, the squatter edge straddling the boundary had a population of more than 10,000 by 1958, or almost 20 percent of the urban population, and this number climbed still higher between 1958 and 1963.

The late colonial regime decried these squatter slums as *ovyo* construction. The main colonial-era Swahili-English dictionary defines *ovyo* as "haphazard or random," but also gives this definition: "useless articles, rubbish, what is common and valueless." This was probably the meaning intended by the colonial state, but these were places given much greater life and meaning by the people living in them and creating them. The names of these *mitaa* say a great deal: Sogea (pack it in), Tumekuja (we have come), Jang'ombe (full of cows, or garbage pit of cows), Raha Kesho (happiness tomorrow: an obvious toponymic reply to Dutton's naming of the civic center as Raha Leo or happiness today), Sebleni (living room) and Makadara (the will of God). From the outset, the absence of *uwezo* for most residents in these *mitaa* left them open to landlords who "packed them in;" left them open in their minds to survive by the will of God alone. Indeed, each of these *mitaa* developed mosques early in the squatting process. Each of them functioned through the 1950s and even into the early independence period by means of customary neighborliness and highly informal voluntary associations. People might have been *packed in* like a *garbage dump of cows,* but in seeking *happiness tomorrow,* people *had come* to share the same crowded *living room.*

The colonial planning and building-control apparatus was remarkably ineffective in most aspects of its mandate during the Time of Politics, perhaps most of all in securing its legitimacy. The urban majority saw themselves locked out of one process after another under colonialism. In spite of the institutionalization of professional planning at the end of the colonial era, residents "had to do for themselves" as Mzee Mandrad put it, in building and planning as in most spheres of their lives.

Conclusion

Colonial spatial planning in Zanzibar had much in common with that in Nairobi or Lusaka besides the person of Eric Dutton. The spatial tactics of enframing, and even to some degree the actual patterns of neighborhood form, were very much the same in these colonies. The ambivalence behind Dutton's sentiment that the British were "there to help" was replicated in Kenya, Zambia, and Zanzibar. Although both of the projects headed by Dutton in Lusaka and Zanzibar dramatically changed the physical land-scape, neither really had its intended social effects. To some degree, the professional attitudes or frames of reference for urban planners in both of those settings as well as in Nairobi today remain influenced by those established on Dutton's watch in the cities. For instance, the tendency to approach planning problems by thinking grandly, to come at the city with a "stupendous hammer to crack a few nuts," as Cumming-Bruce himself described the Dutton project in the 1940s in Zanzibar, predominated in all three cities (Nairobi, Lusaka, and Zanzibar) at least through the 1980s. In chapter 6 I show how much the stupendous hammer of the revolutionary postcolonial reconstruction project relied on Dutton-like approaches. After all, that project's chief protagonist, Abeid Amani Karume, got his political start on the civic center Management Committee and the Ng'ambo Town Council during the Dutton era.

The "finicking path of conduct and action," as the *Zanzibar Gazette* described it in 1928 (Zanzibar Protectorate) that bound the Zanzibar islands' African and Swahili majority to servility and poverty eventually exploded in the 1964 revolution, in which the Afro-Shirazi Party seized power from the month-old ZNP government. Both the ZNP and the colonial state had either misrepresented or misunderstood the aims, values, and motivations of Zanzibar's majority, and this majority ultimately imposed violent retribution on many of their dominators. I have tried to show in this chapter the ways in which the authority and capacity to determine and enframe the course of urban development slipped from the grasp of the powerful. Rhetorically at least, some colonial officers appeared to appreciate the magnitude of this slip: "[T]he process of changing other people's modes of life is either presumptuous or dangerous unless they participate in the change," wrote Cumming-Bruce during the Time of Politics. Moreover, he acknowledged, "participation does not mean the other chap joining in your plan; it means both of you working together to produce a joint plan" (AB

9/9, ZNA). A landscape of domination without legitimation, of rule without goodwill, is a landscape of mere coercion. Zanzibar's urban majority employed what little power it had, held to its faith, and adjusted its customs as best it could as antidotes to that coercive oppression. The lessons its members learned from the late colonial period would serve them well in the new revolutionary order, the subject of chapter 6.

Chapter Six

Revolutionary Zanzibar

> "You know, we had development houses but without development of
> consciousness. We lived the way we were used to living before; it was
> very crowded in those little rooms. But they weren't concerned with
> those things; what they wanted was for everyone to have the same liv-
> ing conditions"
>
> —Ali Talib Ali, Zanzibar, 1992

Introduction

Under the minority leadership of a Zanzibar National Party government, Zanzibar received its independence from Britain on December 12,
1963. A month later, just after midnight on January 12, 1964, cashiered police officers and opposition rank-and-file members of the Afro-Shirazi
Party (ASP) led by a man who called himself Field Marshall John Okello
(1967) seized the police station at Mtoni, north of Zanzibar city. The rebels
proceeded from there, with the seized police weapons, and entered the city.
With one skirmish, they succeeded in capturing control of the city by early
morning. After they took the radio station in the Ng'ambo Civic Center at
Raha Leo, the rebels declared a revolutionary government headed by the
Afro-Shirazi Party. The ASP's main leaders, such as Abeid Amani Karume,
were not even on the island as the revolution unfolded. Karume and others
returned from the mainland early on January 12 and gradually secured
their place at the head of the new Revolutionary Council. It is by no means
certain who masterminded the takeover, and the political situation remained in flux for several weeks. Uncertainty only began to subside when
Karume concluded secret meetings with Tanganyika's president, Julius Ny-
erere, by signing Articles of Union between their two states on April 26.
This signing ceremony created the United Republic of Tanzania, ending
Zanzibar's run of 148 days as an independent country (A. Wilson 1990).

Up to the revolution and even beyond it, Karume had hardly seemed the revolutionary socialist he later sought to appear. The United States consular officer on the island in April 1964, Frank Carlucci, described Karume as "a very decent, somewhat phlegmatic man. . . . a rough-hewn, strong-minded, stubborn—but forthright—politician" (A. Wilson 1990). The last British colonial senior commissioner in Zanzibar, Mervyn Smithyman, despaired in a letter to a fellow colonial official a few days after the revolt: "[E]very member of this Revolutionary Council *except Abeid* is a commie" (Robertson papers 1964, Rhodes House Library; emphasis mine). Lady Mooring, the wife of the last British Resident, George ("Satan") Mooring, said, after an audience with Karume on her return to Zanzibar in 1971, "he was very affable. . . . He was not a bad man really. We had always quite liked him, a rugged fisherman" (Maddocks Papers, Rhodes House Library).

Karume had been the first African on Eric Dutton's Ng'ambo Town Council; he had served on Dutton's Civic Center Management Committee; and Dutton had thanked him personally for his role in defusing the 1948–49 general strike in the city. In the months after the April union with Tanganyika, as he consolidated his power, Karume at least publicly performed a rhetorical conversion to socialism that expanded dramatically on his long-standing commitment to the poor in the city. Yet the program of development that he created for, and partially enacted in Zanzibar city replicated and expanded upon the enframing order of colonialism that he had learned in the Dutton years.

A Socialist City?

Under Karume, revolutionary urban-planning strategy in Zanzibar city was dominated by a grand vision. Ng'ambo, the Other Side of the city, became the physical embodiment of this vision. The principal urban program and most enduring legacy of the revolutionary era (1964–77) was the attempted reconstruction of Ng'ambo into a vast public-housing estate, even as the end of colonialism helped to create what Zanzibaris call "Ng'ambo wa Pili," the Second Other Side, on the outskirts of the first.

Tanzania is often cast as a marginal case of Third World socialism, especially considering the steep rise in overall urbanization and the tremendous growth of its primate city, Dar es Salaam (Coulson 1982; Samoff 1982 and 1979; Shivji 1976; Saul 1979; Hill 1975, 216–54; Mueller 1980; Banyikwa 1989). These analyses are really critiques of socialist urban planning and development in mainland Tanzania, though, and it can be argued that they are not pertinent to Zanzibar, especially for urban policy. Nationalization of land, confiscation and reallocation of the properties of the colonial era's elite, prohibition of all parties other than Karume's Afro-Shirazi Party, centralization of economic planning, and proclamation of socialist goals in urban policy were all accomplished within a year of the revolution. On the mainland such agenda items, when indeed they were even addressed, were taken up fleetingly over two decades. The first postcolonial Master Plan for Zanzibar city was written by planners from the German Democratic Republic (GDR); the second was produced by a team from the People's Republic of China (Scholz 1968; Kequan 1982). The mainland's master planners came from the capitalist West (Alexander 1983; Armstrong 1987).

These factors suggest that Zanzibar's experience be separated out from the critique of mainland Tanzania policy programs and taken more seriously as an attempt at socialist urban planning, in a city that remained capital of its own nation (Zanzibar) despite that nation's union with Tanganyika. This appears to be a situation where, as James Sidaway and Marcus Power put it, "the rhetorics of Marxism-Leninism and state socialism were associated with some distinctive forms of administration and governance" (1998, 410). That said, socialist strategies in Zanzibar in actual practice had more to do with the effort of the Zanzibar state to implant its vision of order and expand its dominance into the domestic environment than with an attempt to create a more equal or just city for its residents. To use Dutton's terms, this was *rule* within a rhetoric of *goodwill*. The Karume regime reproduced the very basic enframing tactics of the colonial state in a socialist garb, via creation of a segmented plan, containerization of inside and outside at various spatial scales, and production of central sites of observation and surveillance. Many in the formerly colonized middle, like Ajit Singh, found themselves in the middle again, used this time by an allegedly revolutionary order. The resilience of Zanzibar's urban majority in subverting or surviving the state's spatial agenda, though, insured that a locally derived urban order endured the state's authoritarian tendencies and reframed them, particularly in the new Second Other Side neighborhoods at the city's edge. Locked out of official planning channels, ordinary residents utilized their own customs and practices to remake the revolutionary city as best they could, albeit under a set of authoritarian constraints and within a highly unequal distribution of power. In the end, much of this reconstruction project's narrative echoes that of the previous chapter.

New Zanzibar

Immediately after the 1964 revolution, the new regime began rebuilding the city, with assistance from the German Democratic Republic. The ASP made its New Zanzibar housing project the centerpiece of an effort to provide the entire population with high-rise apartments. Literally everyone in urban and rural Zanzibar was to be organized in some ten New Towns. The city phase of the project came first. It appeared to be a means of addressing the long-entrenched overcrowding problem in western Ng'ambo and the housing shortage in the city overall.

New economic opportunities, and increased in-migration from rural areas, in Zanzibar as in much of newly independent Africa, fueled great growth in demands for land and housing by new urban migrants. Zanzibar city's official population grew from 49,502 in the 1958 census to 68,490 by 1968, with nearly all of the new population settling on the outer edge of the city. Stone Town's population actually declined from 1958 to 1968, and the older areas of Ng'ambo close to Stone Town expanded by fewer than 600 people. Nearly 20,000 new people arrived in Ng'ambo's outer areas or in neighborhoods outside the colonial city boundary, with most of these migrants coming between 1964 and 1968. After 1968, this urban growth truly exploded, as the official population expanded by 60 percent between 1968 and 1978, from 68,490 to 115,131. Fully 44,000 of the increase of 47,000 were accounted for in neighborhoods outside the colonial town line. The Karume regime anticipated and even encouraged some growth for the city, but this pattern of growth would in the end far outpace the state's capacity to plan for it.

Karume's regime began its urban plans by building 150 apartments at Kikwajuni Juu as a pilot residential development project. They followed this by building another half-dozen larger apartment buildings on vacant land south of the city in Kilimani. Each was intended to be a politically organized "micro-district" (French and Hamilton 1979, 11). Eventually, the first pilot neighborhood was filled by party loyalists from outside the area, but came to be known in much of the city as "New Berlin Street," or "Kikwajuni GDR." In Kilimani, the project became something of a public em-

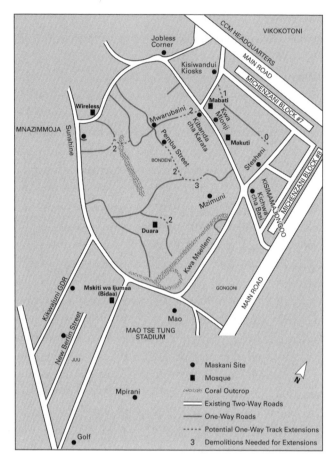

Fig. 13. New Zanzibar. Courtesy of the Kansas
Cartographic Services Office, Geography Department,
University of Kansas.

barrassment when the regime built the community's mosque with a *kibla*
(prayer niche) pointing in the wrong direction—toward Madagascar instead of Mecca.

Enframing Zanzibar Again

In some ways, the Kikwajuni and Kilimani projects presaged what would
come later with the larger enframing program attempted by the revolutionary regime. In 1966, Karume turned once again to the GDR for assistance.
Hubert Scholz and a team of planners, architects, and engineers arrived in

the city in 1967, coming and going through 1969 until they had devised a Master Plan. It was not a plan explicitly segmented by race, but it performed the functions of containerizing in a number of other ways.

The plan begins by stating the revolutionary government's primary goal as the improvement of the standard of living in Ng'ambo. The 1968 plan concentrated on Ng'ambo because the East Germans considered the Stone Town "well-supplied" with amenities in a fashion Scholz identified as "typical" of colonial oppression (1968, 1). Certainly one must not underestimate the extent of inherited inequalities between the two sides of the city. Stone Town had sewage, drainage, street lighting, electricity, and indoor plumbing; with a few exceptions, Ng'ambo had none of these services. Land was valued at more than £14,000 per acre in most of Stone Town, and at much less than £3,000 in the majority of areas in Ng'ambo. Housing values in Stone Town were as much as ten times those of Ng'ambo (Alawi and Yahya 1965).

Still, the new regime exaggerated and codified the differences between the two sides. Where the colonial state used the Ng'ambo-Stone Town divide to containerize and create a racial text of local power relations, the revolutionary state made the division an ideological socialist banner. The divide was often quite literally a banner, since ASP strung banners across the new roadways of its redevelopment project, directly readable from the Creek Road boundary of Stone Town: "Our mother is the revolution, our father is the Afro-Shirazi Party," one read (ASP 1974). In the new ideological representation projected by the state, Stone Town became the embodiment of everything evil about colonialism. The government confiscated the Stone Town homes of Arab and Indian residents who fled the revolution, repackaged them as apartments jammed with new migrants, and then so disregarded their upkeep that complete collapses became commonplace (McQuillan and Lanier 1984). Within this new imaginative order, Ng'ambo was, by contrast, seen as a chaotic mass of underdevelopment, and had to become the shining example of socialism.

Scholz proposed redoing Ng'ambo in five steps: building flats for all or nearly all residents, making a new road system, engineering a sewage system, building schools in the new residential areas, and creating a new industrial area. The new flats were to have been the town's tallest buildings, centered along Ng'ambo's main rise as the public buildings were in Dutton's program. In total, the Scholz plan envisioned 6,992 flats in 229 buildings either five or fourteen stories in height, with thirty thousand residents. The main area to be demolished had 5163 homes in 1966. Thus, the plan called for a modest increase in available housing units (a net gain of 1829 units) as an effort to meet the growing challenge of the city's expansion. However, 81 percent of the homes then standing within the redevelopment area were considered by the regime's own town-planning office to be in good or fair condition (Scholz 1968; Alawi 1966). Once again, as in the Dutton-led reconstruction of colonial times, the areas of the poorest quality housing stock were excluded from the reconstruction efforts, which instead targeted centrally located and therefore highly visible neighborhoods that actually had much less need for the improvement of housing quality.

This plan should not, on paper, be seen as a direct replication of British colonial ideas, since it is illustrative of the alien techniques and concepts of monumental socialist architecture that Scholz brought with him. The Soviet model was still the town-planning paradigm operative in Scholz's East Germany of the 1960s (Bater 1984, 134–62; Kansky 1976). Throughout Eastern Europe in the mid- to late 1960s, a reformulated Soviet model emphasized specific "project plans" (Kansky 1976, 149), and great stress was placed on public housing. Rational distribution, order and control, together with a conception of the city as an ideological instrument, clearly represented a significant part of these projects. Their most identifiable characteristic is the mixture of five-story blocks and fifteen-story high-rises that make the postwar sections of eastern-bloc cities so indistinguishable from one another (French and Hamilton 1979, 15; Szelenyi 1983, 1). That is almost exactly the mixture Scholz's plan called for in Zanzibar.

The 1968 plan was accompanied by a propaganda blitz of posters, banners, and radio broadcasts designed to project its ideological vision of the cityscape. A widely circulated pamphlet in Kiswahili on New Zanzibar came with pictures of the flats at Kikwajuni, which were said to give "the workers better living conditions and save them from living in lousy huts— the poor state in which the colonialist left us" (BA 74/1, ZNA). The broadcast, in English and Kiswahili, of a program called "A Plan for Building the New City of Ng'ambo," echoed the similar broadcast made by Juma Aley and Dutton two decades earlier. Like that earlier piece, it extensively employed passive grammar and agentless change as rhetorical devices (see also Tett and Wolfe 1991). For example, the broadcast began by stating that "it has been decided to have a planned progress in the reconstruction work of Zanzibar town." The people were assured that the "planning scheme has

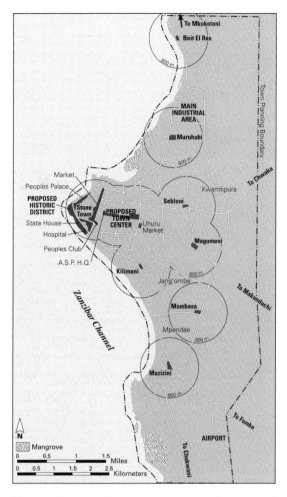

Fig. 14. The 1968 Zanzibar town plan. Courtesy of
the Kansas Cartographic Services Office,
Geography Department, University of Kansas.

already been approved," but they were requested to go and see the Revolutionary Council's architectural model that would show them "how the town
has been laid out" (Town Planning Office, New Zanzibar 1968, ZTPL).
What that model depicts, essentially, is a gray plastic parking lot blanketing
what had been Ng'ambo, and the shining storied blocks of flats along the
new wide roads: the new state's definition of the spatial order.

The New Zanzibar scheme, despite its apparent ideological distinctive-
ness, still replicated the colonial enframing tactics outlined by Mitchell

(1988). First of all, it relied on a segmented plan, where the city was broken down into parts—identified less explicitly with racial containers and instead based around both class and ideology. The plan left intact the zoning strategies of the colonial 1958 town-planning scheme. It found a new use for the "villa zone along the seaside" as the residential area of the party and state leaders along with their new foreign allies. This "elitist milieu," as the plan called it, would not be reconstructed, since it had "good houses" (Scholz 1968). In addition to maintaining the Police Lines separating the villa zone from Ng'ambo, the new regime made the open space between its elitist milieu and the squatter areas around the old Holmwood estates into the main base of the Tanzanian army. Police roadblocks at the boundaries of elite villa zones both north and south of the city continue to operate thirty-nine years after the revolution, an obvious moment of territorial containerizing meant to preserve the "elitist milieu."

These roadblocks are just one of the evident signs that the revolutionary regime continued the enframing project of separating the inside from the outside in spatial terms—here by marking the inside and outside of the rich suburbs. New housing flats were the main sites of this separation of inside from outside as a form of containerizing. Entering and exiting the flats can be accomplished only via a limited number of external and open stairwells, with one's progress up or down clear for all to see. Instead of the struggle to find "the limit between the houses and the street" in neighborhood spatiality in old Ng'ambo (Nilsson et al. 1969), the new flats had clearly delimited, modular houses with no porches or *baraza* (verandahs). Inside and outside behaviors were clearly demarcated. The earliest apartments even had signs on each interior door announcing what the room was: the toilet/bathroom doors had blue signs that said *"choo/*W.C.,*"* as though one had to be told what the rooms inside one's house were to be used for. Since the houses were supplied with electricity, Karume made it unlawful to cook with charcoal on the stairwells or window wells. Residents told stories of him walking by the buildings in the dark, and, if he smelled wood smoke, climbing the stairwells to berate the offending householder to go back and cook in her electric kitchen.

Surveilled central places of objectified space were to be found throughout New Zanzibar. Among the most conspicuous is the Afro-Shirazi Party Headquarters, the city's tallest building, alongside the long strings of flats that were created from the Scholz plan. The main intersection in the center of the completed apartment area is on the very top of old Ng'ambo's highest point. During Karume's time, and long after, banners often crossed the roadways in this area to announce ideological claims of the state. The water fountain within its central roundabout now flows only on Revolution Day, but the marking of Ng'ambo's heart as a reminder of the state's power is as clear as that of Dutton's Ridgeway in Lusaka. When the regime finally built the plan's new central Friday mosque, twenty-five years after it was planned, it took its conspicuous place right across the new main boulevard from Dutton and Singh's Raha Leo Civic Center. And it announced the piety of the revolutionary regime with its gleaming Saudi Arabian minaret—tall enough to afford a view of the whole city.

Admittedly, the ASP government implemented very little of the 1968 plan, even including those buildings like the mosque that it took twenty-five years to build. The strings of flats in the completed area comprise only 8 of the planned 229 residential blocks—and they were not built exactly as Scholz's plan envisioned. Instead, the long blocks that the regime completed, centered on the old Ng'ambo neighborhood of Michenzani (directly between the *mitaa* of Mwembetanga and Kikwajuni), are all between six and eight stories high and three hundred meters long. The total complex contains 1,102 completed flats. Even including the Kikwajuni and Kilimani microdistrict flats, this means the state is still nowhere near the plan's goal of 6,992 units.

New Zanzibar remains unfinished. With 138 flats officially reserved for the party elite and a number of others unofficially doled out as favors, a shortage of flats even as compensation for demolished structures arose, and it has persisted to this day. Zanzibar has, of course, also dramatically changed direction economically, and in some ways politically. Some of the change began with Karume's assassination in 1972. The regime of his successor, Aboud Jumbe (1972–84), was marked by the gradual erosion of the islands' autonomy, signified most forcefully by the 1977 unification of the ASP with the mainland's ruling party, Tanganyika African National Union, to form Chama cha Mapinduzi (CCM, the Revolutionary Party). In 1984, Ali Hassan Mwinyi assumed the Zanzibar presidency, and he rapidly ushered in dramatic political and economic changes before he moved on to the presidency of Tanzania a year later. A new democratically elected (but single-party) House of Representatives soon came into being, rapidly followed by its passage of a Trade Liberalization Act (1986) that paved the way for a privatized economy.

Multiparty politics returned in 1992, with the first elections held in

1995. The new multiparty era is perhaps the only catalyst remaining for Michenzani's completion. One entryway's worth of apartments was opened in 1995, just before the first multiparty elections in Zanzibar since the revolution. Two other New Zanzibar blocks were still unfinished in 1999. I asked the official in charge when he expected to make progress. He did not hesitate: "During the next election campaign [of 2000]." Indeed, one more entryway was completed to coincide with the campaign of Karume's son, Amani Karume, for the Zanzibar presidency in 2000.

Yet throughout the nearly four decades of revolutionary government in Zanzibar city, the state has fallen further and further behind in its rather half-hearted and underfunded efforts to provide land and housing for urban Zanzibaris. By 1988, there were 157,634 residents within the city boundaries. By 2000, that number had grown beyond 200,000, with another 70,000 urbanites living outside the official city limits but within the urban-planning zone demarcated by the Zanzibar government in 1982. Legal and planned allocation of land for residential construction accounts for about 2 percent of actual plot development. The vast majority of urban Zanzibaris therefore develop their plots extralegally, with little help from or knowledge of the state.

The Voices of Poland Again

While Michenzani and New Zanzibar clearly demonstrate the spatiality of state power, these places became the site for the expression of what Denis Cosgrove calls "alternative landscapes" of "excluded groups" (1989, 131). New outer fringe neighborhoods that have developed in the revolutionary era outside of the legal parameters of state control—the Second Other Side—also evidence the deployment of power, faith, and customary practices as the cornerstones for the actual creation of urban space in most of the city. In successive sections below, I explore the responses of Ng'ambo residents to the Michenzani apartments and their multifarious recreations of them as living places, and then demonstrate the operation of *uwezo*, *imani*, and *desturi* in the creation of the Second Other Side.

Getting a flat in Michenzani did not satisfy most of those displaced. It was a very hard adjustment to live in the new buildings. Many practical problems arose that were difficult to overcome. In fact a great deal of bitterness remains about Michenzani among those it affected, just as it remains about the Mwembetanga program of the Dutton era. Interviews revealed much of this bitterness. Unlike the colonial-era reconstruction, though, the revolutionary program is still very much alive in the city, as are some of its protagonists. For this reason, some of the quotations in this section appear anonymously to protect the speakers' privacy.

The flats were more out of character with local customs than Dutton's plan, especially the vital custom of neighborliness, or *ujirani*. One Kikwajuni woman, relocated to the flats by force after the demolition of her home to make way for one of the later flats, explained: "I don't like living here. There are no neighbors. Electricity you can get used to not having. Water— I have never had water up here [on the fifth floor]. And water is important. But you can get water somewhere else. Where do you go to get neighbors? I have lived here since 1977. I will never get used to it. The noise, the sound of the cars, the thieves, the fights, all that nonsense—it is not like that in the single-story houses. [There,] . . . you . . . have your neighbors."

Michenzani was also detrimental to family structure and established gender relations, as one young man described it: "When they built Michenzani, they did not think of the Swahili family. Say I have a brother and two sisters, a family of six. So, where do I sleep in a two-room flat? With my sisters? Where do I change my clothes? Building houses like Michenzani is like taking salt water and pouring it into a fresh water river. It is all water, but you kill all the fish. The stream is dead. People cannot live in Michenzani. Sleep there, yes; but you must go somewhere else to eat, bathe, and to sit with friends."

Bwana Juma Maalim Kombo had been Karume's friend for nearly thirty years when the Michenzani project got under way. They understood one another well. But this was not an area where Juma stood in agreement with his old friend. "Look," he explained one day,

> Karume was a strong man. Karume had three sides. The first was control. He was always in control. He always made the decisions. The second was fear. Everyone from top to bottom was afraid of him. He cared for his friends, he was a friendly man, but he had no mercy for his enemies. The third was that he wanted things to be better for poor people. The results were that he rebuilt the city. He built a new city. . . . We had money back then. He spent it all building the new city. The ones who came after him just ate whatever money was left. (Kombo 1992)

What we see from Bwana Juma is, first, an acknowledgment from a diehard supporter of the revolution that the New Zanzibar project was not necessarily a sensible use of money. Second, we see the tasks of Berman's view of the colonial state repeated in this personalized postcolonial system. It is a rent-seeking state that "eats money" as its means of accumulation, but it still has another aim, to make things "better for poor people" as a means of legitimation. And behind all of this lies domination and the threat of force. Karume himself once said, "[T]here is no civilization if there is no *uwezo*. If you have no *uwezo* you will miss everything in this world" (File BA 68/1, ZNA). In Bwana Juma's view, rebuilding the city was one central way in which he demonstrated his *uwezo*, reinforced with fear.

Yet some of the fish in the stream, as it were, simply refused to die. In Mwembetanga, in the focus group held with residents who experienced the demolition of their homes in both 1946 and 1969, residents clearly identified the project, not with the East German planners or socialist ideology, but with Karume himself (Yahya et al. 1992). Mwembetangans expressed great bitterness over the shortage of flats for compensation, and about the whole manner in which the project was implemented: "[I]t was Poland again," said one, echoing the name used for Mwembetanga during Dutton's reconstruction program in the 1940s. Asked to describe what was different about life in the flats in comparison with life in the old, reconstructed Mwembetanga, Ali Talib Ali replied: "You know, we had development houses but without development of consciousness. We lived the way we were used to living before; it was very crowded in those little rooms. But they weren't concerned with those things; what they wanted was for everyone to have the same living conditions." The disruption of neighborliness and of practical principles of the Islamic faith irritated those impacted: "A whole month might go by without seeing your neighbor. Imagine inquiring about a neighbor and having someone say, 'Oh, he left on a trip two months ago!' Last year someone was dead for three days in one flat without anyone knowing . . . and there were flies everywhere."

These Mwembetanga residents, the victims of two successive programs in this neighborhood to use urban space as an enframing political tool, ultimately condemned both the colonial and the revolutionary regimes. In either case, said one resident, "[T]he citizens were not included in any of the master planning. . . . They survey, they survey, they never tell us why and we are never asked why . . . and we never see any results."

This group did not exhibit unanimity on all issues. Yet from them one can begin to appreciate the pervasive resilience of Ng'ambo's spirit of community that a number of historians have utilized recently as evidence of the

Other Side's collective consciousness, in spite of the diversity of peoples living there (Fair 2001; Bowles 1991). A collective consciousness informs a broad consensus on Michenzani's failings, and it also lies at the heart of many ways this complex community has developed for transforming the flats. In their adjustment to and transformation of the new apartments, residents managed to infuse them with some of the cultural character of the houses below.

The revolutionary regime's original intention, Michenzani residents say, was to give everyone in the city exactly the same living conditions; but the conditions facing those who ended up in Michenzani or Kikwajuni GDR were worse, especially on cultural grounds, than those they had confronted beforehand. Michenzani residents have made the apartment complex recognizable within Zanzibar's rich cultural tapestry. In giving a brief sample of their means for reframing the housing complex, I divide them into adaptations and transformations. The adaptations highlight new uses to which the fixed space of Michenzani and New Zanzibar apartments generally have been put. The transformations refer to cases where the spaces constituting the new housing complex and its surroundings have been altered in efforts to incorporate New Zanzibar into Ng'ambo's cultural landscape.

Adaptations

Michenzani is seen to have five especially valuable adaptations by those living there. The first adaptation may be the most common: the use of flats as starter homes for newlyweds or childless couples more generally. Many extended families employ apartments as homes for couples in the first years of marriage, or for couples without children, mainly because they are viewed as too small for most other family types. A second adaptation is somewhat related. Quite a number of rich men use the flats as homes for their second, third, or fourth wives, or for mistresses. One particular case involved a man whose first and second wives did not wish to acknowledge one another's existence, and by maintaining his second household in a Michenzani flat spatially distant from the first wife's home, the man found a convenient solution to their dispute. There are also some female-headed households of divorced women with a small number of children in Michenzani.

Third, the lower floors are seen as especially good "places to put old people," as one resident put it. Extended families with first- or second-floor flats often allocate them to older family members. Several reasons are given for this phenomenon, but most relate to access. In Ng'ambo's plethora of neighborhoods where single-story houses are jammed together on narrow alleys, older citizens worry that a taxi or other automotive transport to the hospital in the event of an emergency might not reach them. Since there is ready street access from the bottom of Michenzani, their fears are lessened somewhat by living there.

Fourth, many small units are turned into bachelor housing. This enables many extended families to establish a separate domestic setting for young unmarried men, and enhances the young men's feelings of autonomy. At a time when unemployment for school-leavers is virtually assured, families can at least arrange for housing, via Michenzani, for young men. I encountered one case of young unmarried women who share a flat in Michenzani, but this adaptation was substantially less common and quite often carries negative connotations with it. At the end of the 1990s, the Kilimani microdistrict gained a reputation as a haven of prostitution simply because a fairly significant number of mainland-origin single women began inhabiting its flats, regardless of the fact that most were salaried employees of local hotels.

Lastly, some bachelor pads on or near the top floors are notorious for serving as sites of illegal activities, including drug trafficking, prostitution, and money changing. For example, in 1992, Building Number Seven's seventh floor had one unit known locally as the Headquarters. The name came from its status as the office of one of the city's main heroin dealers, but the connection of the name to the flat's unrestricted view of CCM party headquarters, not to mention of the local police station, was unmistakable. Michenzani's exposed stairways and the seventh floor's open access to the roof (and thus to possible escape via another stairway) helped ensure an uninterrupted flow of what residents wryly term *wateja* (customers), the growing addict population.

These flexible housing-use strategies are often talked about by outside observers as evidence that "Zanzibaris love those flats; it seems crazy, but they do" (Meffert 1991). On the contrary, my interviews and discussions with residents suggest that these use patterns are evidence more of Ng'ambo residents making do: "[W]hat else are we going to do; the flats are there," said one man. Just exactly what else Ng'ambo residents are in fact doing to make Michenzani their own can be seen in a brief assessment of five transformations of the material cultural landscape that are associated with Michenzani. These transformations clearly embody the creative evolution of local ways of imbuing places with meaning more than they do any acceptance of the flats as conceived by the state.

Transformations

The first transformation involves the emergence of massive *baraza* built at the base of Michenzani stairwells with the contributions of an entire entryway. The role of *baraza* is deeply embedded in Swahili cultural history, as major loci of social reproduction through neighborliness (Allen 1979; Donley-Reid 1982,63–73). Their reemergence at the base of several apartment buildings as active spaces for what residents refer to as *maskani* ("hangouts" or "homes away from home") points to the endurance of neighborhood consciousness and solidarity in spite of, rather than because of, Michenzani (Hino 1971). The revolutionary party itself even adapted this transformation into its campaign to retain power in the 1995 elections by building elaborate maskani at the base of several Michenzani entryways.

Michenzani was built without regard for any of the multitude of scattered service and grocery shops or storefronts (*duka*) that are fundamental to the built environment and social fabric of Swahili neighborhoods (Hino 1971; Allen 1979). Kikwajuni GDR's government-run supermarket closed by 1980. The second dramatic transformation of New Zanzibar, then, has been the creation of more than fifty *kibanda* (kiosk) shops built to serve the apartments. The kiosks, along with numerous shops carved out of empty ship containers from the city port, violated the building rules of the city and faced decades of harassment and destruction by the government. Yet they became such a vital part of life in Michenzani (not just as ordinary stores, but as real lifelines to the poor and elderly residents, and as *maskani* for others) that, in 1992, two weeks after announcing a plan for finally eradicating them, the state changed its mind. Plans were begun for establishing a shopping center comprised of the container-stores gathered together in front of one Michenzani block. Since the plan still excluded the kiosks, the inevitable result has been a marginal success in concentrating the container-stores and a failure to eliminate the kiosks (Makontena 1992).

The interdependence of the community is a cornerstone of Sunni Shafi'i Islam. This principle of *imani* has, in at least two arenas of everyday life, transformed Michenzani. Michenzani's chronic water shortages are chiefly a function of inadequate pressure, prompting many households to purchase water pumps. In many stairways, use of pumps is held in common. In block areas without pumps, the upper floors enter into cooperative arrangements for supply with friends or relatives in the single-story areas nearby. What Michenzani lacks in water pressure, it compensates for in electrical supply. The blocks are on the same power line as the party headquarters, the post office, the radio station, and the police station; they are the last ones to have their power cut in most circumstances. The very households that supply Michenzani residents with water often depend on the flats for the use of electrical appliances. One young female neighbor of mine in the single-story area of Kikwajuni went to Michenzani one day with a full water jug in one hand and a hand-mixer in the other. Of course, even in these exchanges, residents make compromises with the conditions with which they are faced. It is more common, for example, for households to own a freezer than a refrigerator in the flats: even the best power line in town is so weak that only a freezer keeps perishables from spoiling.

The fourth transformation concerns the very stuff of which Michenzani and Kikwajuni GDR were made. Unfired pressed-earth blocks with a small quantity of cement or lime have figured in the redesign of single-story housing architecture all over the city. Since residents were forced to build the flats, many gained firsthand knowledge of how to work with the materials. Especially the artisans among the volunteered work force saw that blocks would provide the means for more rapid permanent construction than traditional methods or materials. They have also, ironically, seen how well the uncovered blocks of the unfinished buildings have withstood the weather over the years. With the liberalization of Zanzibar's economy, beginning in 1985, has come a lucrative and occasionally illegal trade in the materials that are used to make the building blocks. Indirectly, at least, it can be said that people have used Michenzani in initiating the rapid transformation of Ng'ambo's single-story homes to permanent-material domestic structures. In 1966, only 15 percent of Ng'ambo homes had permanent-material walls; by 1992 that percentage had jumped to an estimated thirty-three, as people worked with the new block style. By 1997, more than half of the new construction in one sample illegal squatter area on the urban fringe had pressed-sand and cement block walls.

The final transformation demonstrates not only the resilience of Ng'ambo's community, but also the ultimate ambivalence with which the story of the New Zanzibar project is greeted on the Other Side. Michenzani's higher proportion of criminal activity motivated many residents, especially on lower floors, to seek protection in window and door bars or gates fashioned with wrought iron. The demand for burglar bars and door gates spread to the houses surrounding the flats and spawned a growth industry in wrought-iron fabrication and engineering. Contracting firms in competition with one another began to experiment with design, and the customary flourishes of Zanzibar's great tradition of carved doors came to be replicated in the iron gates that now covered them. Thus, another of Ng'ambo's customs was put into practice to remake Michenzani, albeit not with the finest of sentiments attached.

Michenzani actually added very little to the total housing stock in the city. Even including the two smaller but similar apartment complexes at Kilimani and Kikwajuni, the New Zanzibar flats only added up to a net gain of less than a thousand homes over the existing housing stock at independence. This meant that the most expensive effort and investment by the state in the urban area in the city's history did next to nothing to solve the problems of overcrowding in older areas and severe land and housing shortages on the city edge. The patterns and processes that actually came to dominate the creation of urban space in postcolonial Zanzibar are amply demonstrated in a visit to the edge of town as it expanded after 1964.

The Second Other Side

By the end of 1964, the ASP state had nationalized all urban land and confiscated the properties of hundreds of former elites and ASP opponents. The revolutionary government represented these mechanisms, along with the new apartments, as means toward addressing the overcrowded housing situation in western Ng'ambo and the shortage of legal building plots to the east inherited from the Time of Politics. These were also potentially useful policies for securing legitimacy by appearing actively and aggressively to seek a just redistribution of wealth and property in very spatial terms. In reality, these new mechanisms seldom addressed genuine housing problems. They rarely fostered either an equitable redistribution or the legitimacy of the state.

Housing development boomed in the outskirts of the city. At first, the town planning office attempted to treat the sprawling of the suburbs generously, in deliberate counterdistinction to colonial policies. On August 28, 1964, the new town planning officer, Abdulwahab Alawi Abdulwahab, who had trained under the creator of the 1958 colonial plan and then served as

his assistant in the colonial planning office for eight years, made a radio an-
nouncement concerning "haphazard building." He began by saying that
"building is necessary—a person must have the opportunity to build a
home where he or she wishes—this is indeed the policy of our government." That alone was a great leap from colonial restrictions. But people
had simply seized parcels on which to build and then built without any co-
ordination. Abdulwahab was concerned: "[L]look, until when will we build
with the uncle south, brother north and father east? There are no roads
passing between; this type of construction is very bad, nor can the government endure seeing our city once again built as it is in Vuga, Kajificheni
[Stone Town *mitaa*] or Vikokotoni [in old Ng'ambo]" (DA 1/261, ZNA).

It soon became clear that Abdulwahab's concern for building control
had little support politically within the state-party machinery. Like postcolonial cities across the continent, Zanzibar was about to expand in population, dramatically. A boom in government and parastatal employment in
town, the construction of several factories in the suburbs along the north
coast, and an increased movement of mainland Tanzanians and Pembans
to the city in search of opportunities made for Zanzibar city's largest
growth in over a hundred years. The main beneficiaries of this boom were
those people who controlled access to building plots and building materials,
the mid-level functionaries of the Afro-Shirazi Party, and they were not interested in orderly neighborhoods. And by 1978, most city dwellers lived in
these disorderly outer areas, places like Kwamtipura (7,617 people), Shau-
rimoyo (10,034), Sogea (9,672) and greater Jang'ombe (14,902) (1978 Census Results, DX 6/2, ZNA).

With little time to build the sort of *ujirani* that was still a major feature of
life in the inner *mitaa*, the new city residents were heavily dependent on the
party branches in the days of single-party rule in Tanzania. They had to
register with the branch even to travel back to relatives on the mainland or
in Pemba. In some cases the party transformed the residents' dependency
and put it to work through highly motivated *mabalozi* (ten-house cell leaders)
for local, grassroots development efforts. Cooperative farms were organized in vacant lowlands. In 1966, the party branch in Jang'ombe had forty-
four acres of the "Urusi" (Russia) and "Angola" subsections planted in
corn, with a further forty-two acres of the branch area in rice. Party leaders
organized cooperative labor teams to bring piped water supply to several
public taps and later did the same thing to bring electricity to the branch
area. They rotated the branch headquarters between the *mitaa* of Angola,

Msumbiji (Mozambique), Urusi, and Holmwood to serve such a huge constituency; otherwise, as the Jang'ombe Branch chair stated on January 2, 1967, the leaders feared that they "could not meet all of [their] new and old members at the same time" (File AK 26/18, ZNA).

Such dynamic organizing was apparently the exception, not the rule. More common were the party branch officials who utilized their newfound powers for their own gain. Acting in a manner little different from that of colonial landowners, branch officials "sold" building plots to the new migrants, even though it was "fully understood that land is government property that cannot be sold" (Documents Commission 1992, 17). Often, these plots were in depressions or along streambeds. Ironically, despite the resultant frequency of damaging floods, severe (potable) water shortages remained unresolved in these branches and were exacerbated as branch leaders crowded new tenants onto their new manors. Inner Ng'ambo branch leaders, too, took to their new powers comfortably and likewise sold building plots that had not existed previously on unsuitable land.

Overcrowding and disorderliness were central features of the neighborhoods developed in the Karume years (1964–72). Michael Ole-Mungaya's case study of the various sections of Kwamtipura, subdivided according to the age of the structures, shows that the section built between 1964 and 1972 is more densely populated and has a higher plot-coverage ratio than the sections built before the revolution or after Karume's death (1990). Lane widths vary dramatically, not unlike those in inner Ng'ambo. The revolutionary-era part of Kwamtipura is also more susceptible to flooding, and more lacking in urban infrastructure, than other sections of the city.

Soon after Karume's death in 1972, the regime of Aboud Jumbe banned haphazard urban development in the "suburbs"—on paper, at least. Jumbe announced in April 1977 that it was no longer "permissible to build *ovyo*," and that the government would again enforce the old Building Rules of colonialism. The Department of Construction (by then simply called Michenzani in ordinary parlance because the whole department had been formed to coordinate the construction of the apartments) went out to the edge of town to mark red *X*s on the doors of the houses, from Angola and Urusi in the south to Mwembemakumbi and Kwamtipura in the north. Radio and television announcements warned of the uses to which the old colonial Building Rules, which had been effectively inoperative since 1969, could be put. These uses included the state's right "to demolish someone's house for them or make them knock it down themselves" and the requirement that evidence of construction be apparent within two years of obtaining a plot (TPO/U-88, vol. 2, ZTPO).

Knocking down people's houses would score few political points unless coupled with a plan to replace them with something better. The Jumbe regime hired an Italian planning team to draw up a master plan, but they only ended up designing a model neighborhood called Mwanakwerekwe. The Italians divided Mwanakwerekwe into two layouts, A and B, in what are presently the constituencies of Mpendae (You have to love it) and Magomeni. The thousand or so original plots in Mpendae and Magomeni ranged from 360 to 400 square meters, and allowable plot coverage was set at no more than 45 percent. This meant plots were very large, and plot coverage was quite small, in comparison to the rest of the city (Building Applications in New Areas, 1978–88, ZTPO).

Although devised by a different team, the Mwanakwerekwe Scheme served as a pilot neighborhood unit (NU) for the later master plan (written in 1982), and what happened there is more or less what has happened in most of the NU development areas laid out on the 1982 plan. From 1978 to 1981, the ministry received over a thousand applications for plots in Mwanakwerekwe A and B. Only fifty of these applicants received plots and still held them in 1984 (A. M. Jiddawi, Town Planning and Development Control, 1977–84, ZTPO). The largest plots by the Amani-Mbweni outer ring road of the city were too large for people to build on to the standard required by planning and building laws. So many people in this part of Mpendae had to sell their plots, or part of their plots, that the area came to be called Maskinihajengi (A poor person can't build). The people who could build were "*wenye* [those having] *uwezo*," who in certain cases obtained three adjoining plots and made veritable estates in the area: As A. M. Jiddawi put it in 1984, "*Wenye uwezo* are in fact many times given aid and loans to get a house and building materials, and while this does ease the problem of permanent housing for those with the ability to help themselves, all those who do not have *uwezo* don't get any help in getting plots in order to build their houses" (Town Planning and Development Control file: 1977–84, ZTPO).

Many residents who did get plots had no money with which to purchase building materials. The revitalized Building Authority, the ministry, or the party branch then often utilized the elusive Building Rules, which demanded evidence of construction progress within two years, to strip the plots from those who had received them. At other times, the allocatee herself sold or subdivided the plot to avoid its being confiscated.

"Private landowners" still claimed some areas of the scheme as plantations. The nationalization of land in the 1960s apparently had not proceeded smoothly in the immediate vicinity of the city. "A large part of the land announced as part of the municipality was not nationalized," and the "owners" of this land did "not want to subdivide their *shamba* [farm]" according to the scheme, or in later years, the 1982 Master Plan (Documents Commission 1992, 18). Instead, these "landowners" subdivided their lands according to their own plans and then sold off parcels at high prices. Many residents who either were allocated plots or purchased them in Mpendae found that the "landowner" required an additional premium as remuneration for the loss of her income from fruit or nut trees.

All other parts of the scheme area and certain stretches around it were invaded long before they could be surveyed or laid out. In some cases squatters bought their squatting rights from the *shamba* owners; others went to the branch: "People come to the branch and say, hey, we need a place to build," said one ten-house cell leader in 1992, as we passed a half-submerged foundation in the swamp at Mpendae.

Mpendae residents, including both squatters and allocatees working together, built a beautiful mosque—right in the carriageway of the Italian plan's main road. The main road on the south of the layout in Kaburi Kikombe "died." It was killed by the squatters on the other side of the layout digging *udongo* (soil) for their homes. "They dug at one or two in the morning, in secret. Then when the rains come, it is a lake, not a road." A set of other roads died in a maze of squatter homes in a depression. "That area there was supposed to be a shopping center, a parking lot, whatever. We waited for years, and then, well, people just decided to build."

It takes time to build the kind of *ujirani*—in Hino's terms (1971), "solidarity consciousness"—found in the older *mitaa*, and Mpendae residents are not always very understanding toward one another. One mainlander who had arrived only recently said in 1992: "[T]he people of Mpendae are half and half: some are well-to-do and have the *uwezo*; the rest are poor and don't. Neighborliness exists, but these days there are also a lot of disputes. My neighbor and I do not speak to each other. I wanted to get his help to make sure we were not flooded, but he wouldn't talk to me. And he is digging a hole for building-soil right in front that is destroying our environment."

Yet in the next breath the man added, "People from the mainland like me and people from the islands get along. In fact the neighborliness is better here than on the mainland." In addition to the mosque construction, *ujirani* has played a positive role in doing for Mpendae what no one else seemed willing to do. In 1992 and 1995, residents frequently recounted examples of neighbor-to-neighbor cooperation to lay water pipes or electricity lines, to dig drainage ditches or plant crops. Small illegal corner shops appeared all over the ward by 1999, whereas the shopping center of the plan has not.

Both in adapting and transforming Michenzani and in creating the new neighborhoods of the Second Other Side, ordinary Zanzibaris in the revolutionary era "have done for themselves" in many matters of urban residential development. Colonial enframing tactics, repackaged in socialism, dominated the strategic interventions of the revolutionary state. Its reach far exceeded its grasp, and in the interstices of its failures the Zanzibar state saw a new city emerge that reframed its efforts within local idioms.

Other Zanzibar residents who were also unaffected by the Michenzani/New Zanzibar scheme had to make other adaptations and transformations, or live from other scripts of power, faith, or custom. This was especially so of those in the formerly colonized middle who remained behind in the new revolutionary space. Ajit Singh, for instance, had a very ambivalent relationship with the Zanzibar Revolution, as the section below details.

Ajit Singh and Revolutionary Zanzibar

Ajit Singh made sure that his political sympathies were always well hidden and never joined a political party or voted in his life. Africans who worked under or beside him consistently spoke to me of their respect for him, his sense of humor and lack of bias, his precision and consistency, but never of his political beliefs. Like many Indian civil servants in Africa during decolonization, he privately supported both sides in little ways, hedging his bets against any outcome and theorizing that a system of checks and balances of contending interests would be better than an all-or-nothing regime. In a 1962 letter to his mentor dated February 12, 1962, Ajit Singh looked back on Dutton's tenure decrying "Labor's . . . sweet dream of independence" (Singh Papers). But at the very same time he retained close contacts with Karume and Thabit Kombo (leader of the Shirazi Association that merged with Karume's African Association in 1957 to form the ASP).

When the ASP seized control in 1964, Ajit Singh, as architectural superintendent, was one of the very few top bureaucrats who worked closely with that first government to retain his post in the revolutionary ASP regime. He held onto that position through the April 1964 union and into the middle of 1965. Ajit served the revolutionary government "wholeheartedly," in his own words. He had grasped, a bit late, the inequities of the colonial system for Africans and started out the revolutionary era with an eagerness to redress them. But Ajit was fond of saying, in the last years of his life, that putting the Michenzani flats onto the urban landscape he had done so much to create in Zanzibar was "like putting a hat on top of my turban" (P. Singh, personal communication, July 1997).

Ajit tried to convince Karume of the inappropriateness of the Kikwajuni GDR designs for Zanzibar's climate and cultural conditions. Karume responded by moving Ajit out of the Kikwajuni project and putting him in charge of designing the "Old Peoples Houses" at Sebleni, Karume's version of an assisted-living facility for the elderly. Wearied by ill health, Singh retired from a state that, as he put it in 1966, he had "served in thick and thin" for more than twenty-seven years (Singh Papers). For a year, he concentrated on the few private architectural contracts he could obtain. The dire financial circumstances of his only daughter and grandchildren, though, soon left Ajit as their only means of support. With Eric Dutton as his main reference, Singh gained employment as a government architect in Malawi just as that country became a republic. This meant that Ajit had to temporarily depart from "pride of possession toward our only property," the home he had completed in Ng'ambo only a few years before the revolution (Singh Papers).

Ajit Singh's grandson Jasjit says of the family home in which the grandchildren still live, "[I]t has a European exterior, an Asian interior, and an African back." Ajit's designs for the Civic Center, the schools, and the hospitals of the colonial era often contained the type of cultural mixing his grandson describes in this home. European models of exterior landscaping and site coverage predominate, as do European engineering principles in the foundations and walls. Ajit's distinctive roof styles emulate the flat roofs of stone houses in Stone Town or the thatching patterns of Ng'ambo Swahili houses, on a larger scale, with different materials. His mixes of even modernism and art deco styles with Indian and African touches hide around corners from more famous historic treasures, in the city's first auto dealership and other mundane office buildings.

But it is in the family home where all of Ajit's talents went to work. It is a marvelous and quirky achievement. Interior-wall windows with Indian-style colored glass adorn doors leading to a Swahili courtyard or a tiny verandah, or rest above an Omani-style wall niche. Ajit designed a swinging kitchen door with a working sink attached to it. Similar moments of apparent structural whimsy surprise the visitor around every turn. Ajit added a bungalow to the front yard and then connected it to the main house. A back entrance to the main house leads upstairs to a self-contained flat behind the home, where, set on an angle, one finds a steep and narrow ladder in an exterior stairwell instead of stairs. Climbing the ladder, one comes to a rooftop patio with a corner loggia perched almost like a minaret designed to look out on Ng'ambo's oldest historically African neighborhood.

The Karume regime confiscated the homes of those it called "Destroyers of National Development" whether they had run away from Zanzibar or not. The state confiscated 611 homes in the town and its suburbs, with Arabs and especially Asians being the primary targets of nationalization. Of these, 371 took place in Stone Town. More than 100 took place in the older Asian stone house commercial areas of northern Ng'ambo (Mchangani, Mbuyuni and Mlandege). More than 50 beachfront and suburban villas to the south of town became government property, as did 35 Asian homes in the middle-class planned suburb of Saateni. Only thirty-one homes in predominantly African neighborhoods were confiscated, and most of these were Arab- or Indian-owned. Ajit Singh did not want his house to be one of them (DX 23/4, ZNA).

Someone in the revolutionary cadre coveted the fine house in Kikwajuni, though, and a confiscation decree was issued for it in late 1966. From Malawi in 1966, in letters to his wife, Ajit detailed what should be done. Karume had to understand that "I have not run away from Zanzibar and have not taken my capital from Zanzibar. My whole family is there and will be there always" (Singh Papers). According to family members' accounts, Ajit's wife went, together with Thabit Kombo, to have an audience with President Karume. As a result of this visit, the confiscation decree was rescinded. Ajit was able to return to his Ng'ambo home in 1979 when his service in Malawi ended.

The story of Ajit and his house shows the inadequacy of reading colonialism through the resistance paradigm alone. The struggles faced by the colonized middle at colonialism's end were very real, as were the consequences of an unsuccessful navigation of the turbulent waters between the rock of the colonial past and the hard place of a postcolonial present. There was little or no wiggle room in Ajit Singh's neocolonized middle position, as this passage from a letter to Eric Dutton, dated August 27, 1962, makes clear: "The position of a foreign civil servant is ever drastic. I don't like India to retire in. England has shut its doors to us. . . . We cannot fit in now at our native place. It has changed so much from us as we have changed as much from it" (Singh Papers). The whole buildup to party politics in Zanzibar—what Ajit Singh termed "the political storm in a teacup"—sickened him and left him deeply troubled for the future: "Everybody is shaky. Many people hardly get a square meal a day. Hatred and unfriendliness among many different communities is on the increase."

Ajit always negotiated a space in between. He was almost, but not quite, Zanzibari. He was almost, but not quite British. He had left his India far behind. His architectural designs physically encapsulated his cultural hybridity, nowhere more than in his own house. His social life and his steady stream of house guests were meant to bring disparate cultures and classes together in continual recombination, the way he had seen his mentors in Punjab do. Instead, what Ajit saw was the gathering of a "political storm in a teacup," a storm from which Zanzibar has yet to recover.

Ultimately, Ajit was uneasy with colonialism and its legacy, and equally uneasy with what he witnessed of both the revolutionary Zanzibari and reactionary Malawian responses to that legacy (see chapter 7). Before the Zanzibar Revolution, and then long after it, Ajit Singh learned and relearned to be wary of British colonial culture. Dutton was one of the few European bosses Ajit ever had in whom he sensed a "friendly and sympathetic and kindly feeling" toward non-Europeans. He once wrote that men of that type were "extinct from the arena." In their place were Europeans with little daring, little humility, little appreciation for Africa or willingness to endure what couldn't be "cured" about it, and little sympathy with his own sort of halfway position (Singh Papers).

Ajit had more than frustration with British bosses to fuel his alienation from the metropole. Since he was not allowed citizenship in either Malawi or Zanzibar after independence, he sought and was denied a British passport. He died as an Indian subject, even though he himself knew he could "never fit in there." He died in Zanzibar, where he had lived half of his life.

Ajit's appreciation for the comfortable "mixture of peoples" that Zanzibar retained even after the revolution came accompanied by a remarkable naïveté about the severity of inequality in Zanzibari society or the degree of bitterness his African neighbors felt toward the colonial regime and the Sultanate and Protectorate he had served. The reality of relations between racial groups, which consisted of humiliation for many Africans in their places of employment or in their daily grind of unemployment, came to be understood by Ajit rather belatedly. Zanzibar's revolutionary moment seems to have been something he eventually came to accept, without completely embracing or even understanding. It was a hat on top of his turban.

Conclusion

The urban programs of Zanzibar's revolutionary era, dominated by the Michenzani project, were publicly proclaimed as a means toward the establishment of a socialist city in postcolonial Zanzibar. Actually, Michenzani, the 1968 plan, and the paltry efforts at planned development for the urban fringe were less about establishing a just and egalitarian balance in the city in terms of housing or infrastructure and more about enframing the landscape within the ASP's vision of power. President Karume oversaw a transformation of the urban environment that failed in its objectives, neither creating a better city nor creating one more defined and maintained by the ideological order of the state. Misuse of funds and an aggressively authoritarian and acquisitive bureaucratic climate combined with a disregard for the needs and wishes of the urban majority to ensure that the New Zanzibar-Michenzani project would not transform society. Yet in making do with the space the state created, residents rewrote the landscape and made it their own through a series of adaptations and transformations that my account, by no means exhaustive, has sought to illustrate. Instead of New Zanzibar, a Second Other Side arose that repeated many of the processes of urban development that brought the first Other Side into being.

As the case of postcolonial Zanzibar suggests, state power in postcolonial Africa often shapes and manipulates the urban landscape in an ideological manner as a part of its struggle for an enframing order, often replicating colonial tactics in the process. It has become common to speak of the landscape as a geographical text bearing the political and ideological impress of the state, but we must recognize that these geographical texts are often read very differently than the state intends in the everyday spatial language of the less powerful. Those on whom such texts are presumed to be written are themselves active and assertive agents in the defining and redefining of spatial boundaries and cultural markers. The Michenzani project began as the centerpiece of a program to make Zanzibar a socialist city and society. Instead, it has ended up as a set of structures into and onto which Ng'ambo residents write their own stories. And, within the constraints of an authoritarian order, the new urban migrants of the Second Other Side created a place "you have to love" that manifested the *uwezo*, *imani*, and *desturi* cornerstones of old Ng'ambo.

Two attempts have been made to totally demolish Ng'ambo and redevelop it according to the orderly precepts of the state, one under colonial rule and the other after colonialism had ended. Despite shifts in the professed ideology of development, little difference can be seen between the two attempts in terms of the purposes of reconstruction. Both were enframing, territorial strategies for achieving dominance activated in the interests of powerful leaders. Although draped in the banners of socialism rather than of imperialism, the postcolonial state inherited from the colonial regime an obsession with spatial order as an ideological tool and means of civic control. The revolutionary regime made a highly segmented plan of the city, containerized notions of inside and outside, and created central spaces of observation and surveillance—often on the exact ground of the colonial order—central to the new postcolonial order it sought to create.

Leadership in these reconstruction efforts was placed in curiously similar hands. The impulsive, impervious Karume dominated the character of his administration as Dutton dominated his, albeit more ruthlessly. It is crucial to remember Karume's strong ties to the colonial government, particularly during Dutton's administration. Archival records and oral sources demonstrate Karume's intimate relationship with the British Protectorate, and his warm relations with Dutton in particular (File AK 20/1, ZNA; File CO 618/83/1, PRO). It is impossible to think that Karume was unaware of the lessons one might have taken from the first remaking of Ng'ambo. He, more than anyone else, was the chief inheritor and transformer of the structures, procedures, and mechanisms of colonial state power during the postcolonial era.

The projects also shared similar outcomes: the state failed to achieve both its practical goals and its hidden aims. The state smashed the homes of Ng'ambo's residents but failed to replace them with an order, let alone a domestic environment, conducive to its goals of legitimation on the Other Side. The chief reasons for a lack of success were similar in both cases. The use of externally derived planning concepts, a precarious financial dependency (on world market prices for cloves and on the whims of external donors), and a marginalization of the interests and ideas of the urban majority were common to both reconstructions. "They survey, they survey, they never tell us why, and we are never asked why," as one Mwembetanga resident said.

The consequences of these projects for city residents were consistent as well. Those people whose homes were destroyed in most cases received a house of equal or lesser size and quality after a profound disruption of their lives. Still others were made permanently homeless and forced to reside with relatives whose houses remained, thus intensifying the densification of Ng'ambo's *mitaa* that both projects suggested it was their aim to decrease. Neither project provided anything of a solution to land and housing shortages that began to emerge in the 1950s and skyrocketed in the 1960s and 1970s. As a consequence, a growing urban majority sought its own solutions in the peripheral edges of the city, circumventing formal processes for residential development. In their circumventions, though, it is possible to see a reframing of both colonial and postcolonial orders that remained reliant on the power, faith, and customs of that urban majority.

This nominally socialist setting for the British colonial legacy presents, on the surface at least, a dramatic contrast with postcolonial Malawi. There, in the former colony of Nyasaland, Hastings Kamuzu Banda also marked the beginning of the postcolonial era by making a new city. In this case, the postcolonial regime did not attempt to undo the colonial city by remaking a new one on top of it. Instead, Banda set out to make what was in essence an entirely new city, as his capital of Lilongwe. As I show in the next chapter, instead of draping the city with the symbols of change toward a socialist order, Banda asked a team of white planners from apartheid South Africa to design the new city for him.

Chapter Seven

Lilongwe

> "We are facing a very huge development program with only four ar-
> chitects, all European save me, and we are going to lick the challenge
> as a team."
>
> —Ajit Singh Hoogan to Eric Dutton,
> December 1966, Singh Papers

Introduction

M̲alawi's new capital project is one of many attempts in Africa in the
1960s and 1970s to address the urban legacy of colonialism by creating
new capital cities for the newly independent states of the continent. In
Mauritania, Rwanda, Botswana, Nigeria, Tanzania, Nigeria, Ivory Coast,
and Malawi, regimes created new national capital cities out of small administrative towns or out of open rural lands. Hamdan (1964, 341) rightly
pointed out that these new capitals in many ways followed the pattern of
the earlier creation of capital cities—such as Nairobi and Lusaka—by colonial regimes. The difference was that those colonial cities were "the most
evident fingerprints of Europe on African life" (Hamdan 1964, 349). The
motivations behind the plans for these new cities varied, but one key justifi-
cation, rhetorically at least, was to wipe away the European fingerprints
and replace them with African ones. The new cities were seen as markers of
change and of the end of colonial rule, and their architecture and design
were meant to convey that break. The wholly new capital cities of postcolonial Africa were clearly intended to stand out on a grander scale than revisions to existing capitals, such as that which the Karume regime produced
in revolutionary Zanzibar. In most cases, attempts were also made to justify
the expense of these new capital cities in directly geographical terms: the
sites were more central, would generate greater efficiency of administration, equitable development, and political balance.

How dramatic was the break between colonial and postcolonial city in the new capitals? The results varied in terms of the meeting of goals or the fulfillment of plans. In the newly created cities, perhaps more than in the reconstructed ones like postcolonial Zanzibar, it proved difficult in most cases to outgrow colonial planning strategies, design features, and design processes. Dodoma, the new capital of the United Republic of Tanzania, is a case in point: a nominally "African socialist" regime paid Western consultants to design an essentially European-style city in a location entirely inappropriate to the purposes of urban growth (Doherty 1977; Hoyle 1979). The case of Lilongwe demonstrates an apparent application of colonial urban enframing even more thorough than that applied to the old colonial capitals. Before we get to the project of creating Lilongwe itself, though, it is vital to appreciate both the colonial and postcolonial context of Malawi as a whole.

"Ruled by Whites, Developed by Indians . . ."

The colony of Nyasaland (today's Malawi) was established in 1891 as an outgrowth of British efforts to combat slave traders linked to Portuguese- and Zanzibar-controlled eastern African ports and to prevent the advance of Portuguese political control up the Shire River and the western shore of Lake Nyasa. Like Northern Rhodesia, Nyasaland had ties to the Cape-to-Cairo vision of the British South Africa Company. The first governor of the territory was Harry Johnston, like Robert Coryndon one of Rhodes's apostles. The missionary-geographer David Livingstone left a deep impact in Malawi: his Church of Scotland's lobbying led the British to proclaim the protectorate, and the most important city economically throughout the twentieth century, Blantyre, is named for his birthplace in Scotland. But it is Johnston's stirring declaration upon taking the helm of the territory that continues to haunt Malawi more than thirty-seven years after independence: "This will be a territory ruled by Whites, developed by Indians, and worked by Blacks" (cited in Patel 1996, 39).

Colonial rule actually did very little to "develop" Nyasaland. In 1924, the Phelps-Stokes Committee investigating British colonialism from the inside went so far as to call Nyasaland the "poorest colony in Africa" (cited in Comment 1993, 7); others labeled it a "colonial slum" (Rotberg 1971). It depended heavily on labor migration to Northern and Southern Rhodesia as well as to South Africa, and its failure to develop as a white settler colony met with little Colonial Office concern for its economic progress. By 1953, disregard had stretched to such a point that Nyasaland was, against the will of its people, incorporated into the ill-fated Federation of Rhodesia and Nyasaland dominated by Southern Rhodesia's white settlers. Activists in the burgeoning nationalist movement spearheaded by the Nyasaland African Congress pushed for the breakup of this federation and the independence of Nyasaland. The Congress's movement was galvanized by their invitation of the exiled Malawian doctor, Hastings Kamuzu Banda, to return and lead them. The British declared a state of emergency in 1959, and they established a pattern of repression and intimidation Banda proved only too willing to copy and expand upon when Nyasaland gained its independence, as Malawi, in 1964. As Guy Mhone put it, Banda rhetorically asked Malawians to "choose . . . between dictatorship and democracy, or what he termed 'chaos.' Dr. Banda won, and the rest has been history" (1992, 4).

Malawi was "one of the most conservative political regimes on the entire continent" from independence until 1994, under Banda's cunning dictatorial hand (Wills 1985, 472). Johnston's outline of Malawi's power hierarchy was one of the things Banda "conserved," albeit with him, his Malawi Congress Party (MCP) elite, and his network of local "traditional" chiefs sharing the top billing with whites. Nowhere is this more evident than in his grandest scheme of all, to create a new capital city in central Malawi's Lilongwe district. The new city's plan came straight from apartheid South Africa and a team of white consultants from the Imex firm in Johannesburg (Connell 1972). The director of the Capital City Development Corporation Banda established to build the city, Geraint Richards, and most of his senior staff, were white Europeans and South Africans. Only one senior architect consultant on the project was not white: Ajit Singh Hoogan. Ajit was one of a very small handful of Asians in Banda's Malawi who, despite their numbers, did much to "develop" the country. Apparently, they did so much to develop it in the form of dominating mid-level business and industry that Banda forcibly removed Asians from rural areas and restricted them to living in four designated towns—Limbe, Blantyre, Zomba, and Lilongwe (Patel 1996, 40). Beneath the MCP power elite, its apartheid allies, and the Asian neocolonized middle, the country's vast majority of citizens struggled with grinding poverty and constant repression.

Ideologically, one could not find two regimes that looked more different on paper than Karume's Zanzibar (from chapter 6) and Banda's Malawi.

At the height of the cold war in 1968, Karume played host to East German, Russian, and Chinese communist development projects and diplomats, while he quite publicly and dramatically deported Frank Carlucci, the American consular officer who had helped forge the union with Tanganyika, for spying. Banda, by contrast, was at that very moment toasting his alliance with apartheid South Africa and forging his deep ties with the government of the United States (where he had earned his bachelor's and medical degrees [Short 1974]). Taiwan created an elaborate central park for the new city Banda built in Lilongwe, whereas mainland China redesigned the "People's Park" in front of the verandahs of the House of Wonders in Zanzibar.

Beneath their rhetoric, though, Karume and Banda had much in common, and internally, their regimes were nearly identical in the fear they inspired among their own people. These strong, authoritarian, one-party dictatorships also shared a grand vision of the city as the emblem of their power. Karume sought to remake the city of Zanzibar in his image; Banda tried to create an entirely new city. For both men, however, the cities stood for their regimes as they stood for their very identities. Eric Dutton's quotation of Byron as an emblematic statement on colonial space in the 1930s echoes back at us: "Survey our Empire, behold our home." Both Karume and Banda asked the world to survey their empires by beholding their capital cities and the homes built there. And both leaders utilized colonial enframing tactics in the design of their cities. Neocolonial Lilongwe, like revolutionary Zanzibar, was laid out as a segmented plan to replace an order without framework, depended upon containerization into insides and outsides at a number of spatial scales, and was characterized by an architecture of surveillance and observation.

Taking Lilongwe "From Vision to Reality"

The Banda regime decided to build a new capital almost immediately upon taking office, in October 1964. Justifications for the chosen site of Lilongwe focused on the geographical centrality of what was then quite a small settlement. Lilongwe, like Lusaka and Nairobi, had begun as a colonial administrative settlement, in this case in 1904. Unlike the cities of chapters 3 and 4, though, Lilongwe had never assumed any greater role than that of a provincial headquarters during the colonial era (Mjojo 1989). The Nyasaland colonial regime had indeed advocated moving the capital from the small southern town of Zomba, but the preferred site in the colonial era was the country's largest city and manufacturing center, Blantyre, a forty-minute drive from Zomba.

Southern Malawi's Shire Highlands and its three main towns, Blantyre, Limbe, and Zomba represented the white settler landscape, and hence, a shift to Lilongwe symbolically made a break from colonialism. Economically, the Banda regime argued, Lilongwe could serve as "a new growth point to stimulate development north of the Southern Region" (Capital City Development Corporation 1972). The government's rhetorical commitment to regionally balanced growth also meant Lilongwe could help redistribute population and resources (Kalipeni 1992, 26). Land control on-site had parallels with Lusaka: the Johannesburg firm that earned the commission for Lilongwe's 1968 Master Plan placed the new city adjacent to "Old Lilongwe," the preexisting administrative center, on lands obtained by the government through a land registration program going on concurrently in the greater Lilongwe district. Overriding any of these logical elements in the geographical decision is the unmistakable stamp of Banda's rule, since Lilongwe was close to his birthplace and the hearth of his Chewa culture group and political power base. If ever someone "ruled the country with a rod of iron" (Eric Dutton's phrase for Governor Maxwell in Northern Rhodesia) it was Hastings Kamuzu Banda. The Lilongwe project was one of the more colossal examples of this rod.

The Banda regime created the Capital City Development Corporation (CCDC) as a quasi-private entity to build the new capital. The money to create CCDC came from an eight million rand loan from the Republic of South Africa. However much this CCDC may have made the project look like it had a life of its own distinct from the Malawi government, the CCDC and the whole project were quite inseparable from Banda's regime. Geraint Richards, the CCDC chairman, served as secretary of the Ministry of Works and Supplies (MWS) and as Ajit Singh's supervisor there. Singh, like most senior staff in the MWS, served as consultant to the CCDC from the drawing of the city plans by the MWS through the completion of the international airport (at least in part a Singh design) in 1977. The epitome of this smokescreen between the Banda regime and the capital project is the fact that Banda himself was, after all, the minister for Works and Supplies. A Malawian MWS draftsman trained by Ajit Singh, whom I interviewed with the promise of anonymity on July 17, 1997, put it this way: "Mr. Clark was Supervisor of Building, Mr. Richards was Principal Secretary, and the

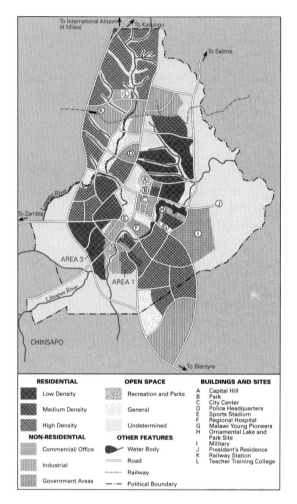

Fig. 15. The Master Plan of Lilongwe. Courtesy of
the Kansas Cartographic Services Office,
Geography Department, University of Kansas.

Chief Architect was always white. But Kamuzu was Minister. He was Minister of Everything."

Ajit Singh arrived in Malawi just prior to the grand celebration of Banda's transformation of Malawi into a republic in 1966, technically the moment of departure for the British overseeing the transition period to outright independence. The pomp and circumstance of the moment impressed him greatly. He wrote to Eric Dutton in 1966 to thank him for having helped get him the job through influential letters. "I'll always remember you with gratitude, for it was only you who afforded me so much experience in the field of architecture, and sincerely speaking I owe you much for the position I hold at present! Thank you very much indeed!" The pending capital development project was much on his mind: "We are facing a very huge development program with only four architects, all European save me, and we are going to lick the challenge as a team" (Singh Papers). It was actually several years later, though, that the actual program even began.

Enframing Lilongwe

In Lilongwe, the CCDC building program initially focused on building Lilongwe's "Capital Hill" and City Center areas. Work began there in January 1969. By January 1972, the first ministerial office building (for MWS) was ready for occupancy, along with eighty houses in what was labeled as "Area 12" reserved for MWS staff. The Town Planning Department did modify the South African consultants' map somewhat. Nevertheless, the new city replaced the old, small town of Lilongwe with a highly segmented plan, the first of Mitchell's elements of enframing. Although race played no explicit factor in the layout of these residential areas, the master plan demarcated low, medium, and high density residential areas that replicated and expanded upon the race-based spatial order of old Lilongwe and of apartheid South Africa, on a class basis that still had implicit racial dynamics. High-density areas were composed entirely of poor and working-class African residents. The low-density areas to this day house all of the city's white and Asian population, joined now by well-to-do blacks. Vast open spaces, swampy lowlands (*dambo*), and the Central Business District all served as buffers between the different types of areas. The Capital Hill and first low density area adjoined one another. The Banda regime constructed the national military headquarters to cover the frontier between the largest high-density area and the monstrous Presidential Residence. Police headquarters straddled the only boundary line where high- and low-density areas meet on the map. Johnston's infamous declaration ("a colony ruled by whites, developed by Indians, and worked by blacks") found its endurance in the areas of the new capital that, even into the late 1990s, maintained something of this hierarchy beneath the veneer of "density" (Potts 1985, 52).

Lilongwe's plan is one where Mitchell's second principle of enframing,

Fig. 16. Capital Hill across the park. From *From
Vision to Reality* by Geraint Richards (Johannesburg:
Lorton Publications, 1974).

that of "containerizing" the inside and outside spaces, is obvious as well.
New Lilongwe's original forty-seven residential areas were laid out with distinct curvilinear road plans that separated one area from another. The plan
relied upon a strict code of zoning between land-use types and a "virtually
clinical degree of orderliness" that deliberately "prevents the intermixture
of functions spatially" (Potts 1986, 226). Each area had one or two defined
entrance or exit points onto the major road network. Many of the areas are
immediately apparent to a visitor as containers.

The paucity of through roads created a city form not dissimilar from
the apartheid suburbs of South Africa. Many South African suburbs of the
post-1948 era display curvilinear or gridlike street patterns with limited exit
and entry points from the neighborhood units. The apartheid mentality
plays into Lilongwe's design, for instance, in the fact that each area—
whether a high- or low-density one—could be easily controlled in any police action. The most easily contained, the low-income Areas, were placed
in "inappropriate" and undesirable locations for reasons Debby Potts
(1986, 232) labels "deliberate" because these Areas were seen as "a potential source of unrest." Likewise, high-income, elite areas like Capital Hill
were designed to be "both aesthetically pleasing and easy to defend" (Potts

1986, 233). Potts (1986, 233) points out that the Capital Hill is "surrounded by a security fence and there is only one guarded entrance." Under apartheid, white and nonwhite areas in South Africa were designed to be defined by what was kept in and what was kept out—the "power of definition" of the spatial order (Western 1996, 8). Potts cautions us to not overemphasize the South African influence, because after all, the Banda regime chose "to continue the policy of urban residential segregation established under colonial rule" (1986, 229). Instead, Lilongwe's enframing order probably ought to be seen as "a result of a combination of these influences" of apartheid and British colonialism (Potts 1986, 229). Since many basic elements of urban apartheid in South Africa, particularly the political power of "apartness" as a spatial tool, were themselves outgrowths of British colonial rule (Robinson 1996), ultimately it is in the empire that the roots of the influence should be located.

As in Dutton's project in Lusaka, the prominent offices of state were constructed first, and on the highest point in the urban area, Capital Hill, the offices of which look down upon the vast outlay of residential zones. Several miles to the east, but on a ridge on the other side of the Lilongwe River and thus visible from the Capital Hill offices, CCDC constructed Banda's lavish Presidential Palace. Directly south of Capital Hill, and again on a small rise, came the City Center. Mitchell's central sites of observation and surveillance in colonial Cairo, as in Baker's Nairobi Government House, the Lusaka Ridgeway Government House, colonial Zanzibar's Raha Leo Civic Center, or revolutionary Zanzibar's Michenzani complex, are replicated in the plan of Lilongwe. The new city center area fulfilled another characteristic of this observational tenet of enframing, because it was designed as a space not only to demonstrate to Lilongwe's residents the greatness and power of the state but also to display for them a modern lifestyle within the enframing order's confines. Its highly visible shopping center and fancy shops—directly across the parking lot from the city council offices—brought into public display an idealized capitalist consumerism within the hypercontrolled politics of the Banda regime. And display is the operative word, since most Lilongwe residents would never be able to afford much of anything they could see in its shop windows.

Lilongwe is extraordinarily spread out, even by comparison with Africa's other low-density urban areas. The city is thirty-eight kilometers long and about sixteen wide, meaning it has an area that is slightly more than half the size of Unguja (Zanzibar) island. It still had an odd, unlived-in feeling in many of its separate corners by the late 1990s. Its cold, rational order continues to gleam through in the extent to which very few of the original plan's Areas have taken on new names. People have grown accustomed to referring to their neighborhoods simply by number, but Lilongwe's area numbers are by now imbued with broad meaning. Area 3, for instance, adjacent to the Golf Club and Sir Glyn Jones Road (named for the last colonial governor-general), is a place-name code word for the elite, often still whites or Asians. If one walks the long and hilly mile or so south across the marshy valley of the Lilongwe River dividing Area 3 from Area 1, it is easy to understand how the latter, most of "Old Lilongwe," has become a place-name code for poverty and violence.

Lilongwe was an incredibly expensive city to build. As Potts has written, "[I]t will never be possible to cost exactly the Lilongwe project" because government and CCDC budgets disguised various costs (1985, 50). Cost factors like the construction of a railway link up to Lilongwe from the south, the new Presidential Palace, or the new international airport, are often not included in official estimates of the city's costs. The airport alone is estimated to have cost more than eighty million kwacha, then equal to about ten million dollars (Potts 1985, 50). It is safe to conclude that one "of the least economically endowed nations on the continent" at the very least made an "intriguing" decision to sink so much of its meager coffers into this new capital (Mlia 1975, 389).

Lilongwe and the Minister of Everything

Relatively little scholarship has been published analyzing Lilongwe. In fact, Malawi's cities continue to be rather under-studied; a search for articles on Malawi on the Internet information service of Article-First generated 932 scholarly articles or papers from 1996 to 1999, and exactly nine (less than 1 percent) had urban issues as their core concern. McCracken notes that there are "good reasons why the remarkable outpouring of work on Southern African urban history that has taken place over the last twenty years has largely bypassed Malawi"(1998, 247). Among the reasons, McCracken cites the obvious facts that both colonial Nyasaland and independent Malawi can be considered "overwhelmingly rural" (an estimated 89 percent of the population in 1994) and that the territory has lacked one single concentrated city of any major size (1998, 247). Malawi is the least urbanized of any of the four former British colonies of this book, for instance. In the case of Lilongwe's postcolonial history, though, we might add the very politics of research on it.

It was difficult to produce any scholarship in Malawi critical in any way of the Banda regime, particularly if one was a Malawi resident and wished to remain so, and the Lilongwe project was inseparable from that regime's politics. As the poet Jack Mapanje has written, the "only way to escape censure was to credit every achievement to Banda" (1997, 70). Banda often receives praise from his supporters for keeping "things in control," but his control was ultimately manipulative and destructive for Malawi's future. "He used to tell people that before he came along they were practically naked. He always wore a six-piece suit. He was Cruel, with a capital C. But outwardly he was the picture of a gentleman," said one Malawian in a 1997 conversation. Despite this chilling, gentlemanly mirage, even outsiders knew that criticisms could jeopardize the possibilities for future work or research in the country. Geraint Richards found a place for no less than fourteen fawning references to Banda as "that quite remarkable man, the Life President," and the like, in his picture-book account of the Lilongwe project, a publication that has the equivalent of nineteen pages of large-print text (1974, 11).

Techno-managerial language often can be used to mask what would in all likelihood have been deeper and more trenchant criticisms. In the early 1980s, Ben Kaluwa couched his criticisms of the Lilongwe capital project in terms of the city's "poor performance relative to the nation as a whole in employment creation" (1982, 73). By making the problems technical ones of "performance" and "employment creation," more controversial aesthetic, political, or cultural issues are buried. Even so, Kaluwa was able to demonstrate that Lilongwe had grown dramatically in population without the corresponding creation of jobs, particularly in manufacturing, thereby replicating a defining feature of Africa's colonial cities. He showed that even when manufacturing firms established themselves in the city, they were typically smaller branch operations of Blantyre-based firms.

The late Malawian geographer J. Ngoleka Mlia admitted that the new city could not really be expected to serve as a growth pole for economic development, and he acknowledged that at least some of the project owed its being to "the personal political objectives of the chief executive" (1975, 389). But two aspects of his analysis are worthy of deeper consideration. First, Mlia saw Lilongwe as ultimately more important for its dramatic and symbolic importance to "national pride" (389). Second, he argued, in essence, that we cannot conclude that Banda acted alone and leave it at that. Lilongwe's creation reflected "changes . . . in the overall spatial distribution of political power," since the country's "proximate policy makers" no longer came from the southern highlands but instead from the central region (390). The "demands of regional interest groups" helped shape the project into being, not Kamuzu alone (397). Some of these arguments are defensive, in the light of what Malawian poet Frank Chipasula refers to as the "nature of our fear" in those days (1984). Banda, with his inseparable companions Mrs. Kadzimira and John Tembo, really did initiate much of this whole project. But Mlia was right to suggest that Banda was not without other allies and at least a partial sense of national pride behind him in going forward with the scheme.

Mlia points us, probably unintentionally, toward an understanding of Banda's Lilongwe project within the overall spatial tactics of the regime Banda led. Banda and the Malawi Congress Party, like Karume and his Afro-Shirazi Party (and a great many other postcolonial regimes in Africa), built their support through patronage and coercion that was highly regional in nature, with the Chewa-dominated central region as its linchpin (Kaspin 1995, 604). The building of Lilongwe in the central region was "the single most important program for economic development" in the "Chewa-ization" of Malawi's "national" pride (Kaspin 1995, 605). The Lilongwe rural land development project in the district around the new city ranked second (Kaspin 1995, 608). The uneven geographical development of "national" pride that Lilongwe encapsulates continued to fester until Malawi finally threw off the yoke of Banda's control in the early 1990s.

Although they now belong to a decidedly different order, the new, post-Banda Malawian cities are still vital symbols of "national" pride. Lilongwe officially became Malawi's capital in 1975; but Malawi's parliament has continued meeting in the old capital of Zomba, and the democratically elected president, Bakili Muluzi, himself a southerner, has chosen to live in Zomba as well. As Potts has commented, Lilongwe's "close association with the Life President, Hastings Banda, meant that the nature of its development was tied up with his prestige, and aesthetic considerations nearly always took priority over the needs of the low-income population" (1994, 215). Muluzi's efforts to assert his concern for low-income people and to make a clean break with Banda's tactics in a sense require him to distance himself from Lilongwe.

Whether the president or parliament choose to continue to ignore it or not, Lilongwe surely still exists, and it continues to expand. It is a city with unmistakable ties to a regime that staked its foreign reputation on an alliance with apartheid. This regime replicated—and improved upon—colonial tactics. Arguably its most famous act, the forcible expulsion of nineteen thousand members of the Jehovah's Witnesses, accomplished the removal of what Eric Dutton (Oldham Papers) had seen in 1935, fifty years beforehand, as "a direct affront to colonial officials' well-laid plans" in Central Africa (Stoler and Cooper 1997, 6).

On first impression, Lilongwe is a rather "boring planned city laid out in a Western way and lived in in an African one," as one of its residents put it in 1997. With a car, it is traversed without great difficulty. Without one, it is one of Africa's more difficult small cities to move across or around. Ronald McGill estimated its population in 1994 at 330,000 people, with a growth rate of 7 percent per year (1994, 35). That estimate would put its population at 495,100 in 2000. Despite its rapid growth, Lilongwe still suffers from "problems of artificiality" with "few of the usual characteristics of urban areas which have grown more or less organically" (Potts 1985, 51).

Ajit Singh's grandson remembers Ajit saying in 1972 that Malawi still had "a colonial government" even after independence. If we assume that by this Ajit meant that the workings of power were little changed from the outline promoted by Harry Johnston at the inception of colonial Nyasaland, then what happened to the Indians who "developed" the neo-colony and its "artificial" capital? Ajit's own experiences provide a pertinent window onto this through the period of Lilongwe's creation as the new capital.

Neocolonized Middle: Ajit Singh's Lilongwe

Ajit Singh was ever eager to please his white superiors in Malawi. But when he first arrived in late 1965, he was only given "small projects, because, as he used to say, 'they were dismissive of me' because he wasn't a European, trained in Britain, and they doubted his abilities" (P. Singh 1997). He was, as he told Dutton, the only non-European beside Banda with any power in the Ministry of Works building services. He owed part of his success in Malawi to his having been already on familiar terms with his immediate superior, Geraint Richards, who arrived in Malawi in 1967 but who had served the Zanzibar Protectorate. But Singh's relationship with Richards never took on the intimacy or trust of his relationship with Dutton. Singh held to a sense of bitterness in the differences between them in status. According to his family, he felt that a number of Richards's designs were inadequate or ill-fitting, and he resented not having been given the chance to develop more of his own ideas.

Little documentary evidence of his bitterness exists, but Singh did retain one letter of censure in his private files from 1966, from the boss who preceded Richards, as well as his reply to that boss. Although he assisted in designing the new campus of the University of Malawi—Chancellor's College at Soche Hill, just southwest of Zomba—he was "disciplined" for drafting mistakes he felt were not his and demanded the situation be taken as a "misunderstanding" and not "misconduct." He even boldly stated that some of the existing design was quite unimaginative: "I deplorably find the general public . . . has been drastically misdirected by the stereotyped and outdated stock designs" (Singh Papers). But for the most part, the Ajit Singh described by his school principal in Punjab in 1932 as a "well behaved gentleman" with "charming manners" showed through in his avoidance of conflicts over office politics. He closed his reply letter in 1966 with: "[I]n any case I will abide by your ruling and will act accordingly. . . . An esteemed ruling from seniors leaves little room for hesitation and doubt with juniors."

Richards, for his part, plays the gentleman, too, in his account of the capital project, entitled *From Vision to Reality.* He focused on administrative challenges faced by the CCDC and the MWS working under "overwhelming financial restraints." He wrote, "many 'sacred cows' became casualties" in Lilongwe's construction (Richards 1974, 24). "I should like to pay tribute to the planners and architects of the Ministry of Works and Supplies for the way in which they accepted control, always determined but I trust never oppressive, from an 'outsider' to their particular disciplines."

Ajit Singh had little or no say in the locating of Lilongwe. He was still Zanzibar's town architect when the choice was made in 1965, and his first six years in Malawi were spent mostly based in the old capital of Zomba. Many of his design assignments concerned posts and telecommunications. Virtually every post office, radio station, telephone exchange building, airport, or other government building created in Malawi between 1966 and 1977 at least bears his influence in its lines. He moved his residence to Lilongwe in 1971, about two years after some of the government office buildings had officially started, and after the first residential neighborhood had been built. Buildings in the new capital for which he is the main contributor included, but were not limited to, its main post office, half of its colossal airport, several of the ministerial office buildings (outside the capital hill complex, which had white South African architects), its city-owned guest house, and a number of its industrial sites.

For Ajit, as we see from his correspondence from 1972, Lilongwe was always "warm and dusty, devoid of friends. It is expensive, too. The land is full of white ants" (Singh Papers). He loved Zomba's environment. The letters he wrote from there are full of phrases like this: "[E]verything looks happy and gay on the ground." His separation from his family, who were still in Zanzibar, caused an anxiety and a bitterness that never left him; but apart from that, Ajit found some moments of happiness in the mountains of southern Malawi.

Southern Malawi contained nearly all of what passed for an Asian community in the country. Nyasaland always had a much smaller Indian population than Zanzibar, with only 2,804 Asians as of 1945. But where Asian migration to Zanzibar peaked around that year, Asians really only began arriving in any number in Nyasaland between 1945 and 1965. By 1966, the country had a little more than 11,000 Asian residents. This was to be the peak population of the Asian community. Soon after Ajit's arrival, in 1967, the Banda regime forcibly removed all Asians from rural areas and denied them any rights of residence or business ownership outside of four urban centers—Limbe, Zomba, Blantyre, and Lilongwe. This forced removal led to the first wave of out-migration of Asians from Malawi, such that only 5,682 remained as of 1977 and 4,927 by 1987. Less than half that number was estimated to still be resident in the country in 1996 (Patel 1996). Almost all of the Asian population lived in the three southern cities when Ajit arrived—the 1966 census listed only 742 Asians in Lilongwe—and very little has changed since then in this geographical pattern.

Sikhs have always been a very small minority in Malawi. Forty Sikhs were among the first contingent of seventy Asian soldiers Johnston brought to "develop" the country in 1891, and two hundred more arrived four years later to help Johnston subdue local Yao and Arab forces. Most of these Sikh soldiers, and many other Sikhs who emigrated in the twentieth century, gained employment in the railway yard and were given housing in the railway engineering works area of Limbe town. Almost all belonged to the Ramgharia (craftsman) caste. Their numbers were sufficient for the formation of a temple community in Limbe. When Ajit arrived, the temple had well over two hundred practicing members (it now has about ten Sikh families and a handful of Hindu attendees). Ajit had only a forty-minute drive from home in Zomba to the temple in Limbe. The move to Lilongwe placed him more than four hours from the Limbe temple in a town that has literally never had more than a handful of Sikh residents. His religious life was instead conducted via the small Hindu temple in Lilongwe, where he was one of two Sikh attendees.

Even in Zomba, Ajit had moments of serious doubt about his position. The 1967 Rural Areas Act expanded these doubts. In 1967, soon after its declaration—and without mentioning the act—Ajit wrote home to his wife, "I am badly lacking my social, spiritual, and religious circle here and often feel 'starving'. I am seriously thinking of leaving this place early next year. Zanzibar though hard to live in now-a-days . . . has retained its mixed society to a greater extent. . . . Although I am well off yet I do not feel happy, as we are split up under two establishments" (Singh Papers). Epilepsy triggered by mounting stress may also be taken as a suggestion of Ajit's uncertain situation. The onset of his epilepsy coincided with his conflict with Abeid Amani Karume over the Old People's Houses in Zanzibar in spring 1965, but his meticulous health diary records no other fits until he came to Malawi ten months later. He had six severe seizures in his first eighteen months in Malawi, and two in the month when Banda declared the Rural Areas Act of 1967.

In Lilongwe, Ajit Singh took up residence in an area reserved for government workers, and in 1972 called it "a dreary place," complaining that, as a result of the extensive land-use plan of Lilongwe, "it must be six or seven miles away" from where he worked (Singh Papers). Despite his long service in Malawi, Ajit remained an architect on contract, and every time his contract came up for renewal he debated long and hard whether he would re-sign, often asking the advice of Dutton or other former colonial officials. His position paid well, but at a cost. He was not only separated from his family in Zanzibar, he had to live and work under what could only have been treacherous and stifling professional conditions for someone of his race and background. In his first year, all Asians had to move to the four cities. In his third year, Banda deported eight hundred Goans—the entire Goan community—because one of them was reported to have asked that the radio in the Goan Club be turned down during a radio broadcast of a Banda speech. A few years after that, one of Ajit's closest friends in the Sikh community was deported for having rented a room to a follower of a banned religious sect. Banda arrested several people Ajit later acknowledged to have been close acquaintances or friends (Singh Papers).

These stresses eventually led Ajit to resign from his contract and return to Zanzibar in 1979. In 1984, once he was safely resident in Zanzibar again and in his seventies, Ajit Singh led a letter-writing campaign in Tanzania for the release of Malawi Freedom Movement leader Orton Chirwa and his wife Vera, whom Banda had condemned to death (Singh Papers). But from within Malawi, from 1965 to 1979, Ajit held silent on all political matters. When friends, including Dutton, wrote with concern from Tanzania, India, or Europe, Ajit inevitably responded as in this letter from 1966: "Things in Africa are not very bright. Next door to us you know how Rhodesia has behaved. . . . Dr. Banda is a very wise and daring politician, and he is saving us by his farsightedness" (Singh Papers). "True," he commented in 1972, "there is a drive against long hair for men, but not against we Sikhs! [Male followers of Sikhism generally are not supposed to cut their hair, which is curled beneath a turban.] The drive is against hippies and other undesirables" (Singh Papers).

Banda "had no inhibitions about leaning on the expertise of the expatriate inhabitants" (Wills 1985, 475). He was especially enamored of whiteness, in spite of the lack of understanding toward African climates or cultures in building design evidenced by his white South African consultants in the building of Lilongwe. Even a casual comparison of Ajit's comfortable mixture of styles and use of local materials in the Lilongwe post office with the alien glass-and-steel office layout of Lilongwe's Capital Hill by the South African designers bears this out. Ajit held that the four cornerstones of successful architecture required attention to materials, climate, culture, and religion in the local setting (J. Singh 1999). Apartheid architecture consistently twisted these cornerstones in the interests of its power, and Lilongwe mirrored this.

Ajit himself understood that twisted power structure. Some of the reasons Banda stuck with Ajit, according to several accounts, were that he gave him credit for understanding Africa and Africans, and that he did his job and kept out of trouble. Chief Maole, who was a draftsman under Singh in Zomba, remembered him as a fair boss. "He liked young people, and he liked mixing with the 'chaps' [meaning Africans]" (Maole 1997). At the same time, he held to standards of punctuality and decorum that gave another suggestion of why his working with Banda was not such an odd pairing: "He was always on time. Look at this MP we are waiting for now, two hours late for our meeting. If it were us with Mister Singh, fifteen minutes late and we knew we'd be sacked" (Maole 1997). Ultimately, though, Maole felt Singh shared his own sense that it was often "a nightmare to work for the Old Man [Banda]. You never knew what would happen next" (Maole 1997).

One of Ajit's drivers in the MWS in Zomba, Wilson Godfrey, remembered that Ajit "always worked hard, he was always drawing plans, and his plans were always correct" (Godfrey 1997). He explained Ajit's apparent friendliness with Banda this way: "With Banda, you couldn't talk politics at all. Banda was very cruel. You couldn't even have a nice car, because Banda would say, '[W]here'd you get your money, you don't deserve this,' and take it away. Now, with [President Bakili] Muluzi, people can do what they want" (Godfrey 1997). Ajit's apolitical demeanor and frugal lifestyle—he used much of his salary to help his family in Zanzibar—helped him fit within Banda's system.

Another African protégé of Ajit Singh, Felix Sapao, formed a bond with Ajit during their years as neighbors in Zomba. "Ajit had a style all his own. We very much admired his work ethic, especially for a man of his age" (Sapao 1997). But even this landscape architect had his misgivings about Banda, and about Lilongwe. The new capital city "is so expensive, so spread out. Transport is a problem, petrol is a problem, telephones are a problem. People who have no money have no cars so they have to walk, and the walks are very long" (Sapao 1997). And the president for life he served "chased away a lot of intelligent and very highly educated people. He used to sit in meetings depending heavily on Aleke Banda, he used to say, 'Where's Banda, where's Aleke?' and then, pop, he put him in jail" (Sapao 1997).

Friends of Singh in the Asian community shared many of the same feelings toward the Banda years. One said, "I admired Banda for his administration. Things worked. I did not like how he conducted politics. His policy toward whites and Asians were full of contradictions" (Mendes 1997). He relied very heavily on white and Asian finance and expertise, and yet he would often turn on white and especially Asian Malawians for the slightest reasons.

Lilongwe, to many of its Asian residents, is a maze and a mess. "We have lived a very sheltered life," said one old friend of Ajit Singh, when talking of the rise on crime in the city in the 1990s. "People say, 'these problems of violence are found in every country,' but we are not living in those countries. We are living in one that has no idea how to handle these problems. This city is filthy, dirty, and rough. The market and bus station area, and

Area 1 [essentially, Old Lilongwe] is an absolute disaster. Cars simply do not move!" (Gautama 1997). Many admitted that, though they had lived in Lilongwe for fifteen or twenty years, they did not know their way around: "The Areas are all numbered out of order—have you noticed?—and some streets have no names" (Gautama 1997).

Of course, this issue of finding one's way by car is of little consequence to its majority African residents, most of whom do not have cars. What is life like for Lilongwe's urban majority? Perhaps unsurprisingly, much of it is lived, it turns out, in "flagrant defiance" of the standards around which the Banda regime intended to create an enframed capital (Potts 1986, 267).

Lilongwe as an African City

It is still difficult to find any scholarship that truly opens up ordinary people's feelings about the city. Even after Banda's 1994 ouster, one senses a reticence on the part of many Malawians to discuss matters that might be construed as political. I certainly sensed this in my 1997 fieldwork. "The atmosphere of terror the threat/submission system entailed was such that the Malawian's mistrust of one's colleagues at work or kith and kin, the Malawian's ability to conceal or suppress political views, no matter how elementary, and the Malawian's inclination to self-censor . . . was almost instinctive or an automatic reflexive response" (Mhone 1992, 8). Such an atmosphere is hard to live down or brush away. Still, there are some works to which we can turn in order to get some sense of Malawian experiences of Lilongwe.

To begin, it must be recognized that at least something of an urban area had existed in Lilongwe prior to the capital project. Old Lilongwe, like old Lusaka before the colonial-era capital project there, "from the very beginning took on the face of differentiated racial advancement" (Mjojo 1989, 11). White, Asian, and African areas were clearly demarcated by physical features in the old town. "The town really was for the European and the periurban was for the African" (Mjojo 1989, 12). Only in 1961 did the British regime develop any program for housing provision in the African areas of the town.

Before this time, Africans in Lilongwe, like so many urban Africans in colonial Nairobi, Lusaka, and Zanzibar, had to do for themselves. That meant that much of colonial Lilongwe—its periurban fringe—looked like an order without framework, developed while disregarded by the colonial regime. In the absence of "formalities of application" to, or standards of construction set by, the colonial state, periurban areas took on a look differentiated by the varied *uwezo* of their residents (Mjojo 1989, 13). Bona Mjojo writes that "most of the people were also attracted because of the social atmosphere. Many liked to identify with their own people where traditional dances and certain traditional practices could be accepted" (1989, 13). Local improvements to these areas were funneled through agencies of this "traditional" associational life, old Lilongwe's *desturi*, the most powerful of which were mission- and church-based, Lilongwe's *imani*.

The Banda regime's project did not, in the end, change the alienated position for Africans in their own city, despite its grand claims to build Lilongwe as a means of supposedly overturning the colonial legacy. Still, the city that the enframing order sought has instead become one that is bursting with periurban communities that literally and figuratively skirt the legal planning boundary. Power, faith, and custom cornerstones of local ways produce much of this urban space at the fringe now, as they did in colonial Lilongwe.

The CCDC, like the colonial regime in Lusaka, really had little interest in providing low-cost housing for low-income residents. Rather than a bias based on racism, here it is the for-profit motive of the CCDC that reduced any regard they may have had for housing the poor. Both the CCDC and the Malawi Housing Corporation that assumed CCDC's assets in the early 1980s developed low-income, site-and-service schemes, called "traditional housing areas" (THAs), in the Lilongwe plan. But they "tended to be located far from the town center, and even from main roads" (Potts 1994, 216; Kaluwa 1994, 249–74). The Banda regime even demolished the largest of its own site-and-service areas entirely a few years after completing it, because it was "too visible, and therefore conflicted with Banda's desire to maintain Lilongwe's garden city image" (Potts 1994, 216). Formal sector housing costs, too, have risen far out of proportion to incomes, as one force pushing Lilongwe toward squatter development outside the THAs (Kaluwa 1994, 249–74).

The ultimate irony of Lilongwe's geography lies in the fact that, despite its spread-out form, most of its African areas (the THAs) and squatter areas are actually severely overcrowded and closely built. In the early 1980s, over half of the urban population lived in areas where the average population per small plot was over fourteen (Potts 1994, 207–23). Unlike squatting in Lusaka, or even in Nairobi and Zanzibar, squatting in Lilongwe was considered exceedingly dangerous until the 1990s because of Banda's harsh policies against it; yet 34 percent of the city's population were estimated to be squatters in 1990 (Kaluwa 1994, 264), and that number had spiraled toward 50 percent ten years later (Englund 2002). One way around the overcrowded planned high-density areas for the urban poor came by means of a loophole in the Lilongwe Land Development Program (LLDP). The LLDP was the government rural-development scheme in the surrounding Lilongwe District, and many of its development areas worked on a system of smallholder land tenure. Many LLDP smallholders and other villagers in areas where land was still under customary (typically matrilineal) tenure on the periurban fringe were willing to rent or sell land to the urban poor at low prices. As these areas tended to be even further from the city, the spread has come out even further. "Street" vendors now operate a good twenty miles outside Lilongwe, serving to commuters on foot, bicycle, or minibus coming from these periurban communities everything from cooking wares to grilled field mice.

Studies by Gillian Roe (1992) and Harri Englund (2002) of one city-edge community, Chinsapo, give us some sense of Lilongwe's version of the power, faith, and custom cornerstones producing much of the urbanized area. As was the case with Karume's Afro-Shirazi Party, Banda's Malawi Congress Party intervened in these ordinary and everyday processes of spatial production. The MCP seems to have been somewhat successful in infiltrating these local ways in order to dominate them. Yet even the Banda regime could not entirely stamp out local ways. Roe's raw-research logbooks from conversations with landlords and tenants in Chinsapo highlight the continuance of such cornerstones, albeit within the authoritarian constraints of the Banda era.

For one example, land control and tenure never came entirely under the sway of the MCP, the city, or the LLDP in Chinsapo. Although Roe found that many tenants complained that landladies and landlords held them "at their mercy," this hold of landladies or landlords lay outside of the MCP apparatus that was supposed to control land transfers and rents. One landlord told Roe "no one here pays anything to the Government because it is a village and it is in the hands of Chief of Chinsapo. The buying of land concerns the chief and the buyer only" (1992, 42). Englund records that even in 2000, six years past the Banda era, the "allocation of land follows the principle of customary land tenure, with the headmen and local families of Chinsapo bearing the responsibility" (2002, 141).

The fact that Chinsapo lies outside the city boundary probably made these under-the-table real estate dealings possible in Banda's time. This also fueled interest in settling there on the part of squatter tenants, since rents were cheaper, the transaction went unregulated, and houses could be built to a lower standard than those required within the city. The fact that Chinsapo, despite being outside of the city border, is not as great a distance from the main African areas for business and industry in the city itself has also helped spur its growth.

To be sure, the headmen's authority would have derived from the Banda regime's heavy reliance on the "decentralized despotism" of late colonialism in Malawi (Mamdani 1996). But Roe's and Englund's studies show that neither the chief nor individual landlords functioned to create an urban order in Chinsapo that would have been in keeping with Areas in Lilongwe proper as planned. In most cases, "the tenants maintain the plot themselves" (Roe 1992, 44). In spite of meager means, both Roe and Englund, as well as the Lilongwe City Council's (1991) socioeconomic survey in Chinsapo, show the residents' eagerness to create the best housing situation their power allowed. More than 80 percent of the houses in the squatter area in 1991 were constructed of permanent or semipermanent material, for instance, and an overwhelming majority of residents expressed willingness to participate in home or community improvement (Lilongwe City Council 1991, 5 and 17). The extraordinary diversity of residents in terms of their place of origin within Malawi was found to produce little in the way of conflict, as most neighborly disputes were resolved in a reasonable manner. Englund claimed that "the idioms of 'ancestral customs' and 'village customs' are . . . widely cited as giving a standard for proper conduct" in Chinsapo (2002, 152).

Customary neighborliness and chiefly power were not the only cornerstones that occasionally surfaced outside of the MCP hierarchy in Roe's study. Faith, in the form of vibrant local churches and mosques, was a central facet of community building available to Chinsapo residents. In marked contrast to the power elite's religious institutions in Banda's Malawi, though, the three strongest churches in Chinsapo, according to Roe, were not member churches of mainstream Protestant denominations (1992, 110–13). Instead, the Zion Church, the Church of Pentecostal Holiness, and the One Cup Church of Christ dominated the lives of Chinsapo's people. The first is a branch of a highly decentralized African church institution, while the latter two are wholly independent churches. This is suggestive of how the marginalized urban majority distinguished itself from the power structure in a number of ways.

All three of these independent churches had at least some community development projects or ideas. Ultimately, Roe argued, the growth of "self-help" or community-based planning in such areas reliant on institutions of faith or any other local cornerstone would never succeed without steps to "empower the community" to break free of the "rigid power structure" of the MCP (1992, 45). Yet it is vital to recognize that within ten years of the community's settlement, its own people had begun to play their part in the production of space in their neighborhoods. In spite of the "straddling and struggling" that Englund saw dominating the lives of Chinsapo residents by 2000 (2002, 149), "a measure of tenacity" (152) remained behind "in the absence of official supervision" (143).

According to Kaluwa (1994, 255), "decades of policy and investment heavily biased toward agriculture as the mainstay of the economy have tended to overshadow the industrial sector and the urban employment situation." Between 30 and 50 percent of Lilongwe's population was considered below a poverty level defined in Kaluwa's work to mean incomes could meet basic food requirements and have 35 percent of the total remaining for other needs (1994, 255). More than 75 percent of Lilongwe residents live in the semiplanned "traditional housing areas" or unplanned squatter areas, where more than 70 percent of households shared a pit latrine with another household in the early 1990s (Lilongwe City Council 1991). Several studies near that time correctly predicted that the situation of urban poverty would only worsen for most Lilongwe residents through the coming decade (Kaluwa 1994, 249–74; Aboagye 1986). The housing and employment crises have roots in the enframing tactics of a postcolonial regime that perpetuated the strategies of colonialism. Still, at least some Malawian squatter settlement residents and other African people in Lilongwe would appear, like those of Pumwani in Nairobi, George in Lusaka, or Ng'ambo in Zanzibar, to be quite practiced in doing for themselves. This resulted, even in the heavily controlled spaces of Banda's Lilongwe, in the production of an urban order that may appear to outsiders as "disorderly" while it conforms to many aspects of customary norms, repressive or inequitable as these customs themselves sometimes may be.

Conclusion

The creation of Lilongwe as Malawi's new capital by the postcolonial dictatorship of Hastings Banda reengineered and magnified the enframing tactics of colonialism. Its enframing spatiality, its spatial language articulating the dominative aims of the state, and its inability to capture the soul of popular consciousness all echo what we have seen in colonial Nairobi and Lusaka, and both colonial and postcolonial Zanzibar. But can Banda's Malawi or Africa's other postcolonial dictatorships be considered at all to be seeking legitimation? Berman saw the colonial state as staking itself to the task of legitimation as well as domination or accumulation, and Berman saw the state as both strong and weak. Isn't this state just strong, or just dominant? Isn't this rule absent of any goodwill? Clearly here we see, probably more than even in Karume's Zanzibar, a case of the rule of force outweighing consensus in the drive for domination. Civil society institutions, such as the labor movement, were all brought under the control of MCP henchmen. Even more than in Tanzania, a "bureaucratic bourgeoisie" formed the main class of beneficiaries from the system (Chipeta 1992, 44).

However, it is highly misleading and ahistorical to not see that Banda's highly centralized and yet highly regional system of rule was a direct inheritance and enhancement of the character of the colonial state in Nyasaland. This is a point driven home by Jonathan Kaunda's careful analysis (1992, 55). Nyasaland's version of British colonial indirect rule "did not make room for the representation and expression of popular opinion," and it worked through the coercive and repressive agency of local chiefs (like the chief in Chinsapo above), just as Banda did. And even in this extremist state Banda did so much to create, his domination was not wholly totalitarian or uncontested. Peter Forster even sees the Banda regime as having had "legitimacy" that was not based "on political repression alone" (1994, 477). He stresses the importance of culture and the invention of tradition to the long run of legitimacy the Banda regime enjoyed. Even within the country, Mapopa Chipeta argues, new social movements, such as informal credit unions, sectarian religious organizations, burial and funeral societies, or even middle-class professional societies can be construed as indicators of Malawians seeking to "cut a niche of political space for themselves" (1992, 47). Part of this niche of political space, I would argue, included the production of neighborhood and domestic space in vast stretches of urban Malawi, including the squatter and high-density areas of Lilongwe.

Chapter Eight

Conclusion

"Many writers lay very great stress upon some definite moral purpose, at which they profess to aim their works. Not to be deficient in this particular, the author has provided himself a moral—the truth, namely, that the wrongdoing of one generation lives into successive ones."
—Nathaniel Hawthorne, *The House of the Seven Gables*

I begin my conclusion by highlighting the parallels I see in design tactics between British colonial urban-planning projects in Nairobi, Lusaka, and Zanzibar and postcolonial urban projects in Zanzibar and Lilongwe. Much of the narrative of these chapters has attempted to tell "the long history of the production of space" in these cities by British colonial and African postcolonial orders, and how Africans have come to live with and reframe these orders (Lefebvre, in Celik 1997, 5). In examining each of these cities, I go inside the design process, to the details of projects and to the level of personalities. My aim is surely to "get beyond treating colonialism as an abstract process, to take apart the shifts and tensions within colonial projects" (Stoler and Cooper 1997, 1–56); but it is just as much to get beyond treating colonialism alone, to look at postcolonial contexts with a critical eye. The transfer of ideas of what a city should be, or how planning and design should take place, was a transfer from real people to real people, not always some ethereal and abstract process. It was also not, at that personal level, a case of formerly colonized people swallowing colonial ideas whole: African and Asian functionaries of state were conscious agents in this transfer. The last few chapters serve as a window on how some essentially colonial ideas of urban form and architectural space were transferred into the independence period. Both the Zanzibar and Malawi postcolonial cases also give rise to an appreciation of some elements of differentiation between the colonial and postcolonial setting.

Obviously, there are many differences between these distinct settings. None of the metaphorical Houses of Wonder of African cities look exactly alike. Still, several key features tie the projects in each city and context to one another. First, the same or very similar geographical justifications were used in all cases for the initial plans and investments, and these concealed more significant political motivations. Each setting manifests in its own way a state seeking to perform the tasks Berman outlined for colonial Kenya— domination, accumulation, and legitimation—with the implementation of specific forms of territoriality. The geographical justifications and the state's motivations are quite similar from Nairobi in the 1920s, Lusaka in the 1930s, Zanzibar in the 1940s and the 1970s, and Lilongwe in the 1970s.

Second, in all of the settings save Nairobi in the 1920s, exceedingly expensive building programs took place at similarly "strange" times of global and local financial stress. All cases involved some version of authoritarian rule attempting to gain the goodwill of the urban majority. The states implementing the plans appear as both weak and strong, as both fragmented and centralized. The colonial heritage has different meanings in each of these former colonies, but the insidious repression of state actions in the urban setting—coupled with the failure of the states to actually follow through on much of this repressive threat—ranks high on the list of inheritances.

Third, the three spatial strategies that Timothy Mitchell (1988) identifies as colonialism's enframing tactics were central to all of these programs. Mitchell characterizes these as: (a) replacing "orders without frameworks" with "segmented plans," typically based on race; (b) solidifying the boundaries between inside and outside at the domestic and neighborhood levels; and (c) providing central spaces of observation and surveillance as part of objectifying space for residents and making it "readable, like a book," for the state. All three strategies can be shown in abundance in these city designs and redesigns, from the various programs in Nairobi in the 1920s, to the colonial capital project for Northern Rhodesia, the colonial and the revolutionary reconstructions of Zanzibar, and the postcolonial capital project in Lilongwe.

Fourth, each of these cities have their chief design failing in land-use planning frameworks that virtually ignore the everyday spatial life-world of the majority of the residents. Lusaka and Lilongwe, in particular, were designed with much fanfare as garden cities of tomorrow, yet the ideal was debased by the segmented plan of separate development divisible by race or class or both, as was the city of Nairobi. The two re-creations of Zanzibar used "stupendous hammers to crack a few nuts," degraded by these same mundane tactics of segmentation and segregation.

Fifth and finally, each of these cities is marked, albeit to varying degrees and under different contemporary conditions of regulation and control, by "the persistence of disorder" and the continued reliance on local customary practices for the production of space in the city. Each state's enframing tactics come undone by internal contradictions and by the circumventions of the urban majority. Perhaps the most striking consequence of the state's failure to establish its dominative order in the cities under examination here is the persistence, albeit in altered form, of local cultural senses of spatial organization. On the collapsing wall of a rental home in the Kikwajuni neighborhood of Zanzibar in 1992, one of its migrant occupants painted the words, in English: "World is a field of chaos, life so hard. People are not planning to fail, they are just failing to plan." In reality, though, many residents plan as fast as they can, with the local framework of understanding, the local variant of what drives spatial production in places like Pumwani, George, Ng'ambo, or Chinsapo, indeed in many settings across urban Africa, as their main guide.

Local ways are often the only alternative for most ordinary residents of Nairobi, Lusaka, Zanzibar, or Lilongwe, to delegitimated governmental urban-planning and building-control processes. Many aspects of *imani* and *desturi* have remained vital to the creation of neighborhood and domestic space in the Ng'ambo area of Zanzibar, for example, while similar cornerstones of local order operate in the other cities. The problem lies in the fact that local ways can only be a solution if they are supported or guided by the state in the progressive interests of the urban majority. As Simone puts it, "the tragedy of the African situation is the resourcefulness of its people finds few expressions at home other than the effort to survive" (1994, 104). In the absence of support or guidance or both toward equitable redistribution, local ways simply come to embody and reproduce *uwezo*—the material inequalities of the city, between men and women, between those with land or power and those without.

I have used several individuals in particular to speak for agency at three levels of power within urban spatial-planning processes. It is fitting to provide closure to their words here at the book's end, because the varied agency at these three levels has much to do with how the four cities I have examined have ended up as they are. Eric Dutton died in November 1973

in Estoril, Portugal, in the home Ajit Singh had helped design, of a heart attack. He was seventy-eight. His wife Myrtle wrote to Ajit in 1974 that he
was "well and interested in life to the end, and did not suffer any long illness" (Singh Papers). In 1971, in one of his last letters to Ajit, Dutton told
his protégé that "Africa is changing very rapidly," but he was "very sorry to
see the plight the whole world is coming to" (Singh Papers). And "well and
interested" or "happy" as he may have been, there were scars on his experiences of Africa that remain unexplained.

Among these scars one must count the disappointment of remaining in
the shadow of power, particularly in Zanzibar. He wrote regularly to
Arthur Creech Jones, the secretary of state for the colonies in the Labor
government of 1945–51, beseeching him with "my special claims" to a
"promotion" to British Resident. In 1948, for instance, he wrote,

> If in your goodness you appointed me as Resident for only one tour
> (which would be rather a shame) you would then see the Development
> Program complete in all its essentials, local government and mass educa-
> tion well under way, the new aerodrome built and the new cocoa industry
> firmly established. I can only hope that you will forgive me for pressing my
> claims to Zanzibar . . . for the sake of my wife and children as well as my-
> self. I am emboldened to go on doing so by the encouragement of every-
> one who knows my work, the centerpiece of which is the remarkable
> progress of development in Zanzibar. (Jones Papers)

He got the airport built (another Ajit Singh design) and local government
under way, but many other tasks in Zanzibar he left abruptly unfinished.
His failure to secure the British Resident position, he had warned Jones,
"might well tempt a reasonable man to consider he had got a life-size griev-
ance—particularly a man who has achievements to his credit and has been
four times decorated." When he was passed over in three consecutive appointments for this post, he gave up. "As [he] had been told that [he] had no
future in [his] own service" (Jones Papers), he retired at the end of 1952.

Whatever the cause, it is apparent that his bitterness lasted quite a
while. When he compiled his memoir and sent it both to his son Charles
and to Elspeth Huxley for deposit at Rhodes House after his death, he
strangely called 1938 (the year he left Northern Rhodesia for a brief post-
ing in Bermuda) his "last year in Africa." Zanzibar, his "other home," the
place where he spent eleven years at the pinnacle of his career and where

he came closest to achieving what he longed for, is hardly even mentioned as a place he visited.

Eric Dutton, like the British colonial system as a whole, failed to grasp fundamental aspects of African cultures and conceptions of the world. He wanted to show Africans that he was "there to help" and to guide them toward "improving themselves in mind and body." He sought "an answer in concrete and bricks," but he had a large wall separating him from comprehension of African views of gender, space, or landscape as though they were truly from the beginning on par with his own in sophistication or legitimacy. He resigned himself to this barrier between him and Africa's people, one where he stood superior in his own mind. In his memoir, Dutton recalled the words about segregation of the governor general of the Belgian Congo, M. Pierre Ryckmans, fresh from an official visit to South Africa, at a dinner in Northern Rhodesia. "These matters were *geographical* in essence [emphasis mine], and all the more racial for that" (1983, 167). Dutton saw this geographical and racial apartness as one not simply built around the segregation of colonial urban space, but one based in fundamentally distinct spatialities and representations of reality that were mutually unintelligible and divisible into superior (white British) and inferior (black African) versions. Eric Dutton's own mind was enframed in a manner he sought to replicate in the enframing of Nairobi, Lusaka, and Zanzibar city. His manner of thinking, though certainly not at all universal among British colonial officers, speaks for the broader sensibilities of the colonial elite verandah in planning African cities. It was a manner of thinking that could "never get the machinery to work properly."

Ajit Singh Hoogan died thirteen years after his mentor, at age seventy-six, after a long and painful illness. He retired to Zanzibar in 1979 after his service in Malawi ended. He was begged by the chief minister of Zanzibar in 1984 to return to work on the development of the city. Reportedly, Ajit's response was something like this: "Look, the people I'd be helping are young. They'd just think I was doing things in a way that took too long, and dismiss me for being old." His grandchildren cared for him in his slow deterioration caused by complications from diabetes, a deterioration they say was brought on by his wife's death a few months before.

Dutton and Singh were both marginal and integral to urban development processes in British and formerly British eastern and southern Africa between the 1920s and 1970s. They were marginal in the sense that neither achieved more than fleeting recognition or status for their achievements.

They were integral in that they spent their careers a heartbeat away from the people who planned to shape the urban spaces for a whole swath of the continent. They were on the colonial elite and colonized middle verandahs of power, respectively—and sometimes literally on verandahs they designed or caused to have built. Yet Dutton was seldom and Ajit was never directly in charge of the cities they spent so much time trying to create.

Both men were integral, in their own ways, to matters of culture and state in British Africa, too. Dutton deliberately ran himself ragged in the inner circles of Britain's African empire. He filled boxes with correspondences with Frederick Lugard, Joseph Oldham, Arthur Creech Jones, Herbert Baker, and Elspeth Huxley, among others. Singh's linkages were, in his world, no less illustrious. He learned to draw from the teachers at Khalsa College in Amritsar and developed deep and long-lasting correspondences with renowned Punjabi artists and Indian intellectuals. Both Thakar Singh and Sohan Singh had a keen eye for architectural painting that clearly fed Ajit's imagination. Ajit's Indian friendships had European and African parallels. Besides Dutton, Singh retained correspondence and close ties with numerous British officers from Zanzibar, particularly those who had played a key role in his training in building design and draftsmanship. Yet Ajit lived the plurality of his years in Africa and sought the company of a broad mix of peoples. He maintained friendships with those who became luminaries and functionaries of the revolutionary Zanzibar government, like Thabit Kombo, Ameir Tajo, Shaaban Mloo, and of course, Abeid Amani Karume, all of whom he could call his neighbors in the polyglot African ward of Kikwajuni Ng'ambo in Zanzibar, where both he and they lived. In Malawi, his friends included the leading early figures of the Malawi Congress Party—not only Hastings Kamuzu Banda, but Aleke Banda, and others. Singh always capitalized on his difference: even as it gave him prominence, it also offered a measure of insulation when used properly. He was proud to be the only non-European architect in the early years of the Banda regime, as he was proud to have played a role in training and mentoring that regime's first African architects and draftsmen.

Ajit Singh cherished the mixture of peoples, religions, and classes in Zanzibar. In contrast to the political leaders on all sides in his time—and ours—he recognized that Zanzibari society had within it a highly cosmopolitan capacity for tolerance of difference. He would no doubt have smiled with satisfaction that Christians, Muslims, Hindus, Sikhs, mainlanders, islanders, and representatives of nearly every Zanzibari community participated in some aspect of his funeral and cremation in 1986. And he would have enjoyed the humor and irony of the Hindu-Sikh crematorium being a few hundred feet from the beachside villas of nearly everyone who ruled Zanzibar during his lifetime. Sadly, as in each of the other cities in this book, the endurance of Zanzibari society's capacity for absorbing and reflecting difference erodes each time leaders attempt to use difference to divide, and loyal functionaries of the state, or indeed of civil society, suffer the consequences of that division.

Perhaps a greater legacy in neighborhood planning than that of the colonial elite or the colonized middle may lie with ordinary people like Bwana Juma, on the metaphorical urban majority verandah. Juma Maalim Kombo outlived both Dutton and Singh, passing away suddenly in November 1993, at eighty-seven, of heart failure. Among his last words to me were these: "When you come back to Zanzibar bring me a good sports coat. A true gentleman needs a jacket to wear over his *kanzu* [gown]." He gave me a gift of his last coins from the Sultanate, some wedding sandals, and an old pair of wooden shoes he'd lined with linoleum to keep them from splintering. In spite of his assertion about gentlemen and jackets, and the pride he had in his old shoes, in the end Juma was puzzled about one particular connection between dress and cultural power. He explained that when he was growing up, "the British told us to dress like gentlemen, to keep our hair cut, wear a sports coat, press our trousers. They made us feel dirty because we had no good clothes. We thought they dressed that way because they had *uwezo* and we didn't. Now, I look at these tourists in short pants and long hair and I think, "We are the ones who dress with respect, who keep ourselves clean." But we still don't have the money. Why is that? What do you think?"

It was not just the colonized middle, but also the urban majority, that learned to "tie the right tie and lift the teacup with the right finger," as Michael Ondaatje's Sikh character put it in *The English Patient* (1992, 283). But folks like Juma wore the "tie" —or in this case the sports coat—differently. Juma wore his jacket over his kanzu, the customary gown of a respected Swahili Muslim. This is a bodily suggestion to me that Juma didn't buy into colonial enframing. Life was not about transcending colonialism to Juma. It had been transcended; the jacket was a proper Swahili thing to wear. In its place came a new order Juma struggled to understand, a little bit socialist, a little bit colonial, yet somewhere underneath, still reliant on power, faith, and custom, the cornerstones of Swahili urban majority society. The city he lived in embodied these cornerstones as much as or more than the oppressive colonialist order or the revolutionary one that replaced it.

Bwana Juma's jacket story relates allegorically to the spatial consciousness of urban majority communities across the cities of Africa. Colonialism has certainly left its imprint, but most cities on the continent, like the four examined in this book, are characterized by majority neighborhoods whose form, function, and character reflect African local conceptions of space or reframings of colonial and neocolonial attempts to enframe them. The people walking through the People's Parks of African cities brush past a hundred crumbling versions of Houses of Wonder. In urban majority communities, "Africans . . . are compelled to interact with definitions of personal and social development engendered by the West. The interaction demonstrates not a lack of capability but of opportunity" (Simone 1994, 104).

During the nineteenth and early twentieth centuries, colonialism galvanized the geographer's art and science of conjuring places that would transform African urban orders without frameworks reliant on these sorts of cornerstones I have spelled out in places much like Ng'ambo, Pumwani, George, or Chinsapo. Geography in this age of imperialism "was not merely engaged in discovering the world, it was making it" (Livingstone 1993, 168). Cities became one of the central places for the making of colonial power through space and geography. In this book I have sought to highlight links—the words, as well as the concrete and bricks—between British colonial conceptions of space in Africa and British colonialism's attempt to forge its particular combination of what Eric Dutton called *goodwill* and *rule*. I've suggested some of the manifestations of the colonial legacy in two very different postcolonial cities, too. In particular, I examined the ways in which both revolutionary Zanzibar and reactionary Malawi replicated and transformed the enframing tactics of colonial states in attempting to perform tasks that are not very much altered from the colonial era. The more immediate experiences of colonial urban space and its aftermath also have been tracked here, on three different verandahs of the power structure: those who created the enframing tactics at the top, those who worked in the middle echelons, and those on whom the urban projects were enacted. Three people have been the primary vehicles for this attempt to personalize the narrative, but others have entered in, particularly on the bottom verandah. The primary lesson that emerges is that, despite all of the varied efforts of power structures draped in different ideological banners, urban majority African conceptions of space not only endure. Within circumscribed arenas and often within repressive parameters of their own, they remain powerful forces in the production of African urbanism.

Glossary

Bibliography

Index

Glossary

The following words are Kiswahili words unless otherwise noted.

balozi (pl. **mabalozi**): ambassador; under the single-party political system of Tanzania from 1967–92, this term referred to the ten-house cell leader in ruling party neighborhood branches

baraza: verandah for receiving visitors just outside a residence; also a public meeting; members of a cabinet

basi: enough, very well; an expression of contentment or resignation

bibi (short form, **bi**): lady, madam, miss, grandmother; a term of respect used to refer to women

Chama cha Mapinduzi: Revolutionary Party, the ruling party of the United Republic of Tanzania since 1977

choo: toilet

dambo (Chichewa/Chinyanja word): a grassy, seasonally flooded depression

desturi: custom

duka: shop

hodi: a polite inquiry before entering a room meaning roughly "Anyone home?"

imani: religious faith

kanzu: a long-sleeved gown

karibu: welcome; come near

kibanda: a small hut

kibla (Arabic word): north; the prayer niche at the north end of a mosque; the direction of Mecca from the Swahili coast

kwacha (Chichewa/Chinyanja word): the currency of Malawi and Zambia

machila (alternately, **machela**): a sling, hammock, or chair for carrying people

masihara mengi: many jests

maskani: dwelling-place, home away from home

Mji Mpya: New Town or New City, the name of both a colonial era model neighborhood and a revolutionary era model housing scheme in Zanzibar

mtaa (pl. **mitaa**): ward or neighborhood

mteja (pl. **wateja**): customer; slang for junkie

mtomo: daub; the style of daub construction common on the Swahili coast

mzee: a term of respect for an elder

mzimu (pl. **mizimu**): a haunted place of spirits; the spirit itself

mzungu: a white person; a stranger

Ng'ambo: literally, "other side"; section of Zanzibar city

Ng'ambo wa Pili: literally, "second other side"; newer outskirts of Zanzibar city

ovyo: useless articles, rubbish, what is common and valueless; recklessly, haphazardly, randomly

Raha Leo: Happiness Today, a neighborhood in Zanzibar City

shamba: plantation, estate, farm, cultivated plot

ua: courtyard, backyard enclosure

uani: in the courtyard

udongo: mud, soil, earth

ujirani: neighborliness

Unguja: Zanzibar island

uwezo: power, strength, or capacity

wenye uwezo: those having power

Bibliography

Archival Sources

Zanzibar National Archives (ZNA)

AB 9/9: Community Development in Zanzibar, 1951–58.

AB 9/47–49: Civic Centre at Ng'ambo, 1943–54.

AB 39/21–22: Housing Shortages and Town Improvement Schemes, 1930–55.

AB 39/24: Major Dutton's Semi-Official Correspondence with the Colonial Office on Town Planning, 1943–50.

AB 39/26: Town Building Rules, 1929–55.

AB 39/36: Numbering of Huts in Native Locations, 1940.

AB 39/37: Central Development Authority, 1947.

AB 40/13A: Acquisition of Property in Ng'ambo, 1940–54.

AB 40/139: The Reconstruction of Mwembetanga.

AB 76/72: Central Development Authority.

AE 5/3 and 5/7: Town Planning Board Minutes and Schemes, 1932–63.

AE 8/10: Land at Mlandege Claimed by Gulamhussein Remtulla Hemani.

AE 8/11: Claim of Land at Ngamboo by Mohammedhussein Tharia Topan, 1926–28.

AE 8/19: Claim of Land at Kisimamajongo by Mr. MH Tharia Topan, 1959–62.

AK 19/17: Senior Commissioner's Office: The Towns Decree (Native Locations Rules), Definition of a Native Hut, 1948–59.

AK 20/1: Unrest in Zanzibar Town, 1948–62.

AK 26/18: Jang'ombe ASP Branch, 1966–77.

AK 26/21: Kikwajuni ASP Branch, 1966–72.

AS 1/77: Ng'ambo Town Improvement, 1947–55.

AW 2/26: Survey of India, Gerald Portal's Plan of Zanzibar.

AW 2/100: The Ngambo Area Folder.

AW 2/113: 1928 Adamson PWD Map of the City.

BA 74/1: Zanzibar Mpya [New Zanzibar].

BA 68/1–15: Speeches of Abeid Amani Karume, 1964–72.

DA 1/163: Town and Country Planning, Housing, General, 1958–63.

DA 1/261: Town Planning Legislation, 1954–64.

DA 1/266: Development Charges, 1958–63.

DA 1/277: Nationalization of Land, 1970–78.

DA 2/3: Confiscated Property, 1967–68.

DA 2/5: GDR Housing Scheme, 1964–68.

DX 6/2: The 1978 Census.

DX 23/4: Records of the Ministry of State on Housing, 1969–84.

HD 3/5: Wakf of Seyyid Suleiman bin Hamed bin Said at Kiunga Ng'ambo, 1915–24.

HD 6/155: Wakf of Seyyid Hamoud bin Ahmed.

Zanzibar Town Planning Office, Zanzibar, Tanzania (ZTPL)

Town Planning Office TP 84: Zanzibar Building Authority, 1957–65.

Town Planning Office TPO/U-88/1: Town Planning and Building Authority, 1969–75.

Town Planning Office TPO/U-154: Housing Policy, 1987.

Town Planning Office TPO/U-159: Project Papers, 1987.

Town Planning Office Social Survey of NU 2 Kikwajuni. Unpublished Report, Town Planning Office, Zanzibar, Tanzania, 1987.

Town Planning Office, Building Applications in New Areas, 1978–88.

Town Planning Office, Town Planning and Development Control, 1977–84.

Town Planning Office, New Zanzibar, 1968.

Rhodes House Library, Oxford University, Oxford, UK (RHL)

Mss Afr s 956: Papers of Vera M. Davies. 1947, 1948, and 1956.

Mss Afr s 1446: R.H.V. Biles. Interview by J. J. Tawney. December 11, 1971.

Mss Afr s 2116: Papers of P. A. P. Robertson.

Mss Brit Emp s 375: Julian Asquith. Interview by I. L. Phillips. Undated.

Mss Brit Emp s 529: The Colonial Service: The Experience of Governors' Wives: Box 2, File 2: Lady Patricia Maddocks, formerly Lady Mooring.

Public Record Office, Kew, Richmond, UK (PRO)

CO 618/83/1–2: Housing and Town Improvement in the Native Town, Zanzibar, 1944–46.

CO/799/13: New Capital at Lusaka; 1934.
CO/795/74/45012: New Capital at Lusaka, 1935.
CO/795/79/45012: Loan G—New Capital at Lusaka, 1936.

National Archives of Zambia, Lusaka (NAZ)

Sec B1/4: Loan Works: Lusaka, New Capital.
Sec B1/5: Chief Secretary, 1930–34, Private and Semi-Official.
Sec B1/474: New Secondary School at Lusaka, 1930–37.

Books and Articles

Aboagye, A. 1986. *Informal Sector in Lilongwe: A Survey of Informal Activities in Garages, Metal Fabricating, Tinsmithing and Woodworking.* Addis Ababa: Jobs and Skills Program for Africa.
Abu Lughod, J. 1967. "Development in North African Urbanism: the Process of Decolonization." In *Urbanization and Counter Urbanization*, edited by B. Berry. London: Urban Affairs Annual Review Volume 2.
Afro-Shirazi Party. 1974. *Maendeleo ya Mapinduzi ya Afro-Shirazi Party, 1964–1974* (The development of the revolution of the Afro-Shirazi Party, 1964–1974). Zanzibar: Afro-Shirazi Party.
Alawi, A. A. 1966. *The Town Planning Office Ng'ambo Housing Survey.* Zanzibar: Town Planning Office.
———. 1986. "Waraka wa Semina juu ya Uendelezaji na Udhibiti wa Master Plan ya Mji wa Zanzibar" (Record of a seminar on the development and control of the master plan for Zanzibar City). Manuscript. Zanzibar: Design Associates.
Alawi, A. A., and S. A. Yahya. 1965. "Some Aspects of Land Use in Zanzibar Town." Manuscript. Zanzibar Town Planning Office.
Alexander, L. 1983. "European Planning Ideology in Tanzania." *Habitat International* 7(1/2):17–36.
Al Falaq. 1946. "Post-War Development." December 7, p. 1.
Ali, A. T. 1992. Interview with author and Ali Hasan Ali. Zanzibar, April 14.
Allen, J. de V. 1979. "The Swahili House: Cultural and Ritual Concepts Underlying Its Plan and Structure." *Art and Archeology Research Papers*, Special Issue: 1–32.
———. 1993. *Swahili Origins.* London: James Currey.
Amin, S. 1972. "Underdevelopment and Dependence in Black Africa—Origins and Contemporary Forms." *Journal of Modern African Studies* 10:503–24.
Anderson, J. 1953. *Islamic Law in Africa.* London: HMSO.

Andriananjanirana-Ruphin, S. 1995. "Zanzibar Town Planning Problems 1890–1939." In *History and Conservation of Zanzibar Stone Town,* edited by A. Sheriff. Athens, Ohio: Ohio Univ. Press.

Armstrong, A. 1987. "Master Plans for Dar es Salaam, Tanzania." *Habitat International* 11(2):133–46.

Arnold, D. 1994. "Public Health and Public Power: Medicine and Hegemony in Colonial India." In *Contesting Colonial Hegemony: State and Society in Africa and India,* edited by D. Engels and S. Marks. London: British Academic Press.

Atkins, K. 1993. *The Moon Is Dead! Give Us Our Money!* Portsmouth, N.H.: Heinemann.

Awadh, G. 1989. "Improving Effectiveness of Urban Management: Zanzibar." Unpublished research paper, Institute for Housing Studies, Rotterdam.

Bachmann, J. 1991. "Reading the Urban Text: The Legibility of Modern Values in the Squatter Settlements of Lusaka, Zambia." Master's thesis, Univ. of California, Berkeley.

Baker, H. 1944. *Architecture and Personalities.* London: Country Life.

Bale, J., and J. Sang. 1996. *Kenyan Running: Movement, Culture, Geography and Global Change.* London: Frank Cass.

Banyikwa, W. 1989. "Effects of Insensitivity in Planning Land for Urban Development in Tanzania: The Case Of Dar es Salaam." *Journal of Eastern African Research and Development* 19:83–94.

Barnow, F., N. Hansen, M. Johnsen, A. Poulsen, V. Ronnow, and K. Solvsten. 1983. *Urban Development in Kenya: The Growth of Nairobi 1900–1970.* Copenhagen: Aurora.

Barrier, N., and V. Dusenbery. 1992. *The Sikh Diaspora: Migration and Experience Beyond Punjab.* Columbia, Mo.: South Asia Books.

Bassett, T. 1994. "Cartography and Empire Building in Nineteenth-Century West Africa." *Geographical Review* 84:316–36.

Bater, J. 1984. "The Soviet City: Continuity and Change in Privilege and Place." In *The City in Cultural Context,* edited by J. Agnew, J. Mercer, and D. Sopher. Boston: Allen and Unwin.

Bates, R. 1974. *Patterns of Uneven Development: Causes and Consequences in Zambia.* Denver: Univ. of Denver Graduate School of International Studies Monograph Series in World Affairs.

Baumann, O. 1897. *Die Insel Zanzibar—Archipel.* Leipsig: Verlag von Duncker und Humblot.

Belloc, H. 1929. Introduction to *Kenya Mountain,* by Eric Dutton. London: Jonathan Cape.

Berman, B. 1984. "Structure and Process in the Bureaucratic States of Colonial Africa." *Development and Change* 15:23–41.

———. 1990. *Control and Crisis in Colonial Kenya: The Dialectic of Domination.* Athens, Ohio: Ohio Univ. Press.

Bhachu, P. 1985. *Twice Migrants: East African Sikh Settlers in Britain.* London: Tavistock.

Blunt, A. 1994. *Travel, Gender, and Imperialism: Mary Kingsley and West Africa.* New York: Guilford Press.

Bowles, B. 1991. "The Struggle for Independence, 1946–1963." In *Zanzibar under Colonial Rule,* edited by A. Sheriff and E. Ferguson. Athens, Ohio: Ohio Univ. Press.

Bozzoli, B. 1991. *Women of Phokeng.* Portsmouth, N.H.: Heinemann.

Bradley, K. 1935. *Lusaka: The New Capital of Northern Rhodesia.* London: Jonathan Cape.

Brunn, S., and J. Williams. 1993. *Cities of the World.* New York: Harper Collins.

Busaidy, S. 1957. Memo to chief secretary, May 22. File AK 19/17, Zanzibar National Archives.

———. 1960. Memo to town planning officer, October 7. File TP 84, Zanzibar Town Planning Office.

———. 1961. Memo to town planning officer, December 22. File TP 84, Zanzibar Town Planning Office.

———. 1962. Memo to provincial commissioner, October 31. File DA 1/261, Zanzibar National Archives.

Capital City Development Corporation (CCDC). 1972. *Lilongwe: New Capital City.* Lilongwe: CCDC.

Carruthers, S. 1995. *Winning Hearts and Minds: British Governments, the Media and Colonial Counter-Insurgency, 1944–1960.* London: Leicester Univ. Press.

Carter, P. 1988. *The Road to Botany Bay.* New York: Knopf.

Celik, Z. 1997. *Urban Forms and Colonial Confrontations: Algiers under French Rule.* Berkeley and Los Angeles: Univ. of California Press.

Chipasula, F. 1984. *O Earth Wait for Me.* Johannesburg: Ravan Press.

Chipeta, M. 1992. "Political Process, Civil Society, and the State." In *Malawi at the Crossroads: The Post-Colonial Political Economy,* edited by G. Mhone. Harare: Sapes Books.

Christie, J. 1876. *Cholera Epidemics in Eastern Africa.* London: MacMillan.

Christopher, A. 1983. *Colonial Africa.* London: Croom Helm.

———. 1988. *The British Empire at Its Zenith.* London: Croom Helm.

———. 1994. "Urbanization and National Capitals in Africa." In *Urbanization in Africa: A Handbook,* edited by J. Tarver. Westport, Conn.: Greenwood Press.

Clark, D. 1978–79. "Unregulated Housing, Vested Interest, and the Development of Community Identity in Nairobi." *African Urban Studies* 3:33–46.

Collins, J. 1977. "Lusaka: Urban Planning in a British Colony." In *Shaping an Urban World,* edited by G. Cherry. New York: St. Martins Press.

Comaroff, J. 1997. "Images of Empire, Contests of Conscience: Models of Colonial Domination in South Africa." In *Tensions of Empire,* edited by F. Cooper and A. Stoler. Berkeley and Los Angeles: Univ. of California Press.

———, J., and J. Comaroff. 1991. *Of Revelation and Revolution: Christianity, Colonialism, and Consciousness in Southern Africa.* Chicago: Univ. of Chicago Press.

Comment. 1993. *Malawi: A Moment of Truth.* London: Catholic Institute for International Relations.

Connell, J. 1972. "Lilongwe: Another New Capital for Africa." *East African Geographical Review* 10:90.

Constantin, F. 1987. Condition Swahili et Identité Politique. *Africa* 57(2):219–33.

Cooper, F. 1983. *Struggle for the City: Migrant Labor, Capital, and the State in Urban Africa.* Beverly Hills: Sage.

———. 1987. *On the African Waterfront: Urban Disorder and the Transformation of Work in Colonial Mombasa.* New Haven: Yale Univ. Press.

Cooper, F., and A. Stoler. 1997. *Tensions of Empire: Colonial Cultures in a Bourgeois World.* Berkeley and Los Angeles: Univ. of California Press.

Coryndon, R. T. Papers of Sir Robert Thorne Coryndon. Boxes 1, 3, and 12, collected by E. Dutton. Rhodes House Library, Oxford.

Cosgrove, D. 1989. "Geography Is Everywhere: Culture and Symbolism in Human Landscapes." In *Horizons in Human Geography,* edited by D. Gregory and R. Walford. Basingstoke: Macmillan Education.

Coulson, A. 1982. *Tanzania: A Political Economy.* Oxford: Clarendon Press.

Coupland, R. 1938. *East Africa and Its Invaders.* Oxford: Clarendon Press.

Crofton, R. 1953. *Zanzibar Affairs, 1914–1933.* London: Francis Edwards.

Crush, J. 1995. *Power of Development.* London: Routledge.

———. 1996. "The Culture of Failure: Racism, Violence and White Farming in Colonial Swaziland." *Journal of Historical Geography* 22:177–97.

Dawaharo, H. A. 1991. Interview with author. Zanzibar, December 19.

Dawson, G. 1994. *Soldier Heroes: British Adventure, Empire and the Imagining of Masculinities.* London: Routledge.

de Bruijne, G. 1985. "The Colonial City and the Post Colonial World." In *Colonial Cities: Essays on Urbanism in a Colonial Context,* edited by R. Ross and R. Telkemp. Dordrecht: Martinus Nijhoff.

de Saissy, E. 1979. "The Role of the Ethnic Factor in the Politics of Pre-Revolutionary Zanzibar." Unpublished paper, Department of Development Studies, Uppsala Univ., Uppsala, Sweden.

de Sechi, L. 1961. Letter to chief secretary, November 15. File DA 1/163, Zanzibar National Archives.

Documents Commission. 1992. *Muhtasari wa Ripoti ya Tume ya Kuchunguza Taratibu na*

Mfumo wa Utoaji wa Nyaraka za Serikali (Summary of the report of the commission investigating the order and system of handling government documents) [translation mine]. Zanzibar: Revolutionary Government of Zanzibar.

Doherty, J. 1977. "Urban Places and Third World Development: The Case of Tanzania." *Antipode* 9 (3):32–42.

Donley-Reid, L. 1982. "House Power: Swahili Space and Symbolic Markers." In *Symbolic and Structural Archeology*, edited by I. Hodder. Cambridge: Cambridge Univ. Press.

Duncan, J. 1990. *The City as Text*. Cambridge: Cambridge Univ. Press.

Dundas, C. 1955. *African Crossroads*. London: Macmillan.

Dutton, E. 1925. *The Basuto of Basutoland*. London: Jonathan Cape.

———. 1929. *Kenya Mountain*. London: Jonathan Cape.

———. 1935. *The Planting of Trees and Shrubs*. Lusaka: Government Printers.

———. 1944a. *Lillibullero, or The Golden Road*. Zanzibar: Privately Published.

———. 1944b. Major Dutton's semi-official correspondence with the Colonial Office, June 10. File AB 39/24, Zanzibar National Archives.

———. 1944c. Major Dutton's semi-official correspondence with the Colonial Office, March 31. File AB 39/24, Zanzibar National Archives.

———. 1949. Introduction to *The Useful and Ornamental Plants of Zanzibar and Pemba*, by R. O. Williams. 5–32. Zanzibar: Government of Zanzibar.

———. 1983. "The Night of the Hyena." Memoirs of Eric Aldhelm Torlogh Dutton, on microfilm. Rhodes House Library, Oxford.

Engels, D. 1994. "Modes of Knowledge, Modes of Power: Universities in 19th-Century India." In *Contesting Colonial Hegemony: State and Society in Africa and India*, edited by D. Engels and S. Marks. London: British Academic Press.

Engels, D., and S. Marks. 1994. *Contesting Colonial Hegemony: State and Society in Africa and India*. London: British Academic Press.

Englund, H. 2002. "The Village in the City, the City in the Village: Migrants in Lilongwe." *Journal of Southern African Studies* 28 (1):137–54.

Fabian, J. 1986. *Language and Colonial Power*. Cambridge: Cambridge Univ. Press.

Fair, L. 2001. *Pastimes and Politics: Culture, Community, and Identity in Post-Abolition Urban Zanzibar, 1890–1945*. Athens, Ohio: Ohio University Press.

Fanon, F. 1979. *The Wretched of the Earth*. Harmondsworth: Penguin.

Fereji, S. F. 1992. Interview with author and Ali Hasan Ali. Zanzibar, March 1.

Forster, P. 1994. "Culture, Nationalism, and the Invention of Tradition in Malawi." *Journal of Modern African Studies* 32 (3):477–97.

French, R., and F. Hamilton. 1979. "Is There a Socialist City?" In *The Socialist City*, edited by R. French and F. Hamilton. New York: John Wiley.

Freund, B. 1995. *Insiders and Outsiders: The Indian Working Class of Durban, 1910–1990*. Portsmouth, N.H.: Heinemann.

Furedi, F. 1977. "The African Crowd in Nairobi: Popular Movements and Elite

Politics." In *Third World Urbanization*, edited by J. Abu-Lughod and R. Hay. Chicago: Maaroufa Press.

Gann, L. 1964. *A History of Northern Rhodesia, Early Days to 1953*. London: Chatto and Windus.

Gautama, D. 1997. Interview with author and P. Singh. Lilongwe, Malawi, July 17.

Ghai, D., and Y. Ghai. 1970. *Portrait of a Minority*. Nairobi: Oxford Univ. Press.

Glenday, V. 1947. Memorandum from British Resident to Chief Secretary, Mar. 19. File AB 39/215, Zanzibar National Archives.

Godfrey, W. 1997. Personal interview with author and P. Singh. Zomba, Malawi, July 9.

Godlewska, A., and N. Smith. 1994. *Geography and Empire*. Oxford: Blackwell.

Gramsci, A. 1971. *Selections from the Prison Notebooks*. New York: International Publishers.

Gregory, D. 1994. *Geographical Imaginations*. Oxford: Blackwell.

Gregory, R. 1971. *India and East Africa*. Oxford: Clarendon.

———. 1992. *The Rise and Fall of Philanthropy in East Africa: The Asian Contribution*. Boulder: Westview.

———. 1993. *South Asians in East Africa*. Boulder: Westview.

Gugler, J. 1970. "Urbanization in East Africa." In *Urban Challenge in East Africa*, edited by J. Hutton. Nairobi: East African Publishing House.

Guillain, M. 1856. *Carte et Album d'un Voyage a la Cote d'Afrique en 1846, 1847 et 1848*. Paris: Société de Géographie.

Hakim, B. 1986. *Arabic-Islamic Cities: Building and Planning Principles*. London: KPI.

Hamdan, G. 1964. "Capitals of the New Africa." *Economic Geography* 40:239–53.

Hamilton, W. 1961. Letter to Chief Secretary, Aug. 4, 1961. File DA 1/163, Zanzibar National Archives.

Hansen, K. 1997. *Keeping House in Lusaka*. New York: Columbia Univ. Press.

Havinden, M., and D. Meredith. 1993. *Colonialism and Development: Britain and Its Tropical Colonies, 1850–1960*. London: Routledge.

Hawthorne, N. 1965. *The House of the Seven Gables*. Columbus: Ohio State Univ. Press.

Heisler, H. 1974. *Urbanization and the Government of Migration: The Inter-relation of Urban and Rural Life in Zambia*. London: C. Hurst and Co.

Helweg, A. 1986. *Sikhs in England*. Delhi: Oxford Univ. Press.

Hetherington, P. 1978. *British Paternalism in Africa, 1920–1940*. London: Frank Cass.

Hill, F. 1975. "Ujamaa: African Socialist Productionism in Tanzania." In *Socialism in the Third World*, edited by H. Desfosses and J. Levesque. New York: Praeger.

Himbara, D. 1994. *Kenyan Capitalists, the State and Development*. Boulder: Lynne Rienner.

Hino, S. 1971. "Neighborhood Groups in African Urban Society: Social Relations and Consciousness of Swahili People of Ujiji, a Small Town of Tanzania, East Africa. *Kyoto University African Studies* 6:9–23.

Hofmeyr, I. 1994. *We Spend Our Years as a Tale That Is Told*. Portsmouth, N.H.: Heinemann.

Holdsworth, D. 1993. "Revaluing the House." In *Place/Culture/Representation*, edited by J. Duncan and D. Ley. London: Routledge.

Home, R. 1990. "Town Planning and Garden Cities in the British Colonial Empire, 1910–1940." *Planning Perspectives* 5:23–37.

———. 1997. *Of Planting and Planning: The Making of British Colonial Cities*. London: Spon.

Hopkins, A. 1987. "Big Business in African Studies." *Journal of African History* 28:136–38.

Horton, M. 1984. "The Early Settlement of the Northern Swahili Coast." Ph.D. diss., Cambridge Univ.

Horvath, R. 1969. "In Search of a Theory of Urbanization: Notes on the Colonial City." *East Lakes Geographer* 5:69–82.

Hoyle, B. 1979. "African Socialism and Urban Development: The Relocation of the Tanzanian Capital." *Tijdschrift voor Economische en Sociale Geographie* 70:207–16.

Hutton, J. 1970. *Urban Challenge in East Africa*. Nairobi: East African Publishing House.

Huxley, E. 1983. Introduction to "The Night of the Hyena," memoirs of Eric Dutton, on microfilm. Rhodes House Library, Oxford.

Hyam, R. 1976. *Britain's Imperial Century, 1815–1914: A Study of Empire and Expansion*. London: Batsford.

Iliffe, J. 1987. *The African Poor*. Cambridge: Cambridge Univ. Press.

Issa, J. 1992. Interview with author and Ali Hasan Ali. Zanzibar, February 23.

Jarosz, L. 1992. "Constructing the Dark Continent: Metaphor as Geographic Representation of Africa." *Geografiska Annaler* 74B (2):105–15.

Jellicoe, G. 1950. "A Plan for Lusaka, Capital of Northern Rhodesia." Unpublished document in file entitled Zambia: Pamphlets on Geography. Rhodes House Library, Oxford.

Johnson, N. 1992. "Nation-Building, Language and Education: The Geography of Teacher Recruitment in Ireland, 1925–45." *Political Geography* 11:170–89.

Jones, A. C. 1946. "Some Current Colonial Problems." An address by Arthur Creech Jones to the Empire Parliamentary Association, May 23. Rhodes House Library Oxford.

———. Papers of Arthur Creech Jones. Box 7: Correspondence with Eric Dutton. Rhodes House Library, Oxford.

Jules-Rosette, B. 1981. *Symbols of Change: Urban Transition in a Zambian Community*. Norwood, N.J.: Ablex Publishing.

Kalipeni, E. 1992. "Population Redistribution in Malawi since 1964." *Geographical Review* 84 (1):13–28.

Kaluwa, B. 1982. "Performance of New Capitals as Regional Economic Measures: A Case Study of Lilongwe in Malawi." *Malawi Journal of Social Science* 9:67–86.

———. 1994. "The Delivery of Urban Services in Malawi: The Case of Housing." In *Planning Urban Economies in Southern and Eastern Africa*, edited by K. Wekwete and C. Rambanapasi. Brookfield, Vt.: Avebury.

Kamau, L. 1978–79. "Semipublic, Private and Hidden Rooms: Symbolic Aspects of Domestic Space in Urban Kenya." *African Urban Studies* 3:105–16.

Kamoche, J. 1981. *Imperial Trusteeship and Political Evolution in Kenya, 1923–1963.* Washington, D.C.: Univ. Press of America.

Kansky, K. 1976. *Urbanization under Socialism.* New York: Praeger.

Kapyongo, A. M. 1992. Interview with author and Ali Hasan Ali. Zanzibar, January 14.

Kaspin, D. 1995. "The Politics of Ethnicity in Malawi's Democratic Transition." *Journal of Modern African Studies* 33 (4):595–620.

Kaunda, J. 1992. "The Administrative Organization and Processes of National Development Planning in Malawi." In *Malawi at the Crossroads: The Post-Colonial Political Economy*, edited by G. Mhone. Harare: Sapes Books.

Kaunda, K. 1962. *Zambia Shall Be Free.* London: Heinemann.

Kayongo-Male, D. 1980. "Community Development in Urban Squatter Areas in Kenya." *African Urban Studies* 8:21–36.

———. 1988. "Slum and Squatter Settlement in Kenya: Housing Problems and Planning Possibilities." In *Slum and Squatter Settlements in Sub-Saharan Africa*, edited by R. Obudho and C. Mhlanga. New York: Praeger.

Kendall, H. 1958. *The Zanzibar Town Planning Scheme.* Zanzibar: Government of Zanzibar.

Kequan, Q. 1982. *The 1982 Zanzibar Town Master Plan.* Zanzibar: Revolutionary Government of Zanzibar.

King, A. 1976. *Colonial Urban Development.* London: Routledge.

Kingoriah, G. 1983. "The Causes of Nairobi's City Structure." *Ekistics* 301:246–54.

Kironde, J.L. 1992. "Received Concepts and Theories in African Urbanization and Management Strategies: The Struggle Continues." *Urban Studies* 29(8):1277–92.

Kiwanuka, M. 1974. "Uganda under the British." In *Zamani: A Survey of East African History*, edited by B. A. Ogot. Nairobi: East African Publishing House/ Longmans.

Kobiah, S. 1984–85. "Urban Development in Kenya." *African Urban Studies* 19–20:9–22.

Kombo, J. M. 1992. Interview by author. Zanzibar, July 7.

Kombo, J. M., and M. A. Jobo. 1992. Personal communication with author. Zanzibar, July 11.

Ladies Committee. 1949. Letter of Ladies Committee of Mwembetanga to Chief Secretary, May 17, 1949. File AB 40/47, Zanzibar National Archives.

Lanchester, H. 1923. *Zanzibar: A Study in Tropical Town Planning*. Cheltonham: Burrow.

Landau, P. 1995. *The Realm of the Word: Language, Gender, and Christianity in a Southern African Kingdom*. Portsmouth, N.H.: Heinemann.

Leach, M., and R. Mearns. 1996. *The Lie of the Land: Challenging Received Wisdom on the African Environment*. Portsmouth, N.H.: Heinemann.

Lilongwe City Council. 1991. *Traditional Housing Area: Socio-Economic Survey*. Lilongwe: Lilongwe City Council Town Planning Section.

Livingstone, D. 1993. *The Geographical Tradition*. Oxford: Blackwell.

Lofchie, M. 1965. *Zanzibar: Background to Revolution*. Princeton: Princeton Univ. Press.

Lugard, F. Papers of Sir Frederick Lugard. Boxes 9 and 10: Correspondence with Eric Dutton. Rhodes House Library, Oxford.

———. 1922. *The Dual Mandate in British Tropical Africa*. London: Blackwood.

Mabogunje, A. 1990. "Urban Planning and the Post-Colonial State in Africa: A Research Overview." *African Studies Review* 33 (2):121–203.

Mackenzie, A. F. 1998. *Land, Ecology and Resistance in Kenya, 1880–1952*. Portsmouth, N.H.: Heinemann.

Makontena Kuondolewa (Containers to be removed). 1992. *Nuru* (The Zanzibar light), June 5, p. 1.

Mamdani, M. 1996. *Citizen and Subject: Contemporary Africa and the Legacy of Late Colonialism*. Princeton: Princeton Univ. Press.

Mandrad, A. T. 1992. Interview with author and Ali Hasan Ali. May 16.

Mangat, J. 1969. *History of the Asians in East Africa, 1886–1945*. Oxford: Clarendon.

Maole, A. 1997. Personal interview with author and P. Singh. Zomba, Malawi, July 10.

Mapanje, J. 1997. "Leaving No Traces of Censure." *Index on Censorship* 26 (5):70.

Mapuri, O. 1996. *Zanzibar, The 1964 Revolution: Achievements and Prospects*. Dar es Salaam: Tema Publishers.

Marks, S. 1987. *Not Either an Experimental Doll*. Bloomington: Indiana Univ. Press.

Maylam, P., and I. Edwards. 1996. *The People's City: African Life in Twentieth Century Durban*. Pietermaritzburg: Univ. of Natal Press.

McClintock, A. 1995. *Imperial Leather: Race, Gender and Sexuality in the Colonial Contest*. New York: Routledge.

McCracken, J. 1989. " 'Marginal Men': The Colonial Experience in Malawi." *Journal of Southern African Studies* 15:537–64.

―――. 1998. "Blantyre Transformed: Class Conflict and Nationalism in Urban Malawi." *Journal of African History* 39:247–69.

McGee, T. 1971. *The Urbanization Process in the Third World*. London: C. Bell.

McGill, R. 1994. "Integrated Urban Management: An Operational Model for Third World City Managers." *Cities* 11(1):35–47.

McQuillan, A., and R. Lanier. 1984. "Urban Upgrading and Historic Preservation: An Integrated Development Plan for Zanzibar's Old Stone Town." *Habitat International* 8(2):43–59.

McVicar, K. 1968. "Twilight of an African Slum: Pumwani and the Evolution of African Settlement in Nairobi." Ph.D. diss., Univ. of California, Los Angeles.

Meffert, E. A. 1991. Personal interview by author. Zanzibar, November 29.

Mendes, C. 1997. Interview with author and P. Singh. Njuli, Malawi, July 13.

Metcalf, T. 1989. *An Imperial Vision: Indian Architecture and Britain's Raj*. Berkeley and Los Angeles: Univ. of California Press.

Mhone, G. 1992. "The Political Economy of Malawi: An Overview." In *Malawi at the Crossroads: The Post-Colonial Political Economy*, edited by G. Mhone. Harare: Sapes Books.

Mill, J. 1965. *Essential Works of John Stuart Mill*. New York: Bantam.

Mitchell, T. 1988. *Colonizing Egypt*. Cambridge: Cambridge Univ. Press.

Mjojo, B. 1989. Urban Development: The Case of Lilongwe 1920–1964. Paper no. 12 presented at the Chancellor College History Department Seminar Series, University of Malawi, Zomba.

Mlia, J. 1975. "Malawi's New Capital City: A Regional Planning Perspective." *Pan-African Journal* 8:387–401.

Mohammed, S. H. 1992. Interview with author and Ali Hasan Ali. March 4.

Moodie, D. 1994. *Going for Gold*. Berkeley and Los Angeles: Univ. of California Press.

Moore, H., and M. Vaughan. 1994. *Cutting Down Trees: Gender, Nutrition, and Agricultural Change in the Northern Province of Zambia, 1890–1990*. Portsmouth, N.H.: Heinemann.

Morgan, W. 1967. *Nairobi: City and Region*. Nairobi: Oxford Univ. Press.

Mueller, C. 1980. *Retarded Capitalism in Tanzania*. London: Merlin Press.

Myers, G. 1994. "From 'Stinkibar' to 'The Island Metropolis': The Geography of British Hegemony in Zanzibar." In *Geography and Empire*, edited by A. Godlewska and N. Smith. Oxford: Blackwell.

―――. 1995. "The Early History of the Other Side of Zanzibar Town." In *History and Conservation of Zanzibar Stone Town*, edited by A. Sheriff. Athens, Ohio: Ohio Univ. Press.

Nast, H. 1994. "The Impact of British Imperialism on the Landscape of Female Slavery in the Kano Palace, Northern Nigeria." *Africa* 64:34–73.

———. 1996. "Islam, Gender, and Slavery in West Africa Circa 1500: A Spatial Archeology of the Kano Palace, Northern Nigeria." *Annals of the Association of American Geographers* 86:44–77.

Neumann, R. 1998. *Imposing Wilderness: Struggles over Livelihood and Nature Preservation in Africa.* Berkeley and Los Angeles: Univ. of California Press.

Nilsson, S. A., M. Glaumann, P. Krabbe, K. Sundstrom, and P. Wisth. 1969. *Tanzania: Zanzibar's Present Conditions and Future Plans: House Building and Planning in Developing Countries.* Research pamphlet, University of Lund Department of Architecture, Lund, Sweden.

Noyes, J. 1992. *Colonial Space: Spatiality in the Discourse of German Southwest Africa, 1884–1915.* Reading: Harwood Academic Publishers.

Obudho, Robert. 1981. *Urbanization and Development Planning in Kenya: A Bottom-Up Approach.* Nairobi: Kenya Literature Bureau.

———. 1994. "Kenya." In *Urbanization in Africa: A Handbook,* edited by J. Tarver. Westport, Conn.: Greenwood Press.

———. 1997. "Nairobi: National Capital and Regional Hub." In *The Urban Challenge in Africa,* edited by C. Rakodi. Tokyo: United Nations Univ. Press.

O'Connor, A. 1983. *The African City.* London: Hutchinson Univ. Library.

Okello, J. 1967. *Revolution in Zanzibar.* Nairobi: East African Publishing House.

Oldham, J. H. Papers of Joseph H. Oldham. Boxes 5, 6, and 7: Correspondence with Eric Dutton. Rhodes House Library, Oxford.

———. 1924. *Christianity and the Race Problem.* London: Student Christian Movement.

Oldham, J., and B. Gibson. 1931. *The Remaking of Man in Africa.* London: Oxford Univ. Press.

Ole-Mungaya, M. 1990. "A Study on the Development of Traditional Settlements in Urban Areas: Zanzibar Case Study." Unpublished diploma project, Ardhi Institute, Dar es Salaam.

Omari, H. 1985. "Zanzibar Administrative History: 1840 to the Post-Revolution Period." Master's thesis, Univ. College, London.

Ondaatje, M. 1992. *The English Patient.* New York: Vintage Books.

Pachai, B. 1971. "The Story of Malawi's Capitals: Old and New, 1891–1969." *Society of Malawi Journal* 24:1–72.

Pakenham, R. 1949. Memorandum from the senior commissioner to chief secretary, Feb. 5. File AK 20/1, Zanzibar National Archives.

Parkinson, C. 1947. *The Colonial Office from Within.* London: HMSO.

Patel, N. 1996. "The Hindus in Malawi." *Religion in Malawi* 6:39–40.

Pearce, F. 1920. *Zanzibar: The Island Metropolis of Eastern Africa.* London: MacMillan.

Pearce, R. 1982. *The Turning Point in Africa: British Colonial Policy, 1938–1948.* London: Frank Cass.

Perham, M. 1970. *Colonial Sequence.* London: Methuen.

Phillips, A. 1989. *The Enigma of Colonialism: British Policy in West Africa.* London: James Currey.

Pilling, G. 1943. Letter to the Colonial Office on Town Planning in Zanzibar, October 22. File AB 39/21, Zanzibar National Archives.

Porter, D. 1995. "Scenes from Childhood: the Homesickness of Development Discourses." In *Power of Development,* edited by J. Crush. London: Routledge.

Potts, D. 1985. "The Development of Malawi's New Capital at Lilongwe: A Comparison with Other New African Capitals." *Comparative Urban Research* 10(2):42–56.

———. 1986. "Urbanization in Malawi with Special Reference to the New Capital City of Lilongwe." Ph.D. diss., Univ. College, London.

———. 1994. "Urban Environmental Controls and Low Income Housing in Southern Africa." In *Environment and Housing in Third World Cities,* edited by H. Main and S. Williams. New York: John Wiley.

Pratt, M. 1992. *Imperial Eyes.* New York: Routledge.

Rakodi, C. 1986. "Colonial Urban Planning in Northern Rhodesia and Its Legacy." *Third World Planning Review* 8:193–218.

———. 1994. "Zambia." In *Urbanization in Africa: A Handbook,* edited by J. Tarver. Westport, Conn.: Greenwood Press.

———. 1995. *Harare: Inheriting a Settler-Colonial City: Change or Continuity?* New York: John Wiley.

———. 1997. *The Urban Challenge in Africa: Growth and Management of Its Large Cities.* Tokyo: United Nations Univ. Press.

Ranger, T. 1995. *Are We Not Also Men?* Portsmouth, N.H.: Heinemann.

Richards, G. 1974. *From Vision to Reality: The Story of Malawi's New Capital.* Johannesburg: Lorton Publications.

Robinson, J. 1990. " 'A Perfect System of Control'? State Power and 'Native Locations' in South Africa." *Environment and Planning D: Society and Space* 8(2):135–62.

———. 1994. "White Women Researching/representing 'Others.' " In *Writing Women and Space,* edited by A. Blunt and G. Rose. New York: Guilford.

———. 1996. *The Power of Apartheid: State, Power and Space in South African Cities.* Oxford: Butterworth-Heinemann.

———. 2000. "Power as Friendship: Spatiality, Femininity and 'Noisy' Surveillance." In *Entanglements of Power,* edited by J. Sharp, C. Philo, and R. Paddison. London: Routledge.

Roe, G. 1992. *Beyond the City Limits: Anatomy of an Unplanned Housing Settlement in Lilongwe, Malawi.* Zomba: Univ. of Malawi Center for Social Research.

Ross, R., and G. Telkamp. 1985. *Colonial Cities: Essays on Urbanism in a Colonial Context.* Dordrecht: Martinus Nijhoff.

Rotberg, R. 1971. *The Rise of Nationalism in Central Africa: The Making of Malawi and Zambia, 1873–1964.* Cambridge, Mass.: Harvard Univ. Press.

Sack, R. 1980. *Conceptions of Space in Social Thought.* Minneapolis: Univ. of Minnesota Press.

Said, E. 1993. *Culture and Imperialism.* New York: Harper and Row.

———. 1995. "Secular Interpretation, the Geographical Element, and the Methodology of Imperialism." In *After Colonialism,* edited by G. Prakash. Princeton: Princeton Univ. Press.

Saleh, B. A. 1992. Interview with author and Ali Hasan Ali. Zanzibar, February 20.

Samachar. 1947. "Opening of the Civic Center in Ng'ambo." *Samachar* (Newspaper of Zanzibar's Indian community in the colonial era). February 1, p. 1.

Samoff, J. 1979. "The Bureaucracy and the Bourgeoisie: Decentralization and Class Structure in Tanzania." *Comparative Studies in Society and History* 21:30–62.

———. 1982. "Class, Class Conflict and the State in Africa." *Political Science Quarterly* 97:105–27.

Sampson, R. 1959. *So This Was Lusaakas: The Story of the Capital of Northern Rhodesia to 1936.* Lusaka: Lusaka Publicity Society.

Sapao, F. 1997. Interview with author and P. Singh. Lilongwe, Malawi, July 20.

Saul, J. 1979. *The State and Revolution in Eastern Africa.* New York: Monthly Review Press.

Schacht, J. 1965. "Notes on Islam in East Africa." *Studia Islamica* 23:91–136.

Schlyter, A. 1981. "Upgraded George Revisited." In *Upgrading in Lusaka: Participation and Physical Changes,* edited by C. Rakodi and A. Schlyter. Stockholm, Sweden: Swedish Council for Building Research.

———. 1984. *Upgrading Reconsidered: The George Studies Retrospective.* Gavle, Sweden: The National Swedish Institute for Building Research.

———. 1987. "Commercialization in an Upgraded Squatter Settlement in Lusaka, Zambia." *African Urban Quarterly*:287–97.

———. 1988. *Women Householders and Housing Strategies: The Case of George, Zambia.* Gavle, Sweden: The National Swedish Institute for Building Research.

Schlyter, A., and T. Schlyter. 1979. *George: The Development of a Squatter Settlement in Lusaka, Zambia.* Gavle, Sweden: The National Swedish Institute for Building Research.

Scholz, H. 1968. *Zanzibar Town Planning Scheme 1968.* Zanzibar: Revolutionary Government of Zanzibar.

Schroeder, R. 1999. *Shady Practices: Agroforestry and Gender Politics in The Gambia.* Berkeley and Los Angeles: Univ. of California Press.

Schuster, I. 1979. *New Women of Lusaka.* Palo Alto, Calif.: Mayfield.

Seymour, T. 1976. "The Causes of Squatter Settlement: The Case of Lusaka, Zambia, in an International Context." In *Slums or Self-Reliance? Urban Growth in*

Zambia, edited by H. Simons, T. Seymour, R. Martin, and M. Muller. Lusaka: Univ. of Zambia Institute for African Studies.

Sharp, J., P. Routledge, C. Philo, and R. Paddison. 2000. *Entanglements of Power.* London: Routledge.

Shaw, C. 1995. *Colonial Inscriptions: Race, Sex and Class in Kenya.* Minneapolis: Univ. of Minnesota Press.

Sheriff, A. 1987. *Slaves, Spices and Ivory: Integration of an East African Commercial Empire into the World Economy, 1770–1873.* London: James Currey.

Sheriff, A., and E. Ferguson. 1991. *Zanzibar under Colonial Rule.* Athens, Ohio: Ohio Univ. Press.

Shivji, I. 1976. *Class Struggles in Tanzania.* London: Heinemann.

———. 1991. "The Politics of Liberalization in Tanzania: Notes on the Crisis of Ideological Hegemony." In *The IMF and Tanzania: The Dynamics of Liberalization,* edited by H. Campbell and H. Stein. Harare: Sapes Books.

Short, P. 1974. *Banda.* London: Routledge and Kegan Paul.

Sidaway, J., and M. Power. 1998. "Sex and Violence on the Wild Frontiers: The Aftermath of State Socialism in the Periphery." In *Theorizing Transition,* edited by J. Pickles and A. Smith. London: Routledge.

Simmance, A. 1972. *Urbanization in Zambia: An International Survey Report to the Ford Foundation.* New York: Ford Foundation.

Simon, D. 1992. *Cities, Capital and Development: African Cities in the World Economy.* London: Belhaven Press.

———. 1997. "Urbanization, Globalization, and Economic Crisis in Africa." In *The Urban Challenge in Africa,* edited by C. Rakodi. Tokyo: United Nations Univ. Press.

Simone, A. M. 1994. *In Whose Image? Political Islam and Urban Practices in Sudan.* Chicago: Univ. of Chicago Press.

Simons, H., T. Seymour, R. Martin, and M. Muller. 1976. *Slums or Self-Reliance? Urban Growth in Zambia.* Lusaka: Univ. of Zambia Institute for African Studies.

Singh, A. Papers of Ajit Singh Hoogan. Privately held collection, Zanzibar, Tanzania.

Singh, J. Personal communications with author. Various dates.

Singh, P. Personal communications with author. Various dates.

Singh, S. n.d. *Thakar Singh Through His Art.* Amritsar: Punjabee Press.

Smith, A., and M. Bull. 1991. *Margery Perham and British Rule in Africa.* London: Frank Cass.

Smith, E. 1984. "The Evolution of Nairobi, Kenya, 1888–1939: A Study in Dependent Urban Development." Ph.D. diss., Univ. of Connecticut.

Smith, J. 1996. "State Formation, Geography and a Gentleman's Education." *Geographical Review* 86(1):91–100.

Soja, E., and C. Weaver. 1976. "Urbanization and Underdevelopment in East Africa." In *Urbanization and Counter-Urbanization*, edited by B. Berry. Beverly Hills: Sage.

Steel, N., and P. Hart. 1994. *Defeat at Gallipoli*. London: Macmillan.

Stoler, A. 1992. "Rethinking Colonial Categories: European Communities and the Boundaries of Rule." In *Colonialism and Culture*, edited by N. Dirks. Ann Arbor: Univ. of Michigan Press.

Stoler, A., and F. Cooper. 1997. "Between Metropole and Colony: Rethinking a Research Agenda." In *Tensions of Empire: Colonial Cultures in a Bourgeois World*, edited by F. Cooper and A. Stoler. Berkeley and Los Angeles: Univ. of California Press.

Szelenyi, I. 1983. *Urban Inequalities under State Socialism*. New York: Oxford Univ. Press.

Tait, J. 1997. *From Self-Help Housing to Sustainable Settlement: Capitalist Development and Urban Planning in Lusaka, Zambia*. Brookfield, Vt.: Avebury.

Tarver, John. 1994. *Urbanization in Africa: A Handbook*. Westport, Conn.: Greenwood Press.

Taylor, R. 1943. "A Survey of Ruinous Huts in Ng'ambo." File AB 40/13A, Zanzibar National Archives.

Tett, A., and J. Wolfe. 1991. "Discourse Analysis and City Plans." *Journal of Planning Education and Research* 10(3):195–200.

United Republic of Tanzania. 1991. *Sensa: The 1988 Census: Preliminary Report*. Dar es Salaam: Tanzania Government Printers.

Usi, M. 1966. *Mheshimiwa Abeid Amani Karume* ((The honorable Abeid Amani Karume). Dar es Salaam: Tanzania Publishing House.

van Onselen, C. 1996. *The Seed Is Mine*. New York: Hill and Wang.

van Zwanenberg, R. 1977. *Colonial Capitalism and Labor in Kenya, 1919–1939*. Nairobi: East African Publishing House.

Walker, R. 1985. *To What End Did They Die? Officers Died at Gallipoli*. London: Macmillan.

Watts, M. 1987. "Powers of Production: Geographers among the Peasants." *Environment and Planning D: Society and Space* 5(2):215–30.

Western, J. 1985. "Undoing the Colonial City?" *Geographical Review* 75:335–57.

———. 1996. *Outcast Cape Town*. 2d ed. Berkeley and Los Angeles: Univ. of California Press.

White, L. 1990. *The Comforts of Home: Prostitution in Colonial Nairobi*. Chicago: Univ. of Chicago Press.

Wilson, A. 1990. *U.S. Foreign Policy and Revolution: The Creation of Tanzania*. New York: Pluto Press.

Wilson, T. 1982. "Spatial Analysis and Settlement Patterns on the East African Coast." *Paideuma* 28:202–19.

Wills, A. 1985. *An Introduction to the History of Central Africa.* 4th ed. New York: Oxford Univ. Press.

Wolff, R. 1974. *The Economics of Colonialism.* New Haven: Yale Univ. Press.

Wright, G. 1991. *The Politics of Design in French Colonial Urbanism.* Chicago: Univ. of Chicago Press.

Yahya, Y. S., A. K. Ali, B. F. Tausir, B. S. Haji, A. I. Juma, M. O. Said, A. T. Yahya, and H. M. Amour. 1992. Focus Group Discussion with author and Ali Hasan Ali. Zanzibar, April 14.

Yeoh, B. 1996. *Contesting Space: Power Relations and the Urban Built Environment in Colonial Singapore.* Oxford: Oxford Univ. Press.

Youe, C. 1986. *Robert Thorne Coryndon: Proconsular Imperialism in Southern and Eastern Africa, 1897–1925.* Waterloo, Ont.: Wilfred Laurier Univ. Press.

Young, R. 1995. *Colonial Desire.* London: Routledge.

Zanzibar Protectorate. 1912. *A Handbook of Zanzibar.* Zanzibar: Government Printers.

———. 1928. Local News Supplement of the Official Gazette. Zanzibar: Government Printers.

———. 1962. *Social Survey of Zanzibar* [conducted in 1948]. Vol. 20. Zanzibar: Government Printers.

Zulu, R. 1998. "Urban Planning and Residential Settlements in Lusaka, Kafue and Chongwe." *Urban Development Research Report,* no. 1. Lusaka: Univ. of Zambia Institute of Economic and Social Research.

Index

Abdulwahab, Abdulwahab Alawi, 123–24
Accumulation, 9–10, 46, 74, 160
Adshead, S. D., 58
African Association (Zanzibar), 128
African cities, xi-xii, xv, xxi, 2, 5–7, 13–14, 15–16, 67, 135–36, 166; gender in, xv, 8, 40, 52, 63–65, 71–72, 82, 90, 117
African paramountcy, 38, 59, 67
Afro-Shirazi Party (ASP) of Zanzibar, 29, 100–101, 106, 109, 111, 114–15, 123–24, 128–29, 132, 155; headquarters of, 114; merger with Tanganyika African National Union of, 29
Aley, Juma, 85, 112
Ali, Ali Khalil, 97
Ali, Ali Talib, 106, 118
Amani-Mbweni road (Zanzibar), 126
Amour, Hamid Mohammed, 97
Amour, Salmin, 96
Amritsar (British India), 25
Anticolonial movements, 14, 38–39, 71, 98
Apartheid (South Africa), 134, 137–38, 142–43, 151
Arabs, 2, 5. *See also* Omani
Architecture, 7, 9, 11–12, 26, 35, 42, 48–49, 58, 62; of Ajit Singh, 89–93, 129–30, 148–49
Area 1 (Lilongwe), 144, 153
Area 3 (Lilongwe), 144
Area 12 (Lilongwe), 141
Articles of Union between Zanzibar and Tanganyika, 106

Asians: in East Africa, 12–13, 23–24, 27, 35; in Lusaka, 68, 74; in Malawi, 136, 144, 149–50, 152; in Nairobi, 35–37; in Zanzibar, 23–24, 130
Asquith, Julian, 77, 92

Bachmann, Jon, 73
Baker, Herbert, 19, 26, 35, 47–49, 54, 58, 143
Banda, Aleke, 152, 164
Banda, Hastings Kamuzu, xiv, 26–27, 134, 137–41, 143, 145–47, 150–58, 164
Barghash bin Said Sultan, 1
Barotseland Protectorate, 56
Basutoland. *See* Lesotho
Baumann, Oskar, 31
Bemba, 70–71
Berman, Bruce, 9–10, 46, 118, 158, 160
Blantyre (Malawi), 6, 136–37, 139, 145, 149
Bowling, P. J., 55
Bradley, Kenneth, 64–65
British (colonial) Africa, xi-xii, 4–6, 12, 18–20, 24, 31, 53, 74, 76, 136, 143, 159, 164. *See also* British Empire; British imperial power; Colonialism (British).
British Empire, 10, 20, 25, 33, 53, 74
British imperial power, 49, 56
British India, 23. *See also* Punjab